HACKING GROWTH

HACKING GROWTH

HOW TODAY'S FASTEST-GROWING COMPANIES DRIVE BREAKOUT SUCCESS

SEAN ELLIS AND MORGAN BROWN

CROWN
BUSINESS
NEW YORK

CROWN BUSINESS is a trademark and CROWN and the Rising Sun
colophon are registered trademarks of Penguin Random House LLC.

Crown Business books are available at special discounts for bulk purchases
for sales promotions or corporate use. Special editions, including personalized
covers, excerpts of existing books, or books with corporate logos, can be created
in large quantities for special needs. For more information, contact Premium
Sales at (212) 572-2232 or e-mail specialmarkets@penguinrandomhouse.com.

Library of Congress Cataloging-in-Publication Data
Names: Ellis, Sean, author. | Brown, Morgan, author.
Title: Hacking growth : how today's fastest-growing companies drive breakout
success / Sean Ellis, Morgan Brown.
Description: First Edition. | New York : Crown Business, 2017.
Identifiers: LCCN 2016044987 | ISBN 9780451497215 (hardback)
Subjects: LCSH: Success in business. | Consumer behavior. | Marketing. |
BISAC: BUSINESS & ECONOMICS / Development / Business Development. |
BUSINESS & ECONOMICS / Consumer Behavior. |
BUSINESS & ECONOMICS / Marketing / Direct.
Classification: LCC HF5386 .E434 2017 | DDC 658—dc23
LC record available at https://lccn.loc.gov/2016044987

ISBN 978-0-451-49721-5
Ebook ISBN 978-0-451-49722-2
International edition ISBN 978-1-5247-6000-7

Printed in the United States of America

Book design by Anna Thompson
Illustrations by Mapping Specialists, Ltd.
Jacket design by Oliver Munday

10 9 8 7 6 5 4 3 2 1

First Edition

*SE: Dedicated with love to my amazing wife Svetlana
and our talented daughters Natasha and Anna.*

MB: For Erika, Banks, and Audrey Grace

CONTENTS

HACKING GROWTH

When I (Sean) got a call from Dropbox founder Drew Houston in 2008, I was immediately intrigued by the predicament the one-year-old start-up was in. The company's cloud-based file storage and sharing service had built up a good early fan base, concentrated primarily among the tech-savvy community centered in Silicon Valley. Even before the product was completely built, Houston had pushed a video prototype online illustrating how the service would work, which had earned him the backing of the powerful Y Combinator start-up incubator and drawn a flood of early adopters.

It became pretty clear that Houston was on to something when the waiting list he was keeping for the beta version grew from 5,000 to 75,000 in a blink of an eye when a second video was posted on news aggregator site Digg and went viral.[1] The next wave of users who signed up after the public launch were happy with the service, but Houston was still running into a wall trying to break out beyond the tech elite. And he didn't have much time. The competition was fierce. One start-up, Mozy, had a three-year head start, while another, Carbonite, had raised $48 million in funding—versus the $1.2 million in seed capital raised by Houston. Meanwhile, behemoths Microsoft and Google were gearing up to enter the cloud storage arena. How could Dropbox grow their customer base in the shadow of such formidable competitors?

When Houston called me, he wanted to explore what I could do to help them grow beyond their very solid but not-yet-big-enough pool of early adopters. I was just wrapping up an interim VP of marketing role at Xobni, a start-up run by Drew's good friend Adam Smith, when Adam suggested that we meet to discuss Dropbox's challenges. I had developed a reputation in Silicon Valley as someone who could figure out how to help companies take off, particularly those facing fierce competition and limited budgets such as Dropbox was. I'd first had success driving growth at the online game pioneer Uproar, growing the site to one of the 10 largest on the Web, with more 5.2 million gamers at the time of IPO in March of 2000, all in the face of an aggressive push into gaming from Sony, Microsoft, and Yahoo![2] I'd then moved over to work on growth initiatives at LogMeIn, an innovative service started by the Uproar founder. There I'd managed to help turn the company into the market leader despite a massive marketing campaign waged by its main competitor, GoToMyPC. What was the secret? I worked with the engineers to utilize technology for what was, to them, an unconventional purpose: to craft novel methods for finding, reaching, and learning from customers in order to hone our targeting, grow our customer base, and get more value from our marketing dollars. I knew nothing about software engineering when I started my career in 1994 selling print ad space for a business journal at a time when businesses were just starting to move to the Web. But I saw the promise of the future in Web business, and so when I got to know the founder of Uproar, I decided to invest some of my hard-won sales commissions and hop over to work for the gaming portal, once again, selling ads. It wasn't long before I caught on to the dangers of relying only on traditional marketing methods—even the newer, Internet-era versions of old methods, like online banner ads—to drive growth. My big wake-up moment was probably when the leading advertising firms I was trying to sell to, such as Saatchi and Ogilvy, declined to recommend banner ads on Uproar to their clients, on the grounds that the site didn't have a large enough user base. Short on cash and in danger of missing out on much-needed sales commissions, I suddenly found myself tasked by the founder with figuring out how to bring in more users, fast. My first approach was paid advertising on Internet portals, like Yahoo!, and that stoked growth nicely. But it was costly, and, just as Drew Houston later discovered with Dropbox, the ads weren't bringing in enough bang for the buck. Meanwhile, Sony, Yahoo!, and Microsoft started making their big push, flooding the Web with gaming ads, and as a young start-up, Uproar didn't have anywhere close to the money needed to compete with them head to head. I knew I had to find another way.

That's when I got the idea of creating an entirely new type of advertisement that allowed Web proprietors to offer Uproar games for free on their site, meaning the site got fun new features to offer their visitors, and Uproar got exposure to everyone who visited those pages. The founder gave the go-ahead, and within a few weeks, the engineers and I had created a new single-player game that could be added to any website, with just a small snippet of code: one of the first embeddable widgets. The site proprietors would become Uproar affiliates, paid just $.50 for each new game player the company acquired through their sites. The low cost made it highly affordable for us and, because the game was so engaging, the affiliates were happy to feature it. In addition to sending new gamers to Uproar, we experimented with adding an "add this game to your site" link, which made it easy for other website owners to make the game available on their sites, too.

As we saw the game start to take off, we tested different versions of the copy, calls to action, and which free game we offered to find the most potent combination. The result for Uproar was explosive growth; the free games were soon on 40,000 sites and Uproar shot to the top of the online gaming world, beating out the behemoths and their splashy marketing campaigns. Many other companies have since used the same strategy to grow, the most famous example being YouTube, who later supercharged its growth by creating its embeddable video player widget, which landed YouTube videos all over the Web and turned online video into a phenomenon.

It was this success that led the founder of Uproar to ask me to come help grow his next venture, LogMeIn. LogMeIn was an ingenious product that let users access their files, email, and software on their home or work desktop computer from any other PC connected to the Internet. Yet while an aggressive search engine marketing campaign led to a good initial burst of customer sign-ups, they soon plateaued, and I realized that ads were once again proving far too costly for the payoff—especially since, at my suggestion, LogMeIn had pivoted from a paid to a freemium model in an effort to differentiate the service from its fierce competitor, GoToMyPC. At over $10,000 in ad spend per month, the customer acquisition costs no longer generated a positive return on the investment. Despite lots of ad copy testing and playing around with different keywords and advertising platforms, the conversion rate was woefully low—and this for a service that was clearly incredibly helpful, and was free, to boot. So once again I turned to technology to find a novel way to try to solve the problem.

I decided that we should try to get feedback from people who had signed up but had then abandoned the service. We had collected their email addresses as part of the sign-up process, and we sent out an email asking them why they weren't using LogMeIn. Seems obvious, but it was a radical idea at the time. After just a few days, the collective responses offered an absolutely unequivocal explanation: people didn't believe the service was really free. At the time, the freemium software model was new and it still seemed too good to be true to lots of people. So with that realization, I got my marketing and engineering teams in a room to brainstorm ideas for how to change the landing page, to better communicate to customers that there was no "catch"—that LogMeIn did, in fact, offer a completely free version of the product. We experimented with many iterations of marketing copy and page designs, and yet even this led to very little meaningful improvement. We then decided to test adding a simple link to buy the paid version to the page. And with that, we found a winning combination of design, message, and offer that led to a tripling of the conversion rate. That was just the start, though. Upon digging into the data, we discovered an even bigger drop-off among users who downloaded the software but then didn't follow through and use it. We kept experimenting, such as with changes in the install process, the sign-up steps, and more, and ultimately we improved the conversion rate to the point that search ads not only became cost effective again, they could be profitably scaled by over 700 percent. So scale up the company did, and immediately growth took off.

Once again, the solution had been found in just weeks, using a recipe that included healthy doses of out-of-the-box thinking, cross-company collaboration and problem solving, real-time market testing and experimentation (conducted at little or no cost), and a commitment to being nimble and responsive in acting on the results. These are the very ingredients that I later codified into the growth hacking methodology you'll read about in the pages that follow.

Of course, Uproar and LogMeIn weren't the only start-ups in town combining programming and marketing know-how with the emerging characteristics of the Web to drive growth. Hotmail, for example, was one of the first to tap into the viral quality of Web products—and their ability to "sell themselves"—when it added the simple tagline "P.S.: Get Your Free Email at Hotmail" at the bottom of every email that users sent, with a link to a landing page to set up an account.[3] At the same time, PayPal had demonstrated the extraordinary growth potential in creating the synergy between a product and a popular Web platform—in their case, eBay. When the team noticed auction owners promoting the PayPal service as an easy way for winners to pay, they created AutoLink, a tool that automatically added the PayPal logo and a link to sign up to all of their active auction listings. This tool tripled the number of auctions using PayPal on eBay and ignited its viral growth on the platform.[4] LinkedIn, which had struggled to gain traction in its first year, saw their growth begin to skyrocket in late 2003, when the engineering team worked out an ingenious way for members to painlessly upload and invite their email contacts stored in their Outlook address book, kicking network effects growth into high gear.[5] And in each of these cases, growth was achieved not with traditional advertising, but rather with a dash of programming smarts and on a shoestring budget.

Approaches like these to building, growing, and retaining a customer base that relied not on traditional marketing plans, a pricey launch, and a big ad spend, but rather on harnessing software development to build marketing into products themselves, were proving both extraordinarily powerful *and* incredibly cost effective. Perhaps more important, companies' growing ability to collect, store, and analyze vast amounts of user data, and to track it in real time, was now enabling even small start-ups to experiment with new features, new messaging or branding, or other new marketing efforts—at an increasingly low cost, much higher speed, and greater level of precision. The result was the emergence of a rigorous approach to fueling rapid market growth through high-speed, cross-functional experimentation, for which I soon coined the term *growth hacking*.

After the success of my growth strategy at LogMeIn, I decided to focus on helping early stage companies accelerate their growth through experimentation. So when Drew Houston reached out to me to discuss how I could work with Dropbox, I couldn't wait to implement the method that I'd developed. My first step was to get Houston's buy-in to conduct a simple survey of the current users to calculate what I called (and what you'll read about in more detail later in the book) the product's must-have score. The survey asked the simple question "How would you feel if you could no longer use Dropbox?" Users could respond "Very disappointed," "Somewhat disappointed," "Not disappointed," or "N/A no longer using the product" (I wrote the question this way because I found that asking people if they were satisfied with a product didn't deliver meaningful insights; disappointment was a much better gauge of product loyalty than satisfaction). Having already run this survey at numerous start-ups, I had found that companies where more than 40 percent of respondents said they would be "very disappointed" if they could no longer use the product had very strong growth potential, where those that fell under that 40 percent threshold tended to face a much harder path in growing the business (due to user apathy). When I saw the results of the survey, though, even I was blown away. Dropbox's score was off the charts, particularly for users who had fully explored the features of the product.

This indicated that there was enormous potential for growth here, and the next challenge was to figure out how to tap into it. So I proposed to Houston that we experiment with finding alternate ways to ignite it other than more paid ads. Houston agreed, and brought me in as interim head of marketing for a six-month term. An engineering graduate of MIT, Houston had already put his skills to good use in building the Dropbox product; now we would apply that prowess to helping put the product in front of many more customers—and ensure they loved it.

Then came the second step in the growth process: a dive into Dropbox's user data. One discovery this yielded was that a full third of Dropbox users came from referrals of current users of the product. That meant word of mouth was strong, even if it wasn't yet driving

growth fast enough. In other words, Houston had created a product people truly loved, and that they were raving about to their friends, and yet
it wasn't coming close to its potential for signing up new customers. This
was a striking example of the *Field of Dreams* fallacy, still too popular
in the start-up community; that is, the belief that all that's needed is to
build a standout product and "they [the customers] will come."

What if, I wondered, Dropbox could find a way to harness and amplify their strong word of mouth, making it easy and appealing for the
early fans to evangelize to many more of their friends? Drew and I brainstormed with an intern Drew had roped into the effort, Albert Ni, and
together we decided to create a referral program like the one PayPal had
implemented to great success. The only catch was that the PayPal program had offered to deposit $10 into the user's PayPal account, in ex-
change for referrals, and though the total cost had not been disclosed
(cofounder Elon Musk has since revealed that it amounted to some $60
to $70 million), there was no way Dropbox could afford to "buy" users to
achieve the level of growth they were looking for.[6] Then it hit us: What
if we could offer people something else they clearly valued highly—more
storage space—in exchange for referrals? At the time Dropbox was using
Amazon's low-cost S3 Web servers (which launched a couple of years
earlier) for its data storage, which meant that it would be pretty simple
(and cheap) to add more space to their infrastructure. Using PayPal's
program as a template, our small team quickly crafted a referral program
that offered users an extra 250 megabytes of space in exchange for refer-
ring a new friend to the service, who would also get 250 megabytes added
to their own account. At the time, 250 megabytes was the equivalent of
offering a whole hard drive of storage for free, so as far as incentives go,
it was pretty powerful.

Once the referral program went live, we immediately saw invites
flooding out via email and social media, resulting in a 60 percent increase in referral sign-ups. The plan was working, no doubt about it, but
we didn't stop there; determined to make the most of the opportunity,
our team worked furiously for weeks to optimize every element of the
program, from the messaging, to the specifics of the offer, to the email
invites, to the user experience and interface elements. Implementing a
method I call high-tempo testing, we began evaluating the efficacy of

our experiments almost in real time. Twice a week we'd look at the results of each new experiment, see what was working and what wasn't,
and use that data to decide what changes to test next. Over the course
of many iterations, the results got better and better and by early 2010,
Dropbox users were sending more than 2.8 million invites *per month* to
their friends—and the company had grown from just 100,000 users at
the time of launch to more than 4,000,000. All this in just 14 months,
and all achieved *with no traditional marketing spend*, no banner ads, no
paid promotions, no purchasing of email lists, and, in fact, Dropbox
didn't even bring in a full-time marketer for another 9 months after I left
at the end of my engagement with them in the spring of 2009.[7]

As all this was going on, this new approach to market growth and
customer acquisition—one that discarded the old model of big marketing budgets and unscientific, unmeasurable tactics in favor of more cost-
effective, consistent, and data-driven ones—was spreading across Silicon
Valley. Innovators at other companies began developing similar approaches that involved rapidly generating and testing inventive growth
ideas. In late 2007, Facebook set up a formal growth team of five people,
called The Growth Circle, bringing together experts in product management (including their most tenured product manager, Naomi Gleit),
Internet marketing, data analytics, and engineering. The team was run
by a hard-charging executive and former head of product marketing on
the Facebook Platform and Ads products named Chamath Palihapitiya,
who recommended to Mark Zuckerberg that he refocus his efforts on
helping the site grow its number of users. Though Facebook, who had
by this time about 70 million users, had already achieved remarkable
growth, it looked like the company might be hitting a wall. So Mark
Zuckerberg tasked the team to focus exclusively on experimenting with
ways to break through that plateau. As the team racked up success after
success, Zuckerberg saw that the investment in the new unit was paying
off, and continued to add more manpower, enabling the team to experiment more and grow the site even faster.[8]

One of their biggest breakthroughs, the creation of a translation engine to spur international growth, provides a sharp contrast as to how the
growth hacking method is so different from the traditional marketing

approach. At the time, the majority of Facebook's 70 million users lived in North America, making it clear that drawing in international users was one of the biggest growth opportunities. But that would require translating the product into every conceivable language—a daunting task. The old way would have been to identify the 10 most spoken languages and hire local teams to do the translation, country by country. Instead the growth team engineers, led by Javier Olivan, built a translation engine that allowed Facebook's own users to translate the site into any language via a crowdsourcing model. As Andy Johns, who is a leading authority on growth hacking and worked on the growth team at Facebook, said of the effort, "Growth was not about hiring 10 people per country and putting them in the 20 most important countries and expecting it to grow. Growth was about engineer[ing] systems of scale and enabling our users to grow the product for us." Johns has called it one of the most significant levers in scaling Facebook to the massive reach it enjoys today.[9]

As Facebook's user base was spreading, so was the growth hacking method (albeit on a much smaller scale). This was in part due to the number of Facebook employees who moved to new start-ups, including Quora, Uber, Asana, and Twitter, bringing these methods with them. And while I was implementing growth hacking with great success at two more start-ups—Eventbrite and Lookout—a number of other companies including LinkedIn, Airbnb, and Yelp, were adopting similar experiment-driven approaches.

Take the case of Airbnb. Its founders struggled so much to attract customers that they launched the site *three times* before growth started to take off. In the meantime, they were so strapped for cash that at one point, during the 2008 presidential election, they resorted to selling boxes of cereal—cleverly branded as "Obama O's" and "Cap'n McCain's"—to make ends meet (their cash situation became so dire that Brian Chesky and Joe Gebbia actually lived off the unsold cereal until they could raise more money). The team tried all sorts of ideas to grow the user base, all of which proved unsuccessful. That is, until they finally hit upon an untapped-growth gold mine with a brilliant growth hack, which has since become Silicon Valley legend. Using some sophisticated programming, and lots of experimentation to get it right, the team figured out a seamless way to cross-publish Airbnb listings on Craigslist, free of cost, so that whenever someone searched the popular classifieds site for a vacation rental, listings for properties on Airbnb popped up.

The cleverness of this hack cannot be understated. Because Craigslist did not offer any sanctioned way for Airbnb (or anyone) to post new listings, the team had to reverse engineer how Craigslist managed new listings, and then re-create those steps with their own program. This meant understanding how the Craigslist posting system worked, which categories vacation rentals were posted in in different cities, figuring out the limitations of what could be posted on Craigslist, such as rules around images and formatting the listings, and much more. As Andrew Chen, who leads rider growth at Uber, commented when analyzing the hack, "Long story short, this kind of integration is not trivial. There's many little details to notice, and I wouldn't be surprised if the initial integration took some very smart people a lot of time to perfect." He concluded, "Let's be honest, a traditional marketer would not even be close to imagining the integration above—there's too many technical details needed for it to happen. As a result, it could only have come out of the mind of an engineer tasked with the problem of acquiring more users from Craigslist."[10]

This intricate integration meant that Airbnb listings flowed quickly onto Craigslist, where millions clicked over to Airbnb, and (without a dime spent on advertising) room bookings skyrocketed. Once they had the integration built, the team worked to capitalize on the uncontested "blue ocean," measuring and optimizing the response to the listings, including how they looked on Craigslist, the headlines used, and more.[11] Though eventually Craigslist blocked the unauthorized access, Airbnb had generated powerful momentum, and the team continued to experiment with additional ways to fuel their growth. The company continues to do so today, and we'll introduce some of their more recent successful experiments in later chapters.

By breaking down the traditional business silos and assembling cross-functional, collaborative teams that bring together staff with expertise in analytics, engineering, product management, and marketing, growth hacking allows companies to efficiently marry powerful data analysis and technical know-how with marketing savvy, to quickly devise more promising ways to fuel growth. By rapidly testing promising ideas and evaluating them according to objective metrics, growth hacking facilitates much quicker discovery of which ideas are valuable and which should be dismissed. It is the solution to the misplaced, often quite stubborn, devotion to features or marketing approaches that don't work, replacing wasteful, outdated, and unproven approaches with market-tested and data-driven alternatives.

WHO CAN BECOME A GROWTH HACKER?

Growth hacking is not just a tool for marketers. It can be applied to new product innovation and to the continuous improvement of products as well as to growing an existing customer base. As such, it's equally useful to everyone from product developers, to engineers, to designers, to salespeople, to managers.

Nor is it just a tool for entrepreneurs; in fact, it can be implemented just as effectively at a large established company as at a small fledgling start-up. Indeed, if you work for a large company, you don't need some big corporate mandate to implement growth hacking. It is designed to work on the largest scale (company-wide) or the smallest (a single campaign or project). What that means is that any department or project team can run the growth hacking playbook by following the process we'll outline in the coming chapters.

This method is the engine that's driven the phenomenal success not only of all of the companies you just read about, but many other of the fastest-growing Silicon Valley "unicorns," including Pinterest, BitTorrent, Uber, LinkedIn, and dozens more. The popular mythology about the breakout growth of these companies is that they simply came up with a business idea that was "lightning in a bottle"—one idea that was so brilliant and transformative that it took the market by storm. Yet that version of history is patently false. Mass adoption was achieved neither quickly nor easily for all of these powerhouses; far from it. It wasn't the immaculate conception of a world-changing product nor any single insight, lucky break, or stroke of genius that rocketed these companies to success. In reality, their success was driven by the methodical, rapid-fire generation and testing of new ideas for product development and marketing, and the use of data on user behavior to find the winning ideas that drove growth.

If this iterative process sounds familiar, it's likely because you've encountered a similar approach in agile software development or the Lean Startup methodology. *What those two approaches have done for new business models and product development, respectively, growth hacking does for customer acquisition, retention, and revenue growth.* Building on these methods was natural for Sean and other start-up teams, because the companies that Sean advised and others that developed the method were stacked with great engineering talent familiar with the methods, and because the founders were inclined to apply a similar approach to customer growth as the engineers applied to their software and product development. Central to agile development is increasing the speed of development, working in short "sprints" of coding, and regularly testing and iterating on the product over time. The Lean Startup adopted the practice of rapid development and frequent testing, and added the practice of getting a *minimum viable product* out on the market and into the hands of actual users as soon as possible, to get real user feedback and establish a viable business. Growth hacking adopted the continuous cycle of improvement and the rapid iterative approach of both methods and applied them to customer and revenue growth. In the process, the growth hacking method broke down the traditional walls between marketing and engineering in order to discover novel methods of marketing that are built into the product itself, and can only be tapped with more technical know-how.

The growth hacking practices innovated by these early practitioners and others who have followed have been honed into a finely tuned business methodology—and spawned a powerful movement with hundreds of thousands of practitioners (and growing) across the globe. This vibrant community of growth hackers includes entrepreneurs, marketers, engineers, product managers, data scientists, and more, not just from the tech start-up world but from all walks of industry, from technology, retail, business-to-business, professional services, entertainment, and even the political arena.

And while the details of how it is implemented vary somewhat from company to company, the core elements of the method are:

- the creation of a cross-functional team, or a set of teams that break down the traditional silos of marketing and product development and combine talents;
- the use of qualitative research and quantitative data analysis to gain deep insights into user behavior and preferences; and
- the rapid generation and testing of ideas, and the use of rigorous metrics to evaluate—and then act on—those results.

Yet despite growth hacking's proven effectiveness, growing ubiquity, and the ease with which it can be applied and adopted in almost any field or industry, no definitive, authoritative, step-by-step playbook has yet existed to walk practitioners at companies of all shapes and sizes through the process.

This book is designed to be just that.

A DEFINITIVE GUIDE

We decided to write this book because we saw both the enormous potential for growth hacking to serve all of these purposes, for all types of businesses, and because we perceived the pressing need for a better understanding of the process and a guide to the best practices for implementing it. Growth hacking is a fundamental new approach to market development with enormous power, but the truth of how it should be managed for optimal effect is as of yet poorly understood.

Not only has Sean been one of the leading innovators of the practice, he's also the founder of the GrowthHackers.com website, which is the leading source of information about growth hacking and has become the home of a thriving community, with members from all over the world, attracting millions of visitors. The fact that we are barraged every day with questions about best practices is clear indication about just how much confusion there is about how growth hacking works and how exactly to implement it. So we decided to write the definitive guide, one that marketers, managers, project developers, founders, and innovators at businesses of all stripes can follow to put growth hacking to work within their teams or companies.

Along the way we share insights into the process from Sean's experiences at Dropbox, Uproar, LogMeIn, and many other hugely successful companies, as well as in growing both the GrowthHackers .com community and his own start-up, Qualaroo, a user research and survey company that achieved rapid growth and resulted in a successful acquisition. We have also canvassed the insights of the growth team innovators responsible for the surging growth of many of today's other fastest-growing firms, including Facebook, Evernote, LinkedIn, Yelp, Pinterest, HubSpot, Stripe, Etsy, BitTorrent, and Upworthy, and draw on the interviews we have conducted with the leaders who are bringing growth hacking to a number of the largest established firms, including Walmart, IBM, and Microsoft. We synthesize our own experiences with the wisdom of all of these expert practitioners and their stories to offer a "playbook" of growth hacks that readers can draw inspiration from and tailor to their own business goals.

The result is the first practical, accessible, step-by-step playbook to hacking growth—written by one of its founders in collaboration with one of its most expert practitioners, that can be adopted by any team, department, or company of any stripe.

AN UNSTOPPABLE GROWTH MACHINE

There is no question that stalled growth is one of the most pernicious and pressing problems for today's businesses, and that's not just true for start-ups, but for just about any business, large or small, in just about any industry you can think of. A *Harvard Business Review* article about growth stalls reported that 87 percent of the companies in a large study had run into one or more periods in which growth slowed dramatically, and that "on average, companies lose 74 percent of their market capitalization . . . in the decade surrounding a growth stall." What's more, the authors emphasized that the problem will be getting worse in the future, writing that "all signs point to an increasing risk of stalls in the near future," due to the "shrinking half-life of established business models." Among the causes of stalled growth they cite are problems "in managing the internal business processes for updating existing products and services and creating new ones," and "premature core abandonment: the failure to fully exploit growth opportunities in the existing core business."[12] Growth hacking is a powerful solution to both of these problems.

Put simply, every company needs to grow their base of customers in order to survive and thrive. But growth hacking isn't just about how to get new customers. It's about how to engage, activate, and win them over so they keep coming back for more. It's about how to adapt nimbly to their ever-changing needs and desires and turn them not only into a growing source of revenue, but also passionate ambassadors and an engine of word-of-mouth growth for your brand or product.

A core mandate for growth teams is to find every last bit of growth potential through a laserlike focus on continuous testing of lots of tweaks to a product, its features, the messaging to users, as well as the means by which they're acquired, retained, and generate revenue. Intrinsic to the method is also the search for new opportunities for product development, whether by assessing customer behavior or feedback, or perhaps experimenting with ways to capitalize on new technologies such as machine learning and artificial intelligence.

At many of the firms that pioneered the method, it has been so instrumental to their success that growth teams have evolved to well over a hundred members, often broken down into subteams focused on specific missions, such as customer retention or building a mobile following. Different companies have even formed subteams of different sizes and have modulated the mix of personnel and the breakdown of responsibilities to best fit their specific business needs. At LinkedIn, for example, the growth team has evolved from an initial 15-person unit to comprise 120-plus members, broken down into five units dedicated to: network growth; SEO/SEM operations; onboarding; international growth; and engagement and resurrection of users.[13] At Uber, by contrast, the growth team is divided into groups, including those who focus on adding more drivers, growing the pool of riders, expanding internationally, and more.[14]

No company today has any reason *not* to establish a growth team—or multiple teams as the case may be—and doing so doesn't require abandoning traditional organizational structures or traditional marketing strategies. Growth teams don't necessarily replace more traditional departments, but rather complement them, and help them optimize their approaches. At early stage start-ups, avoiding these silos from the start is advised, but as a start-up grows, more traditional marketing groups can be established alongside a dedicated growth team. And at larger, established firms, teams can complement the existing product, marketing, engineering, and business intelligence groups, collaborating with them and helping to open up more effective communication across them.

As Sean's experience with Dropbox shows, the process can be implemented by even the smallest of teams, which for many start-ups, especially in the early growth phase, should be run by the founder and comprise the entire company. For larger firms that must contend with existing structures and cultures resistant to change, small teams can be set up independently and even for finite projects, like perhaps the launch of a new product or a specific marketing channel, such as mobile. Teams can range from dedicated units built from the ground up, to groups made up of existing staff from different parts of the organization, to ad hoc groups that form as needed. Many evolve in size, scope, and responsibility over time to meet the specific needs of the company at any given moment.

Growth hacking is a method designed to be easily tailored and adapted to the specific needs of any team or company, large or small, at any stage of growth. And its rewards are many. Here are a few benefits of growth hacking and why they are so essential now, more than ever.

SURVIVING DISRUPTION

Every kind of company must today be implementing the growth hacking method, from the scrappiest start-ups to the most established firms. If they don't, they risk being disrupted by a competitor who has.

It is telling that even large legacy companies like IBM and Walmart are beginning to see growth hacking as a critical tool for survival. All companies today are, after all, in some sense Internet tech companies, even if their Web involvement is limited to marketing and sales rather than product development. In addition, in today's business landscape, where market leaders are being disrupted seemingly overnight, the need for rapid adoption of new technological tools and continuous experimentation with product development and marketing is rapidly spreading from the domain of digital products to business of all kinds.

This process will only be accelerating with the advent of the fast-developing Internet of Things, as more and more products are being made "smart" through connectivity to the Web and to other products. With the worlds of physical products and software rapidly merging, it will soon not only become possible to continuously monitor and update products, in real time, it will be vital to do so in order to remain competitive. General Electric CEO Jeffrey Immelt recently said that "every industrial company will become a software company," and the same can be said for consumer goods companies, media companies, financial services firms, and more.[15] Leading business strategy analyst Michael Porter and his coauthor James Heppelmann, CEO of software firm PTC, argue in a *Harvard Business Review* article that the ability of companies to stay connected to their products after sale "shifts the focus of a company's customer relationship from selling—often a predominantly onetime transaction—to maximizing the customer's value from the product over time." They emphasize that this shift leads to "the need to coordinate across product design, cloud operation, service improvement, and customer engagement." In our experience, building a cross-functional growth team is the best—and most cost effective—way to do so.[16]

One company that is smartly using technology to continuously test and update and improve its product—and fend off new market entrants in the process—is electric car pioneer Tesla Motors. The company doesn't put model years on its cars, sending regular updates to the cars' software, upgrading cars' capabilities (such as adding self-driving technology) in real time rather than waiting for a new model release. The company also monitors cars' performance and sends word to owners when repairs are advised. With plans to greatly expand sales in the coming years, the company has brought in talent from both the Facebook and Uber growth teams, and has announced, "We're building a growth team from scratch to design, build and optimize scalable solutions to accelerate adoption."[17]

THE NEED FOR SPEED

Growth hacking is also the answer to the urgent need for speed experienced by all businesses today. Finding growth solutions *fast* is crucial in today's ever-more-competitive and rapidly changing business landscape.

By revolutionizing the long-established business processes for developing and launching products, institutionalizing continuous market testing, and systematically responding to the demands of the market in real time, growth hacking makes companies much more fleet-footed. It enables them to seize new opportunities and correct for problems—fast. This gives those who adopt the method a powerful competitive advantage, one that will become even more powerful as the pace of business continues to accelerate.

The need today for great agility in adapting to new technologies and platforms cannot be overestimated. In the traditional business model that still prevails at most companies, product management, marketing, sales, and engineering are siloed in respective business units with different priorities and limited cross-functional interaction. Product teams do the market research, develop the product specifications, and assess the market size. Then, only once the product is properly defined, do they turn it over to the production side of the house—engineering or manufacturing—who then return the finished product ready for market. At the same time, marketers begin working on marketing plans once they've received the research and specs from the product team—often contracting with outside agencies, who are even further removed from key personnel, to plan the advertising and promotion. Only once the product ships does the company work to maximize sales, and sales reports from the field are fed back to the product and marketing teams to guide the next product release. This highly inefficient cycle can take quarters or even years to complete, creating a debilitating lag in both responding to changing consumer demands or technological developments, and in rolling out the new capabilities, product improvements, and marketing channels through which to reach customers.

Start-ups and established companies alike, in other words, simply can't afford to be slowed down by organizational silos. By breaking down those barriers growth hacking enables teams and companies to become more nimble and responsive to the ever-changing demands in the market, accelerating the rollout of new products and features as well as the crafting and implementation of marketing and sales strategies critical to attracting, activating, and monetizing customers. This need for speed is why a key feature of growth hacking is to experiment at the fastest possible tempo. As Facebook's vice president of growth Alex Schultz puts it: "If you're pushing code once every two weeks and your competitor is pushing code every week, just after two months that competitor will have done 10 times as many tests as you. That competitor will have learned 10 times, an order of magnitude more about their product [than you]."[18]

MINING DATA GOLD

Indeed, yet another way growth hacking gives companies a vital competitive edge is by helping them make good use of the mountains of customer data that today's new tech tools make it easier than ever to gather. Within all of that data is growth gold waiting to be mined, yet today's companies from big to small are struggling mightily to capitalize on its potential by extracting the valuable nuggets buried deep in those mountains of information. For the most part, companies have yet to develop methods for collecting data from customers in an *integrated* way. Product managers may conduct surveys and run tests in isolation from marketing departments, who are often gathering their own data and using it independently of other teams. Advertising agencies are hired to run campaigns and collect data without input from other departments on what information is most useful to collect. Meanwhile, programming teams are spoon-fed requirements based on yesterday's data, which meet outdated customer needs.

As a result, companies are either acting on the wrong data, relying on surface level, vanity metrics (like page views), or have such internal fragmentation that the most powerful growth ideas and opportunities are missed because dots can't be connected.

Growth hacking provides a method for more effectively tapping into data, and using it to extract specific, relevant, real-time insights into user behavior that can be used to inform strategy and craft more effective and targeted growth initiatives.

A great case in point is the Savings Catcher mobile app by Walmart, which arose from assessing user behavior around the company's price matching policy. To capitalize on the boom in ad matching, a practice whereby retailers agree to match the lowest price on the market for an item, Walmart's growth team enlisted the engineers to build an app that could allow customers to upload their receipts from shopping at Walmart via their phone's camera and automatically receive cash refunds from the company if another chain had advertised any of their purchases for less. In addition, the engineering team realized that it could marry the data Walmart was collecting as part of its price matching program with the ad campaigns being run by their paid search teams, leading to big savings in ad spend by only bidding aggressively on items where they were the clear price leader.

Recognizing that Walmart's greatest asset is its data, Brian Monahan, the company's former VP of marketing, pushed forward a unification of the company's data platforms across all divisions, one that would allow all teams, from engineering, to merchandising, to marketing, and even external agencies and suppliers, to capitalize on the data generated and collected. Growth hacking cultivates the maximization of *big data* through collaboration and information sharing. Monahan highlighted the business need this approach solves: "You need marketers who can appreciate what it takes to actually write software and you need data scientists who can really appreciate consumer insights and understand business problems," he explained.[19]

THE RISING COSTS AND DUBIOUS RETURNS OF TRADITIONAL MARKETING

The techniques of traditional marketing—both print and television advertising, and the newer online versions that have become essential parts of the traditional marketing toolkit—are in crisis, as markets are becoming more and more fragmented and ephemeral, while advertising is becoming both more expensive and less viewed. One key problem is that the growth of the Internet audience in major markets, particularly the US and Europe, is plateauing: with nearly 89 percent of the US population online and 93 percent of the UK's population connected, the audience is growing barely faster than the population.[20] Even in the fast-growing mobile space, 64 percent of the US population has mobile Internet connectivity.[21] This means that as more ad dollars continue to shift online, each ad has more competition for the same eyeballs, and that's been driving prices up at an alarming rate.

At the same time, increasingly tech-savvy consumers are tuning out. In fact, 69.8 million Internet users in the US (up 34 percent year over year), including nearly two out of three millennials, report using ad blocking software.[22] Add to that the fact that due to the ubiquity of streaming services like Netflix, Hulu, and Amazon Prime that are now a staple in 50 percent of American homes, not to mention TiVo and other DVR technology, the notion of watching TV—and by extension TV commercials—has become as quaint and old-fashioned as the 1950s-era Swanson TV dinner.[23] In short, ads have become, at worst, completely invisible, and at best, little more than white noise.

How bad has the crisis of traditional marketing become? A recent McKinsey study of publicly traded software companies showed absolutely no correlation between marketing investment and growth rates. Zero.[24] Another study, of CEOs' views of traditional marketing, conducted by the Fournaise Marketing Group, reported that "73 percent of CEOs think marketers lack business credibility and are not effectiveness-focused enough," and 72 percent of CEOs agreed with the statement that marketers "are always asking for money but can rarely explain how much incremental business this money will generate."[25]

Growth hacking empowers companies to achieve breakout growth without pouring money into outdated and horribly expensive marketing campaigns of questionable business value. Devising features that get consumers to love a product or service and spread the word to their friends, and creative hacks to reach customers in new, measurable ways, is taking the place of cash-guzzling marketing and ad plans, and the upside is enormous.

GETTING THE JUMP ON NEW TECHNOLOGY

The ways in which consumers discover new content and products are evolving at a dizzying pace. This reality is perfectly captured in the following graph of the rise and fall of digital marketing channels created by venture capitalist and growth expert James Currier. In a world where new online platforms are springing up (and disappearing) virtually overnight, early adoption of new technology and new online platforms is of vital importance for companies looking for a growth edge.

VIRAL CHANNEL EFFECTIVENESS

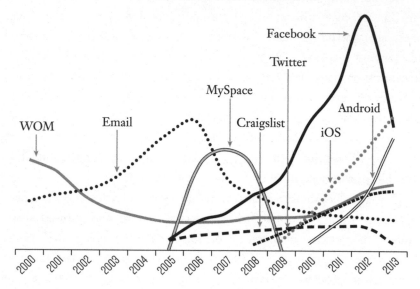

Seizing these opportunities requires tech and marketing teams to work closely together. Yet most companies are far too slow to adopt promising platforms, trapped by legacy planning, budgeting, and organizational norms. By the time they are ready to act, evanescent early advantages are long gone. And the pace of change is only accelerating.

MYTH BUSTING

Before we delve into what exactly a growth team is, and how to build one, we'd like to correct a number of misconceptions that exist about growth hacking. First, the process is not, as it's been misunderstood by some, about discovering one "silver bullet" solution. The press coverage of many of the widely celebrated growth hacks, such as the Dropbox customer referral program and Airbnb's integration into Craigslist, has encouraged this notion that one great hack is all you need to ignite growth. But while finding such big breakthrough ideas—like Dropbox's referral program—is absolutely a goal of the process, in truth, most growth is due to an accumulation of small wins. Like compounding interest in a savings account, these gains stack on top of one another to create liftoff. And the best growth teams continue to experiment with improvements even once growth takeoff has been achieved. Later in the book we'll profile how leading growth teams, such as those at Facebook, LinkedIn, Uber, Pinterest, and the team at Dropbox, continue to work furiously every day on generating, testing, and refining ideas for new growth hacks.

Second, many companies believe they can simply hire a single Lone Ranger to be *the* growth hacker, who will swoop in with a bag of magic tricks to bring growth to their business. This, too, is badly misguided. Throughout the book we show that, in reality, growth hacking is a team effort, that the greatest successes come from combining programming know-how with expertise in data analytics and strong marketing experience, and very few individuals are proficient in all of these skills.

Growth hacking is also too often thought to be all about devising clever work-arounds that break the rules of existing websites and social platforms. But despite what the well-publicized story of Airbnb's Craigslist hack would have you believe, flouting rules is by no means required and in fact plays no part in most growth success. That *was* a stroke of genius, but such "backdoor" tactics are not core to the method; and most growth professionals groan at the mention of the case. The real story in the Airbnb case is that they ran a host of experiments to find growth, most of which failed, before they came up with the Craigslist hack, and they have continued to grow the business through rigorous experimentation and testing with strategies that are completely aboveboard.

When I (Scan) coined the term *growth hacking* for the method, I did so in the broader and positive sense that it's now come to be understood—as in "hack space," "hackathon," and in the address of Facebook headquarters, 1 Hacker Way—meaning creative, collaborative idea generation and problem solving to thorny challenges that are the essential characteristics of growth hacking.

One final misconception must be addressed. Growth hacking is often characterized as being specifically about bringing in new users or customers. But in fact, growth teams are, and should be, tasked with much broader responsibilities. They should also work on *customer activation*, meaning making those customers more active users and buyers, and figuring out how to turn them into evangelists. In addition, growth teams should work on finding ways to *retain* and *monetize* customers—that is, both keeping them coming back and increasing the revenue generated from them—in order to sustain long-term growth. So often, too much effort is focused only on acquisition of new users and customers, who then, in so many cases, quickly disengage. Much too much dumb money is spent this way. For example, a 2012 *Econsultancy* report revealed that for every $92 spent on acquiring more Web traffic, only $1 was spent on converting those visitors into actual paying customers.[26] Customer disengagement and flight, known as *bounces* for website visitors, and *churn* for paying customers, are two of the biggest problems for start-ups and established firms alike and consequently represent some of the best immediate opportunities for growth.

Then there is the misconception that growth hacking is all about marketing. As we mentioned earlier, growth teams should also be involved in new product development, to analyze whether or not a product is optimized for its intended market—whether it's offering what we call a must-have experience, and whether it has figured out how to deliver that experience to the right customers, what is often referred to as achieving *product/market fit*. They should then work on generating a wealth of ideas for continuous product improvements, prioritizing which to try and implementing tests to see which are driving growth and revenue, and which are not. Growth teams may even be instrumental in the strategic development of the business. For example, at Facebook the growth team has steered the company toward strategic acquisitions to fuel growth, such as that of Octazen, which had developed services for importing users' contacts from whatever email they used. Indeed it was the Facebook growth team who initially recognized that Octazen's technology would make it easier for users to invite their contacts to the social network.[27]

In short, growth teams should be involved in all stages and all levers of growth, from attaining product/market fit to customer/user acquisition, activation, retention, and monetization. In the chapters that follow, we'll offer specific instruction on how.

HOW THE BOOK IS ORGANIZED

We have divided the book into two parts. The first, titled "The Method," offers a general introduction to the process, showing how to set up growth teams, who is needed on a team and what skills are required, how they should be managed, and how the high-tempo growth hacking process used by these teams creates the idea generation and testing that produce such quick and powerful results. We'll present the highly effective process I (Sean) and other growth team leaders have developed for facilitating smooth-running and cross-divisional collaboration to create growth, demystifying it and showing how easy it is to adapt to the specific needs of any business. In short, Part I details the method and makes the business case for implementing it.

The second part, titled "The Growth Hacking Playbook," offers a detailed set of tactics for how exactly to implement the method, with individual chapters on how to acquire, activate, retain, and monetize users or customers—and how to sustain and accelerate growth once it has been achieved. We will share stories demonstrating how growth teams from a wide variety of companies and industries—ranging from unicorn companies like Pinterest and Twitter, to consumer apps like Spotify and Evernote, to business software companies like HubSpot and Salesforce.com, to Web portals like Hotels.com and Zillow, to e-commerce retailers like Amazon and Etsy, to brick-and-mortar retailers like Walmart and a grocery chain—have used these various methods to drive growth. And we will also point readers to a set of online tools for teams to use, including GrowthHackers Projects, which enables growth teams to manage the growth process outlined in the first half of the book, as well as customer survey tools, templates for prioritizing hacks to try to keep track of results, guidelines for running growth meetings, and scores of testable experiments in each area of focus, continually updated by the GrowthHackers.com community.

Businesses of all shapes and sizes, in every industry and all around the globe, are struggling mightily to find ways to grow. Growth hacking provides a rigorous methodology for driving the discovery of opportunities through collaboration across functions and at a rapid-fire pace. It insists upon data-driven analysis and experimentation, providing the answer for how companies can systematically tap the power of the wealth of data they have invested so heavily in accumulating. As we'll demonstrate throughout the course of this book, businesses of all kinds can implement these strategies, whether they start small or decide to incorporate the method company-wide. Growth hacking is a new fundamental business methodology that all companies, and every founder, every corporate team leader, and every department head and CEO who wishes to meet high expectations, produce meaningful results, and achieve their business goals with limited investment and maximum return on their marketing dollars must adopt. In the coming pages we'll show you exactly how to do so.

PART I:
THE METHOD

CHAPTER ONE

BUILDING GROWTH TEAMS

When Pramod Sokke joined BitTorrent as the new senior director of product management in 2012, the once-red-hot start-up was at a crossroads. Growth of their popular desktop software, which lets users find and download files from all around the Web, had stalled. More worrisome was the fact that the company had no mobile version of the product—a huge disadvantage at a time where people were rapidly migrating away from their desktops to their smartphones. Making matters worse, YouTube, Netflix, and other streaming services were gobbling up users' time and attention both on their phones and across other devices, leaving BitTorrent behind. Pramod was brought in to build the mobile product and reignite growth.

The 50-person company was organized around the traditional silos of marketing, product management, engineering, and data science. The product team and engineers were divided up into subgroups dedicated to different products, such as the desktop versions for Mac and Windows, and now the newly minted mobile team. Both the data team and the marketing group served all of these product groups, and as is typical at all kinds of businesses, the process of product development was completely separated from marketing. The product managers would inform the marketers about upcoming launches or releases and all marketing efforts were then conducted by the marketing group—with no collaboration from those actually making the product.

THE CUSTOMER FUNNEL & TYPICAL DEPARTMENT OWNERSHIP

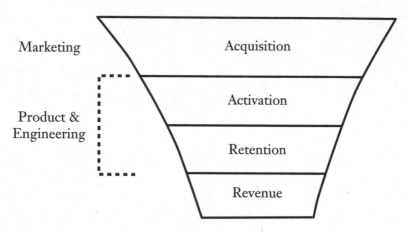

As is also typical for many companies, the BitTorrent marketing team was focused on efforts exclusively at the "top of the funnel" (depicted above), meaning raising customer awareness and bringing users to the products through branding, advertising, and digital marketing with the goal of acquiring new customers. At most software or Web-based companies, the work of increasing the activation and retention of those who've visited a website or app is done not by marketers but by the product and engineering teams, who focus on building features to make users fall in love with the products. The two groups rarely collaborate with each other, with each focused on their own priorities and often having little or no interaction. Sometimes they're not even located in the same building—or even the same country.

Per this standard organizational playbook, once the BitTorrent mobile app was ready for launch, the marketing group crafted a launch plan, which, as usual, included a range of traditional marketing activities, with an emphasis on social media, public relations, and paid customer acquisition campaigns. The app was solid, the plan was strong, and yet, adoption was still sluggish.

Pramod decided to ask the marketing group to hire a dedicated product marketing manager (PMM) to help stoke acquisitions. These marketing specialists are often described as being the "voice of the customer" inside the company, working to gain insights into customers' needs and desires, often conducting interviews, surveys, or focus groups, and helping to craft the messaging in order to make the marketing efforts more alluring and ensure they are conveying the value of the product most effectively. At some companies, these specialists might also be tasked with contributing to the product development, for example, by conducting competitive research to identify new features to consider, or assisting with product testing.

An experienced PMM, Annabell Satterfield, joined the BitTorrent marketing team to assist in boosting adoption of the newly minted mobile product. In addition to focusing on the awareness and acquisition efforts she was charged with, she requested that she be allowed to work with the product team on driving growth throughout the rest of the funnel, including user retention and monetization strategies, rather than being restricted to just efforts at the very top of the funnel. The head of marketing granted her permission to do so, but only after she first focused on user acquisition programs and only once they'd achieved their marketing team objectives.

Yet upon conducting some customer research—which included both customer surveys and analysis of the company's data on user behavior—in order to generate ideas for new marketing campaigns, she discovered something that seemed directly at odds with her boss's instructions: many of the best growth opportunities appeared to lie farther down the funnel. For example, she knew that many users of the mobile app, which was a free product, had not chosen to upgrade to a paid Pro version, so she conducted a survey to ask those who had not upgraded why that was. If the team could get more users to do so, she knew that would be a big revenue generator, which could be as important—if not more so—as getting more people to download the app. As the results rolled in, it became clear to her that the most promising strategy for growth wasn't to focus exclusively on building the company's customer base, but also on *making the most of the customers they already had.*

She took the insights she'd uncovered to the product team, thinking they could work together to find ways to improve the app. In doing so, she caught the product team a bit off guard; this was the first time a marketing person at the company had ever come to them with such input. But Pramod, who believed in a data-driven approach to product development, was impressed, and he quickly gave her free rein to continue mining the user research for product insights, and to keep communicating those insights across the divisional sand lines of the then-siloed company.

One of the discoveries from Annabell's surveying stunned the product team, and led to a rapid increase in revenue. The team had lots of theories about why many users hadn't upgraded to the paid, Pro version of the app, but the most frequent response to the question of why a customer hadn't purchased the paid version took them completely by surprise. The number one answer? The users had no idea there *was* a paid version. The team couldn't believe it. They thought they had been aggressively promoting the Pro version to those using the free app, but apparently they were missing the mark. Even their most active users hadn't noticed the attempts to get them to upgrade. So the team prioritized adding a highly visual button to the app's home screen encouraging users to upgrade, and, almost incredibly, that one simple change resulted in an instant 92 percent increase in revenue per day from upgrades. It cost virtually nothing, took virtually no time to execute (the time from the discussion of the survey data to deployment of the button was just days), and resulted in immediate, significant gains. And all from an idea they likely would never have come up with if not for the input and feedback from their customers.

Another success came from what Annabell and Pramod called their "love hack." Looking into user data to try to identify the drivers of increases and decreases in the number of downloads of the app day to day, Annabell noticed a clear pattern. The app was only available from the Google Play store, and she noticed that whenever the first several reviews of the app in the store were negative, the daily installs of the app would dip. She experimented with pushing up positive reviews into those top positions, and found that it instantly improved the number of installs. So she and Pramod decided to encourage users to write reviews, right after they had downloaded their first torrent, when they had seen how easy the app was to use. They expected that this would be a moment when users would be most happy with the app and most inclined to write a favorable review, if asked. They ran an experiment to test the hypothesis, having the engineers program a request that would pop onto the user's screen right after the first torrent was downloaded. Sure enough, positive reviews came flooding in. They went ahead and deployed the prompt to all new users based on the initial strong results, and that led to a 900 percent increase in four- and five-star reviews, followed by a huge boost of installs. Her credibility officially established, it wasn't long before one engineer came to her and said, "Do you have any more ideas? What else can we do?"

This kind of collaboration between marketing and product teams is woefully uncommon. Generally, the product team is in charge of the process of building the product, as well as of making updates, such as improving the sign-up experience or adding a new feature, and the team establishes a schedule, commonly referred to as a roadmap, for making those improvements. Often, ideas for changes that aren't part of the preestablished roadmap are met with resistance. Sometimes it's because timing is already tight for making the planned enhancements, and sometimes because the changes being asked for are poorly conceived, much more difficult, time-consuming, and therefore costly, to enact than the person making the requests is aware of. Yet other times the product team might also determine that a request isn't aligned with the strategic vision for the product (or some combination of all these factors and others).

Even if you don't work for a tech company, you may be familiar with this kind of tension between departments, maybe with marketing teams pushing back on suggestions from sales, or the R&D team resisting a request to build a prototype for a new product that marketing has recommended. This is one of the chief problems with the practice of siloing responsibilities by departments, and it's primarily why, as you'll learn more about in a minute, growth teams must necessarily include members across a range of specialties and departments. As the BitTorrent team soon realized, often the best ideas come from this type of cross-functional collaboration, which, again, is why it's a fundamental feature of the growth hacking process.

SILOS BREACHED AT LAST

Buoyed by the successes they were seeing, everyone on the BitTorrent mobile team eagerly began brainstorming about more hacks to try. One hack they tested could only have been thought up by a bona fide techie: stopping the app automatically to save the phone's battery life. The team discovered this opportunity through another survey targeted specifically at the power users of the free app—ones who were using it all the time but who had yet to upgrade to the paid Pro version. The survey revealed that these users had a major pain point around the drain of the phone's battery power from their heavy use of the app. So the engineers quickly proposed they build a feature for just the Pro version, one that would turn off battery-draining background file transfers when the app detected that the user's battery had less than 35 percent charge remaining. They cleverly promoted the feature in the app to free users when their phone battery started to dwindle, enticing them to upgrade on the spot. The feature proved so popular that it resulted in a 47 percent increase in revenue.

This string of hits didn't go unnoticed around the rest of the company. For one thing, Annabell was officially moved from marketing to the mobile team, reporting to Pramod, and eventually her title was changed to Senior Product Manager for Growth. At the same time, other engineers working on other projects were fascinated by how the team continued to churn out big wins, leading two of the more senior engineers on other product teams to leave their posts just for the chance of working on a high-performing, growth-oriented team. Annabell explains that "[f]rom speaking to our engineers this was because, besides the fact that we seemed to be having fun and enjoying each other so much, they saw us as 'doing things right,' being 'data-driven.'"

As the team continued to hack their way to growth, they leaned more and more heavily on data analysis (provided by a member of the data group), to both set up and evaluate the results of their experiments. The data analyst worked with the engineers to ensure that they were tracking the *right* data about customers' response to their experiments—and providing the most useful reports on that information as it rolled in. The analyst had the expertise to know when they had enough data to call the experiments either winners or losers, and worked with the team to review results and to help plot their next steps for follow-up experiments. The team relied so heavily on the analysis that eventually the analyst was also moved over full-time to the team, just as Annabell had been.

The success of this data-driven approach to growth and product development prompted the BitTorrent executives to invest more heavily in data science and staff up its analytics team. At the same time, word of how the mobile team was growing prompted other product teams to start tapping the data analysts more frequently, and collaborate with them more closely to develop experiments and insights of their own.

The mobile team went on to discover dozens of other high-impact improvements that rocketed the product to 100 million installs through its two and a half years of rapid-fire growth hacking. With that mission accomplished, the team was reorganized and put to work on other company product priorities. It's hard to understate the impact that this small team had on the previously growth-challenged company. It wasn't just that their efforts boosted their teams' revenue by 300 percent in a single year, but also, and perhaps more important, that the team fundamentally altered the culture at BitTorrent from one constricted by traditional marketing and product silos to an open and collaborative one in which everyone, from marketers, to data analysts, to engineers and executives, was aligned around the fast-paced, collaborative growth hacking process. Annabell fondly recalls how faith in the growth process rippled out across the organization, describing how "two of my favorite moments were seeing our old tech lead present a growth experiment at Palooza [which is BitTorrent's term for regular hackathons it holds], and meeting with an old engineering colleague who wanted to dive into the process with me. He's an ambassador for the approach now."

This collaborative approach is unfortunately the exception, rather than the rule, at companies of all types and sizes. The all too common practice of siloing business units into isolated groups that rarely talk, share information, or, God forbid, actually collaborate, has been a widely acknowledged organizational Achilles' heel at many companies for many years. As highlighted by a McKinsey report, one of the most damaging effects of departmental silos is that they slow innovation that drives growth. But while, as the authors explain, "research shows that the ability to collaborate in networks is more important than raw individual talent to innovativeness," a survey McKinsey conducted found that "only 25 percent of senior executives would describe their organizations as effective at sharing knowledge across boundaries, even though nearly 80 percent acknowledged such coordination was crucial to growth."[1]

Similarly, a team of Harvard Business School professors who conducted a study of communication across business units reported that they were "taken aback" by how little interaction there was among units they uncovered. Even more shocking: they reported that "two people who are in the same SBU [strategic business unit], function, and office interact about 1,000 times more frequently than two people at the company who are in different business units, functions, and offices, but are otherwise similar. Practically speaking, this means that there is very little interaction across these boundaries."[2]

One specialist on the silo problem, Professor Ranjay Gulati of Northwestern University's Kellogg School of Management, notes that this lack of cross-departmental communication impedes efforts to make product development and marketing more customer focused—an increasingly important mandate as technology and social media facilitate, even demand, ever more substantive and continuous interaction with customers. Put simply, engineers and product designers are quite capable of coming up with marvelous ways to satisfy customers' needs and desires, but they most often are simply not privy to what those needs and desires are. Gulati reports that in a survey of executives he conducted, over two-thirds of them identified the need to make product development more customer-centric as a priority in the coming decade, but he also writes that his research shows that companies' "knowledge and expertise are housed within organizational silos, and they have trouble harnessing their resources across those internal boundaries in a way that customers truly value and are willing to pay for."[3]

Creating cross-functional growth teams is a way to break down these barriers. Cross-functional teams not only smooth and accelerate collaboration between the product, engineering, data, and marketing groups, they motivate team members to appreciate and learn more about the perspectives of the others and the work they do. So how, exactly, does one set up a growth team to meet the strategic needs and priorities of a specific project or initiative? We'll address the key steps in the pages that follow.

THE WHO

Growth teams should bring together staff who have a deep understanding of the strategy and business goals, those with the expertise to conduct data analysis, and those with the engineering chops to implement changes in the design, functionality, or marketing of the product and program experiments to test those changes. Of course, the specific makeup of growth teams varies from company to company and product to product. The size of teams also varies widely, as does how narrow or broad-ranging the scope of their work is. They can be as small as four or five members or as large as one hundred or more, as is true at LinkedIn. Regardless of size, the personnel they comprise should include many, if not all, of the following roles.

THE GROWTH LEAD

In every case, a growth team needs a leader, who is like a battalion commander, with her boots on the ground, both managing the team and participating actively in the idea generation and experimentation process. The growth lead sets the course for experimentation as well as the tempo of experiments to be run, and monitors whether or not the team is meeting their goals. Growth teams should generally convene once a week, and the growth lead should run those meetings (which we'll offer guidance on how to do shortly).

Regardless of specialty or background, he or she plays a role that is part manager, part product owner, and part scientist. A key responsibility for the growth lead is choosing the core focus area and objectives for the team to work on and for what period of time. As we'll explore more fully in subsequent chapters, focusing experiments on a main goal is vital to optimizing results. A growth lead might establish a monthly, quarterly, or even annual focus area, such as to get more users to upgrade from a free version of a product to a premium version, or to determine which would be the best new marketing channel for a product. The growth lead then ensures that the team is not derailed by pursuing ideas that don't contribute to their stated goal, tabling those for when the focus changes and those ideas will serve the new objective.

The growth lead also ensures that the specific metrics the team has chosen to measure and work to improve are appropriate to the growth goals established. Often, marketing and product teams are not systematically tracking data on key user behavior that can lead to discoveries of improvements to make or can be early warning signals that users are becoming less active or defecting from the product altogether. Too many companies focus lots of attention on vanity metrics that might look good on paper (like number of eyeballs to a website), but ultimately do not indicate actual growth, whether in product use or revenue generated. We go into detail about how to choose the right metrics to measure in Chapter Three.

All growth leads require a basic set of skills: fluency in data analysis; expertise or fluency in product management (meaning the process of developing and launching a product); and an understanding of how to design and run experiments. Every lead must also have familiarity with the methods for growing adoption and use of the type of product or service the team is working on. A social network, for example, should have a growth lead who understands the dynamics of viral word of mouth and of network effects—that is, how the value of the network keeps improving as more people join it—which are key mechanisms by which many (though of course not all) social products grow. He or she should also have the relevant industry or product expertise: a growth lead for an online retailer, for example, should have a keen grasp on shopping cart optimization, merchandising, and pricing and marketing strategy. Strong leadership skills are also needed to keep a team focused and to push to accelerate the tempo of experimentation moving forward, even in the face of the (entirely to be expected) regular failure of growth experiments. Dead ends, inconclusive tests, and abject duds are a part of the reality of growth experimentation. A strong growth lead keeps enthusiasm going, while providing air cover for the team to be experimental and fail without undue scrutiny and pressure from management to deliver more wins.

There is no one best career background for a growth lead. Some people are now specializing in the role, most of whom have moved into the job from some other area of specialty, such as engineering, product management, data science, or marketing. People with expertise in each of these areas are good candidates for the role, because they each bring strengths key to the growth hacking process. For start-ups, especially in the early stage of growth, often the founder should play the role of growth lead. Or, if not to run the team, the founder should appoint the growth lead and make him or her a direct report. At larger companies, which may have one growth team or multiple teams, the growth leads should be appointed by an executive with authority over the work of the team, to whom the growth lead should report.

The role may sound daunting, and simply too much for one person to manage, but with the tools and formal methods for prioritizing experiments, tracking, and sharing results that we will introduce in the following chapters, the process can be managed with great efficiency.

PRODUCT MANAGER

The ways in which businesses organize product development teams vary, and this will affect the personnel who are assigned to work on a growth team, and may also determine how the team fits into the organizational structure of a company, which we'll discuss more later in the chapter. In general product managers oversee how the product and its various features are brought to life. As venture capitalist Ben Horowitz put it simply, "A good product manager is the CEO of the product."[4]

In most types of company, the role is well suited to assisting in the growth hacking mission of breaking down the silos between departments and identifying good candidates in engineering and marketing to help start the growth team. This is in large part because product managers' experience with customer surveying and interviewing, as well as with product development, allows them to make vital contributions to the idea generation and experimentation process. If you have this role at your company, this person should absolutely be on your growth team.

Depending on the size of a company, the functions of product management may be filled by other staff, and at start-ups, especially in the early stages of growth, the role may be played by the founder. But at larger companies, there may be multiple levels of staff within product management, from product manager, director of product management, VP of product management, or chief product officer. The level of product management staff appointed to a growth team can vary, but as we'll discuss more fully in a moment, at many software companies, the product manager who oversees the particular product that a growth team is formed to work on should be assigned to the team and reports to the head of the product group, often a VP of product management.

SOFTWARE ENGINEERS

The people who write the code for the product features, mobile screens, and webpages that teams experiment with making changes to are cornerstone members of a growth team. Yet all too often they are left out of the ideation process as companies work to plan new products and features, or are relegated to simply taking orders, implementing whatever product and business teams have come up with. Not only does this sap morale of some of your most highly skilled and precious staff, it also stunts the ideation process by failing to tap into the creativity engineers can bring as well as their expertise about new technologies that might drive growth. Recall that at BitTorrent, the engineers were invaluable in recommending the development of the lucrative battery saver feature. The very essence of growth hacking is the hacker spirit that emerged out of software development and design of solving problems with novel engineering approaches. Growth teams simply don't work without software engineers being a part of them.

MARKETING SPECIALISTS

While we should be clear that some growth teams operate without a dedicated member who is a marketing professional, we advocate including a marketing specialist for optimal results. The cross-pollination of expertise between engineering and marketing can be particularly fruitful in generating ideas for hacks to try. The type of marketing expertise the team needs may vary depending on the type of company or product. For example, a content growth team, working to build readership, would clearly benefit from having a content marketing specialist onboard. For example, at Inman News, a trade journal for real estate professionals, where Morgan is COO, the growth team includes the email marketing director, because the company's growth is heavily reliant on email as a channel for acquiring, monetizing, and retaining customers. Other companies may rely heavily on search engine optimization and elect to have a specialist in that field on the team. Teams might also include several marketing specialists to cover a wide range of expertise. Marketers can also be brought in for stints focusing on an area of their expertise and then leave the growth team once the goal is achieved.

DATA ANALYSTS

Understanding how to collect, organize, and then perform sophisticated analysis on customer data to gain insights that lead to ideas for experiments, is another of the cornerstone requirements for teams. A growth team might not include an analyst as a full-time member, but rather have an analyst assigned to it who collaborates with the team but performs other work for the company as well. That was the case in the beginning for the BitTorrent team. But if a company can afford to appoint an analyst full-time to the team, that's ideal.

A team's data representative needs to understand how to design experiments in a rigorous and statistically valid way; how to access your various customer and business data sources and connect them to one another in order to draw insights into user behavior; and how to quickly compile the results of experiments and provide insights into them. Depending on the degree of sophistication of the experiments a team is running, it might be possible for the marketing or engineering team member to play this role, as in both of those fields, a certain level of data analytics aptitude has become important. At more technically advanced companies, analysts with expertise in reporting of experiments as well as data scientists, who are mining for deep insight, should both play a role.

What is essential is that data analysis not be farmed out to the intern who knows how to use Google Analytics or to a digital agency, to cite extreme but all too frequent realities. As we will discuss in detail coming up in Chapter Three, too many companies do not place enough emphasis on data analysis, and rely too heavily on prepackaged programs, such as

Google Analytics, with limited capacity for combining various pools of data, such as from sales and from customer service, and limited ability to delve into that data to make discoveries. A standout data analyst can make the difference between a growth team squandering its time and mining data gold.

PRODUCT DESIGNERS

Here again the job titles and specific functions vary according to the type of business. In software development, the specialty field of user experience designer is responsible for developing the screens and sequences that users experience with the software. For manufactured goods, this designer might be responsible for the product drawings and specifications, while at other companies, designers might be chiefly involved in graphic design of advertisements and promotions. Having design experience on a team often improves the speed of execution of experiments, because the team has a dedicated staff person to immediately produce whatever design work may be involved. User experience designers can also offer important insight into user psychology, interface design, and user research techniques that can help to generate great ideas for testing.

THE SIZE AND SCOPE

At start-ups and small established companies, a growth team might comprise only one staff member in each of the abovementioned areas, or even just a few people, each of whom takes charge of more than one of these roles. At large companies, growth teams may include many engineers, marketers, data analysts, and designers. The composition of growth teams and the mandates they are charged with must be tailored to your company: its size, its organizational structure, and its specific challenges and priorities. The scope of a growth team's work might also be quite general, such as to work on growing all areas of the business, or highly specific, such as to oversee improvement of a specific part of the product, such as the shopping cart feature. Some growth teams are permanent fixtures, like those at Zillow and Twitter, and others are formed for specific tasks, such as a product launch, and are disbanded after goals are achieved. Some companies have created multiple growth teams with different areas of focus, such as at LinkedIn and Pinterest, which has four teams dedicated to new user acquisition, viral growth, engagement of users, and activation of newly acquired users. Other companies have just a single growth organization responsible for many initiatives, such as at Facebook and Uber.

If you're just starting to form a growth team, then bringing over one or two individuals from different departments to get the team started may be a good way to get the ball rolling, and the size of the team can grow over time. In some cases, as the process is learned, additional teams can be formed. At IBM, for example, a growth team was formed to work specifically on growing the adoption of its Bluemix DevOps product, a software development package for engineers, by assigning five engineers and five other staff, from business operations and marketing, to make up the team. At Inman, Morgan comprised his growth team of a data scientist, three marketers, and their Web developer to start the growth hacking process. Morgan is also the head of product development, and he fills the spot for product management on the team. As COO he is also the highest-ranking executive on the team, but he is not the growth lead. Rather a marketing manager runs the process, and Morgan plays a contributing and guiding role.

THE HOW

Once you've chosen your team members, what, exactly, should they do? The growth hacking process provides a specific set of activities that growth teams should undertake to find new, and amplify existing, growth opportunities through rapid experimentation to find the top performers. The process is a continuous cycle comprising four key steps: (1) data analysis and insight gathering; (2) idea generation; (3) experiment prioritization; and (4) running the experiments, and then circles back to the analyze step to review results and decide the next steps. At this stage the team will look for early winners and invest further in areas of promise, while quickly abandoning those that show lackluster results. By continuing to move through the process, the growth team will compound wins big and small over time, creating a virtuous cycle of ever improved results.

THE GROWTH HACKING PROCESS

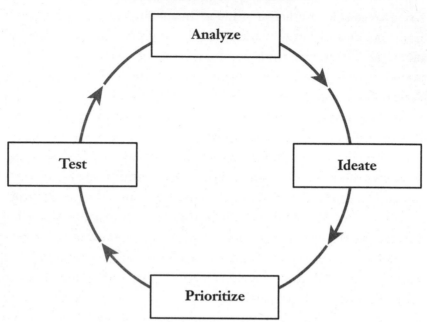

The team keeps the process on track by coming together for a regular growth meeting. Team meetings, which should generally be held once a week, provide a rigorous forum for managing the team's testing activity, reviewing results, and determining which hacks to try next. The standing meeting practice, which is a well-established part of the agile software development method, can be easily adapted for growth hacking. Much like in agile software development, where the team uses sprint planning meetings to organize their upcoming work, growth meetings allow the growth team to similarly review progress to date, prioritize experiments to try, and maintain their experiment velocity.

During the meeting, ideas identified for experiments are assigned to various team members to take charge of implementing, analyzing, or researching to garner more information about whether an idea is worth trying. The team lead stays in regular communication with each team member in between meetings, checking in on the progress of their work and helping to deal with any problems or delays that might come up.

This weekly meeting keeps the team on track and focused, and ensures the high level of coordination and communication required to keep up the high-speed nature of the process; think of it speeding along like a Formula One racing car making precision adjustments, in contrast to a runaway truck whose brakes have gone out. In addition, the deeply collaborative nature of the meeting leads to a 1+1=3 dynamic, where the expertise of the various members is amplified to turn promising ideas into powerhouse winners and often generate unpredictable ideas that team members couldn't possibly have come up with on their own.

So, for example, an in-depth analysis of customer churn (meaning identifying those who recently abandoned the product) might reveal that the people who are defecting haven't made use of a particular feature of the product that is popular with avid users. That discovery might lead the team to experiment with ways to get more people to try that specific feature out. Or take another example from the work of our growth team at GrowthHackers.com. In looking at our user data, we found that content submitted by the community that included rich media (such as presentation decks from conferences and videos from YouTube) sparked greater engagement and led to more repeat visits from viewers than posts that simply link to stories elsewhere on the Web. So growth team members came up with a series of ideas for adding more rich media items, such as podcasts and videos, to the site. This course of action seemed obvious and predictable enough; that is, until the engineer on the team chimed in to explain that not only could we support many, many more types of media on the site with a simple plug-in, but that we could also build in code to automatically recognize links from popular media sites like YouTube, SoundCloud, and SlideShare and instantly embed that content into the discussion pages on the website. Rather than simply adding video from one or two additional media sources, we were now able to support more than a dozen, while making the process for adding that media to GrowthHackers dramatically easier. After this discovery, one that likely would not have been made without the input of the engineer in the group, the experiment was redesigned and it proved even more powerful in growing the community than we had initially expected. We will introduce specific procedures for running meetings for the greatest efficiency in Chapter Four, including a recommended meeting agenda.

WHO DOES WHAT

In terms of the tasks that team members are charged with, team members will still take on specialty tasks according to their area of expertise, sometimes working independently at least at first. For example, the engineers will take charge of any coding needed for an experiment; the designer will craft any design elements needed; the data analyst will work on selecting the sets of users with whom a change will be tested; and the marketing member will take charge of implementing any experiments with promotional channels, such as with a new Facebook ad campaign. If there is a user experience designer on the team, that person might be charged with collecting and evaluating user feedback about the types of features they find most valuable, and bringing that qualitative information back to the team. That research might lead to an idea for a change to a feature or to a new feature to experiment with. An engineer might be asked to program a change to the shopping cart page if research indicates that users are finding it difficult to navigate, as an example.

Yet other initiatives will require close collaboration among all team members, such as the creation of a new product feature, which should involve cross-functional agreement about how it will be designed and implemented, how it will be messaged or delivered to customers, and how its success will be measured. For example, the team responsible for a business mobile app may decide that an improvement in the rate at which new users become regular, successful customers is their key priority, and they might decide that an experiment consisting of a substantial redesign of the first several screens that greet users and the messaging on those should be conducted.

Throughout the rest of the book we'll describe specific experiments conducted by actual growth teams, and we will introduce tools for keeping track of the results and establishing priorities for which experiments to run, as well as for designating the follow-up steps to take once experiment results are in hand.

EXECUTIVE SPONSORSHIP REQUIRED

Growth teams must be worked into the organizational reporting structure of a company with total clarity about to whom the growth lead reports. It is imperative that a high-level executive is given responsibility for the team, in order to assure that the team has the authority to cross the bounds of the established departmental responsibilities. Growth cannot be a side project. Without clear and forceful commitment from leadership, growth teams will find themselves battling bureaucracy, turf wars, inefficiency, and inertia. At start-ups, if the founder or CEO isn't personally leading the growth efforts directly, then the team or teams should report directly to him or her. In larger companies, which may have multiple growth teams, the teams should report to a vice president or C-level executive who can champion their work with the rest of the C-suite. Support for these methods at the highest rungs of the organization is critical to the team's sustained success.

Mark Zuckerberg is an outstanding model of the leadership required. He was relentlessly focused on growth in the early days of Facebook, and his enthusiasm hasn't waned since. In 2005, two years before Facebook formally established the growth team, Noah Kagan, a digital marketer who was employee number 30, brought a revenue generating idea to Zuckerberg. Kagan was concerned that the social network needed to prove to investors that it could make serious money. Standing in a company conference room, Zuckerberg stopped Kagan mid-pitch, stood up, picked up a marker, and wrote on the whiteboard in big letters one word, "Growth." He would not entertain any ideas outside of growing the total number of users on Facebook. His crystal clear prioritization of growth over all other business concerns—even revenue—in the early days was the linchpin of Facebook's incredible success.[5]

Even today, as the company invests in future technologies such as virtual reality and artificial intelligence, the understanding is crystal clear that the health of its core customer base is what creates the opportunity to invest in the future. As Mike Schroepfer, Facebook's CTO, told *Fast Company:* "I have one hand in the day-to-day and one hand in the future. It's a little bit crazy-making at times, but it's important that our core business continues to do well. Because that is what allows us to aggressively invest in these longer-term things."[6]

Another founder who has been a fervent champion of the growth process is Spencer Rascoff, CEO of Zillow, the world's largest real estate site. Nate Moch, employee number 40, who is now the Vice President of Product Teams, recalls that Rascoff and his executive team made growth a priority from day one, and as the company has grown, Zillow has built a dedicated team around Moch to ensure that the company is constantly keeping its sights on sustaining that growth. Moch's team works in a similar fashion to Facebook's, focusing on the core company KPIs and working with other product teams to drive customer acquisition and retention and hit their respective business goals.

Rascoff has rallied the whole company around the growth mission by establishing a focus for growth efforts that he calls Zillow's "Play," a recurring nine-to-twelve-month growth initiative that the entire company aligns around. In 2008, for example, the company realized that it was losing traffic to a rival upstart, Trulia, largely due to Trulia's smart use of search engine optimization to rank its home listing data higher than Zillow's in Google search results. So the Zillow executive team decided that SEO would be that year's Play, and every team in the company was mandated to make becoming world class at search a priority. This involved a major cultural shift, as the company had previously ignored SEO in favor of other tactics. But in the end every team managed to find ways to improve their SEO efforts, and as a result Zillow was able to catch and surpass Trulia, ultimately buying the competitor in 2015 for $3 billion.[7]

THE REPORTING STRUCTURES FOR TEAMS

There are two common reporting structures for growth teams, as a survey of Silicon Valley firms by researchers Andrew McInnes and Daisuke Miyoshi revealed.[8] The first, which McInnes and Miyoshi call the functional (or product-led) model, is to create teams that report to a product management executive, in charge of the product or set of products that the growth team will be working on.

THE PRODUCT-LED MODEL

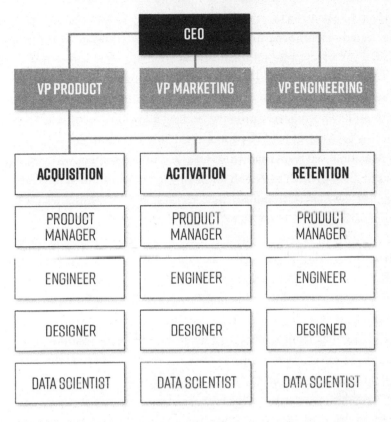

A product-led team, for example, might be dedicated entirely to growing the user base for the company's mobile app, while another might be assigned to helping to drive readers of an online news service to upgrade to a paid subscription. In some cases the mandate of teams dedicated to a particular product will be limited to improving the performance of one aspect of the product, such as activating new users of an online learning software by optimizing the *onboarding process*, the term for orienting new users on how to use a product. At Pinterest, John Egan runs a growth team that is dedicated entirely to testing the frequency, content, and calls to action in the email messages and mobile push notifications aimed at getting users to come back more frequently. That scope might sound impossibly narrow, but this intense focus allows the team to really drill down on a key component of the company's growth. For example, in one of their recent growth efforts, the team built Copytune, a highly sophisticated machine learning algorithm, which allowed them to rapidly test dozens of variants of notifications sent to users, across more than 30 languages, and have the software pick winning versions and tee up subsequent tests in search of even better performance. The results of the program have been extraordinary, adding additional people to the site's monthly active user (MAU, pronounced "mao") count.[9]

A product-led team might also be asked to experiment with a range of ways to drive growth across all levels of the growth funnel, from attracting more customers, to improving retention, to increasing the amount of revenue being made from them.

Typically in organizations that use this model, each product manager runs a small product team that includes engineers, user experience designers, and data analysts, and it's not uncommon for a product group to have a handful of such small teams. This model is easier to implement in an established firm or a later stage start-up because it fits into the already existing management structure. This not only means that less reorganization is required, but it helps to mitigate friction in scheduling growth experiments into the existing roadmap for testing product features in development.

In addition to Pinterest, companies that follow this model include LinkedIn, Twitter, and Dropbox.

The other structure is that of a stand-alone team—so not part of an existing product development team—with the growth team lead reporting to a VP of growth, who typically reports directly to senior management, such as the CEO or other executive leader. The VP of growth role itself is often created to assure that an executive level employee has ownership of the team's results, such as at Uber and Facebook. In contrast to product-led teams' specific dedication to a particular product, independent teams have the authority to conduct experiments across the full range of the company's products, and even to look for strategic opportunities for growth outside of the scope of the current product lineup. An example of the latter is the Facebook growth team's role in advising the company to purchase Octazen once the team recognized that Octazen's technology would help the performance of the social network's friend referral product. And in fact the Facebook growth team has worked on an incredibly broad range of growth initiatives, from helping to optimize existing products and features, such as improving the sign-up flow for new users, to even building some of its own products, such as Facebook Lite, which was designed to run on a globe with poor data connectivity. The team has also provided support to product teams, acting as both an internal analyst group and a SWAT team that can parachute in to help identify optimization and growth opportunities and show them how to deploy the growth experimentation process.

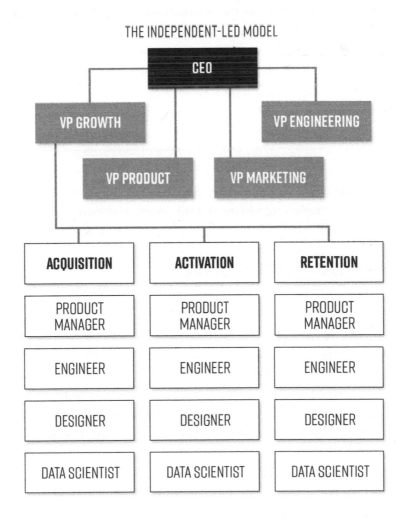

THE INDEPENDENT-LED MODEL

Independent teams are most easily established early in a company's development before corporate structures have crystallized and ownership battles over resources and reporting formalize. When the turf isn't yet claimed, there are fewer complaints against redistributing responsibility and headcount to a growth team. That said, it's not impossible to introduce independent growth teams in established, larger companies. One approach is that taken by Walmart, which created its stand-alone growth operation in 2011 by acquiring an innovation center in the well-regarded Silicon Valley start-up Kosmix, which became @WalmartLabs.[10] Run as an independent division focused on e-commerce, this team focuses on digital innovation initiatives for Walmart websites and mobile applications, like the successful Savings Catcher app we described in the introduction. It also leads the acquisition of promising digital start-ups, such as mobile fashion search app Stylr, and social recipe aggregator Yumprint, and works to integrate their technology and talent into Walmart's digital offerings.

It's important to emphasize that even when teams are given independent authority, they need the strong backing of top management in order to navigate the internal sensitivities and frictions that can arise between product, marketing, design, and engineering specialists who have their own notions of what's important and the "right way" to do things.

MELDING MINDS AND DISMISSING LORE

It's not unusual for someone setting up a growth team for the first time within a company to encounter some initial resistance. For most companies—the exception being the earliest stage start-ups where organizational silos and norms have yet to crystallize—setting up a growth team, or set of teams, will involve either a significant realignment of personnel and reporting structures or a rededication of some of people's time and shifting of their responsibilities, either in an ongoing capacity or for the duration of a specific growth mission. As anyone who's worked in any kind of organization knows, making such changes can be quite a challenge, for a few reasons.

At their heart, most of these sources of friction are cultural. Many people in marketing, product development, and software engineering have preconceived notions about the ownership of initiatives: what teams are "supposed" to do—and how they are supposed to do it. At BitTorrent, marketing's original intent was to concentrate solely on user acquisition. Data analysis was done by the company's data team, specifically at the request of the product teams, and experimentation had no home and had mostly fallen by the wayside. So when the growth team came in and knocked down these divisional silos, it took some adjustment.

Stories of such friction caused in the process of establishing growth teams abound. After Josh Schwarzapel joined Yahoo! to create and lead a growth team tasked with growing the company's mobile products, he recalls that when his team began running experiments to promote Yahoo!'s apps to visitors, they got pushback from the brand team because they had departed from the established style and voice guidelines in some of their experimental messaging. The product managers were also leery because of the broad reach and implications of what the growth team was building; their messaging would be seen by every single person who came to the Yahoo! site on a mobile device. Overcoming this resistance required lots of cross-team collaboration and trust building. "We had to do a lot of work to get support from the partner teams," he recounts.[11]

Another source of friction is the fact that growth experiments—and the resources needed to pull them off—can interfere with, or come at the expense of, time or resources needed to deliver on already established projects and priorities. For example, some friction was created at BitTorrent when Annabell's work designing tests and analyzing results took her time away from more immediate acquisition efforts. In addition, as the data demands from the team increased, strain on the resources of the data team became an issue until the executive team decided to expand the data analytics group.

A final cause of potential strife lies in the fact that when you bring together people from such a diverse range of fields and backgrounds, there are almost certain to be differing and sometimes conflicting perspectives and priorities. Engineers tend to be most interested in working on the most technically challenging jobs, whether or not the solutions they come up with will have a meaningful impact on growth. Product managers are typically obsessed with product development and launches and can be infuriated by marketing and sales teams making last-minute requests for changes with poor business rationales. User experience designers often resist the introduction of experimental features for testing because they don't want to upset happy users with annoyances. Marketers can become focused on vanity metrics such as the number of website visitors or leads and lose sight of the need to drive up the performance indicators in other parts of the funnel (such as user retention).

Moreover, these perspectives tend to be deeply ingrained among members of each of these groups, not only in terms of the design of organizations, but also in people's training for their jobs as well as in their individual psychologies and the incentives that drive them. Thus even at early stage start-ups, getting people to work collaboratively across these specialties can be a mighty challenge.

Growth teams can ease these tensions if they are managed correctly and if the whole team is incentivized, and rewarded, for achieving shared goals that create meaningful results for the company. Another way to mitigate conflict is to ensure that the decisions about which growth hacks to prioritize (and the evaluation of how successful they are) are made strictly on the basis of hard data rather than assumptions, or what Chamath Palihapitiya, the original leader of the Facebook growth team, calls the "lore" that holds sway about how products should be designed or what customers want. Every company, large or small, has entrenched lore that should be blasted away by data-driven experimentation. At Qualaroo, for example, growth was held back for a time by company lore that maintained we couldn't raise our prices and still succeed. Yet when we conducted pricing tests, the data showed that we could raise prices by more than 400 percent and still grow by attracting a new type of clientele.

When data analysis provides a strong rationale for trying a hack, dissent is much easier to counter. The results of well-crafted experiments are also extremely difficult to disagree with, which helps to defang the emotional commitment people often feel to their particular vision or strategy. And when experimentation is data driven, team members also generally respect the rigor of the learning process and appreciate the latitude it gives them to rack up a string of failures in order to achieve a win.

Finally, few things are more effective for squashing conflict and dissent than success. Many growth team members have described how enthusiasm for the method built not only within their teams but all around their companies as they began to see the method working, and leading to impressive gains.

TEAMS EVOLVE

As companies grow and evolve, so should their growth teams. At Facebook, the growth team has exploded from its early days of five people to a now sprawling unit with multiple focus points such as international and emerging markets phone units.

The composition and focus of growth teams will generally change over time as well, as the company develops and brings on more staff. When this happens, growth teams might add more people from specific departments, create new departments, or spin off into separate teams to focus on more specific growth initiatives in various parts of the business, as the Pinterest growth team did when it evolved from one independent team into the four subteams within the product group that are now focused on different parts of the user experience.[12] At Twitter, Josh Elman's initial onboarding team morphed into a larger growth team with greater responsibility for growth beyond just new user activation.[13] Other specialists can also be pulled in to provide expertise in a specific area, whether permanent members from within the company, or temporary ones through outside consultants or agencies. Retaining, and even continuing to grow the team or teams as the company scales, assures that the fixation on growth stays in its DNA. Even the most inspired products and ideas can, and often do, stall out and ultimately crash and burn due to the failure to continuously improve them. Growth teams are the best hedge against this painful potential outcome.

For early stage start-ups, for whom growth teams will almost certainly be small, bringing in outside experts who are specialists in one area of user growth (such as acquisition or retention) to add bench strength to the team can pay big dividends, as Dropbox found in hiring Sean. Such small growth teams can reap great rewards by combining their deep internal knowledge of the product and company with external expertise. One cautionary note is that it's vital not to outsource the core responsibility for growth, at this or any stage. The fact is, growth is too important to delegate, and consultants often lack the organizational authority, time, or intrinsic motivation to get the hard work done that results in sustainable growth.

A GROWTH HACK TO START GROWTH HACKING

Implementing the growth hacking process can seem daunting. Creating a cross-functional team can be tricky, as managers of groups may push back about rededicating the time of some of their staff. The notion of so much experimenting can also be uncomfortable for people. Inevitably, there will be naysayers and resisters. The good news is that there is also a virtuous growth cycle in the adoption of growth hacking. A small team with a narrow focus that begins running the growth hacking process and generates a series of wins can spark growing enthusiasm for the process around a company. Once people see the power of the data-driven approach to experimentation—and the growth ideas that come out of it—enthusiasm for the process tends to be infectious.

Implementing growth hacking across a company or even a department won't happen overnight; so think about starting with a team working on just one product, and perhaps even just one important aspect of how it is being adopted, such as the sign-up page on your website. Or you could create a team to work on optimizing the company's customer acquisition in a single channel, such as Facebook, or improving the readership of the company's blog, or the performance of the company's email marketing. Or you can launch the growth team with a sole focus in one metric, such as on improving conversion rates in activation, or shoring up your customer retention. As successes are achieved, the growth team can take on a wider range of initiatives, or more growth teams can be created.

If you are the head of a small team and want to give the process a try, it's best to set your team up for success by getting buy-in first, even if it is just with a few peers and a supervisor. You will make mistakes, experiments will fail, webpages will break—it's an inevitable part of the experimentation process. Having the support of higher-ups can alleviate the blowback from such eventualities. Lauren Schaefer, who was the growth hacking lead on the Bluemix DevOps team at IBM, launched a test early in the process of experimenting with growth hacking that crippled the product's home page. But her boss was a supporter of the effort, and she and her growth team got past that stumble.[14]

It's just as important that the growth team machine not be put into drive too early. Because all the rapid experimentation in the world won't ignite lasting growth if the product isn't loved by the people who use it. While plenty of companies manage to eke out enough sales or user loyalty to stay alive with products that are merely satisfactory, or even sometimes clearly inferior, they're on a trajectory to fail sooner or later.

This is why, as we'll discuss more fully in the next chapter, no overly ambitious growth scaling plans should be instituted until a company has determined whether the product it's bringing to market is a "must-have" or a "just okay but can live without." So now that you know how to set up a growth team, let's move on to the next step in the process: how the team can use customer feedback, rigorous experimentation and testing, and a deep dive into data to evaluate if a product has in fact achieved product/market fit.

CHAPTER TWO

DETERMINING IF YOUR PRODUCT IS MUST-HAVE

All fast-growth companies share one thing in common. Regardless of who their customers are, their business model, and the type of product, industry, or region of the globe they're operating in, they all make a product that a large group of people love. They've built products that, in the eyes of their customers, are simply *must-have*.

While creating a must-have product alone is not sufficient for breakout success, it *is* the baseline requirement for rapid and sustainable growth. Of course, building a must-have product isn't easy, and one result is that too often those launching new businesses or products put the cart before the horse, pouring resources and staff into trying to drive more customers to a product that isn't actually loved, or sometimes even understood, by its target market. This is one of the most common, and deadly, mistakes start-up founders make, and it's also a huge problem that often surfaces when established firms, even those known for their innovation prowess, launch new products. Just think of Google Glass and Amazon's Fire Phone—both innovative products . . . that nobody wanted. Or the infamous Microsoft Zune media player, launched in November 2006, which Microsoft reportedly spent at least $26 million to promote but which never generated more than a tepid response.[1] The Zune was not a bad product; many critics considered it quite well designed. But it added no "wow factor" to make it more appealing than Apple's already ubiquitous iPods. Despite continued efforts to stoke sales, including the release of an improved version, the Zune HD, in 2009, the Zune was never able to garner more than a single-digit share of the market and was discontinued in 2011.[2]

One of the cardinal rules of growth hacking is that you must not move into the high-tempo growth experimentation push until you know your product is must-have, why it's must-have, and to whom it is a must-have: in other words, what is its core value, to which customers, and why. (The exception to this rule being businesses such as social networks, where the core value is the people on the platform.) This may sound blindingly obvious, but the fact is that it can sometimes take enormous patience, because the pressure to start pushing for growth is intense. For start-ups, that's often due to demands from taking venture capital or, on the flip side, because the company needs to prove itself in order to raise capital, or generate revenue to keep the lights on. Even in established firms, where products are generally assigned a target revenue contribution by a specified date, there is pressure to start demonstrating growth, yesterday. And as this pressure mounts, the belief that growth can be forced, usually by increasing spending on marketing, becomes increasingly alluring.

But the hard truth is that no amount of marketing and advertising—no matter how clever—can make people love a substandard product. If you haven't created and identified core value *before* you make your growth push, you'll either end up with illusory growth at best or market rejection at worst. Sure, a glitzy launch can create some initial interest, but if your product doesn't wow people, all the celebrity spokespeople and multimillion-dollar ad campaigns in the world won't result in sustainable growth.

The opportunity costs of pushing for growth too soon are twofold. First, you're spending precious money and time on the wrong efforts (i.e., on promoting a product that no one wants); and second, rather than turning early customers into fans, you're making them disillusioned, even angry, critics. Remember that viral word of mouth can work two ways; it can supercharge growth or it can stop it in its tracks.

A pernicious misconception about growth hacking is that it is primarily about building virality into products. That is indeed one of the key tactics, but like other growth efforts, it must only be deployed *after* the product has been determined a must-have. As Chamath Palihapitiya, the original head of the Facebook growth team, recalls stressing in launching the team's growth efforts, "I don't want you to give me any product plans that revolve around this idea of virality. I don't want to hear about it."[3]

Growth teams need to adopt rigorous methods for probing into user behavior in order to discover the core value of their product or service, and we'll introduce these methods shortly. Additionally, growth teams need to recognize that sometimes establishing what the core value is, or should be, isn't about the features of the product or service itself, but rather a matter of connecting with the right core market, which, again, as we'll explore, might be quite different from the originally envisioned one.

Finally, it's important to note that identifying core value does not necessarily follow directly from having created it. Often those of us building and marketing new products *think* we know what aspect of our product consumers will love—and often we are wrong. Sometimes it's a feature or user experience that was built into the product that is quite different from what was hypothesized in the original product vision as the core value; other times it's one that was built into the product somewhere along the way as almost an afterthought. Whichever the case, it's up to the growth team to find out. In this chapter we'll learn how.

THE FLAMEOUT OF BRANCHOUT

One of the fastest-growing Facebook apps of all time serves as a cringe-inducing reminder of the danger of pushing too hard, too soon, for growth. Founded in 2010, and designed to let Facebook users build up a professional network on the site by connecting them with business contacts, BranchOut was hailed in the press as a LinkedIn killer.[4] After all, the pundits posited, once you had your professional network in place on Facebook, what would you need LinkedIn for? To hasten the app's viral growth, the team, led by Zack Onisko, devised a brilliant hack of Facebook's invite system to get more users to share the app with their Facebook friends.

At the time, Facebook allowed users who installed a new app to invite other friends to use it, too (and, in fact, many of the apps that grew virally on Facebook took advantage of this mechanism, such as the wildly popular game Farmville). But the base invite mechanism in Facebook only allowed you to invite a maximum of 50 friends at once, and the BranchOut team knew that the conversion rate for Facebook invites was extremely low. The only sure way to drive viral growth, they decided, was simply to prompt users to send more invites. Onisko says they tried hundreds of experiments for how to do so, until they "stumbled upon" a solution. The team had figured out how to allow users to overcome the 50-invite limitation by repeatedly clicking the Next button in a specially designed window, which triggered Facebook's invite system to suggest another 50 of the user's friends, and then yet another 50. The tactic supercharged referrals, and BranchOut grew from four million users to twenty-five million in about three months.[5]

The only problem was, it turned out that when people tried to use the app, they were generally disappointed to find that there wasn't much they could do with it. Pretty soon, the tidal wave of new users turned—turned, that is, into an equally rapid deluge of users leaving. At one point, the app was losing more than 4 percent of its monthly active users every day, prompting ERE Media, a recruiting intelligence publication, to describe the app as nothing more than a digital Ponzi scheme.[6]

BranchOut's founder, Rick Marini, conceded in a 2012 talk that the company had erred in trying to rush user acquisition without delivering on the product experience. "Often people think there's a silver bullet to getting traffic and going viral," he said. "What we've learned is that there are times when you can get some spike of virality, but if you really want that long-term major user growth it's got to start with a good product. We realized, OK, we've got to really enhance the product and get users back every day. Don't be an episodic utility, be a community. And now we've got to make that shift."[7]

But that desire to shift turned out to be little more than wishful thinking. Despite raising nearly $50 million in venture capital, Branch-Out never became more than a viral one-hit wonder; its wild ride ended in a resounding thud when the company sold its assets to a relatively obscure human resources company, 1-Page, for $2 million in cash and some stock.[8]

Many other products that achieved rocket-like growth by pushing too hard too soon for adoption have flamed out in similarly spectacular fashion. Which is why all growth hackers must always keep in mind that, as the growth team at Airbnb says, "love creates growth, not the other way around." And for there to be love, there needs to be that aha moment.[9]

WHAT'S THE AHA MOMENT?

Having reached a $2 billion valuation as a publicly traded company in 2016, Yelp's success might today seem preordained. But in fact its growth was sluggish at first as Yelp struggled against stiff competition from the much larger Citysearch, which in 2005 was a top 50 site on the Web and enjoyed the backing of its massive parent company, media mogul Barry Diller's InterActiveCorp. Yelp, by contrast, which had launched as a proof of concept in October of 2004, was barely getting its feet under itself. Even founder Jeremy Stoppelman thought the service was of questionable value. Then Stoppelman's team discovered, by poring through user data, that a surprisingly large number of users were taking advantage of a feature buried almost laughably deep within the site—a feature that allowed users to post reviews of local businesses.

The team ran some tests to see how visitors would respond when reviews were put front and center, and when they saw good results, they pivoted from the original business model of friends asking friends for business recommendations and put the reviews at the heart of the experience. But they didn't stop there. The team then created 20 million profiles for small businesses in the Bay Area on the site and encouraged users to add their reviews. Growth took off. Meanwhile Citysearch is now little more than a footnote, having been folded into CityGrid Media in 2010.[10]

Yelp had found its *aha moment*. This is the moment that the utility of the product really clicks for the users; when the users really *get* the core value—what the product is for, why they need it, and what benefit they derive from using it. Or in other words, why that product is a "must-have." This experience is what turns early adopters into power users and evangelists. For Yelp, that experience was the ability to discover promising local restaurants and businesses through trusted community reviews. For eBay, the aha moment was finding and winning one-of-a-kind items at auction from people all over the world. For Facebook, it was instantly seeing photos and updates from friends and family and sharing what you were up to. For Dropbox, it was the concept of easy file sharing and unlimited file storage. Or take Uber's aha moment, which Uber cofounder and CEO Travis Kalanick explained as, "You push a button and a black car comes up. Who's the baller? It was a baller move to get a black car to arrive in 8 minutes."[11] An aha experience is a necessary ingredient of sustainable growth because it is one that is simply too remarkable *not* to value, to return to often, and to share.

Thus the key to knowing when it's time to start the high-tempo push for growth is simple: Can you identify an aha moment that users love? New products are generally built on the premise of delivering an aha experience that customers will find irresistible and that fills a meaningful need for a big audience. Sometimes things are going very much according to plan, and as soon as people begin using a product, they have the aha moment and then they tell two friends, and word of mouth takes off from there. But many times, delivering a standout aha experience takes extra work beyond just offering the product and hoping for the best.

Sometimes a product isn't yet offering a true aha experience and more product development is needed to create it. But in others, the product already has what it needs to give people an aha experience, and the work is in leading them more effectively to it. Often, people have to use a product a certain amount of time before they truly have this experience with it, or perhaps they have to use a certain feature to really get the full-force aha hit. For example, Twitter struggled to sustain growth in its early days until it learned (from doing extensive analysis of its user data) that users who quickly started following at least 30 other users were much more engaged and likely to continue using the service. Digging into why following 30 people seemed to be the tipping point, the Twitter growth team found that getting a steady stream of news and updates from people they were interested in was the aha moment for people. Following 30 people created a stream of updates that made the service "must-have."

Similarly, at Qualaroo, the website survey company where Sean and Morgan worked together, we identified that trial users who received 50 or more responses to one individual survey were three times as likely to pay for their subscription at the end of their trial when compared with users who did not get a survey with 50 responses during the same period. Here, 50 responses was what it took to deliver the aha moment of seeing how the product delivered new and valuable feedback. At Slack, a team chat and messaging product designed to eliminate internal corporate email threads (and one of the fastest-growing business applications of all time), data showed that once team members had sent and received 2,000 messages to one another, the team became far more likely to make Slack a core part of their communication workflow and upgrade to a paid plan with premium features. This number of messages seemed to be the threshold at which Slack's value in improving team communication over email became profoundly clear to them.

Identifying what a product's aha moment is can sometimes be quite tricky. It's entirely possible to launch a product and conclude, because you're experiencing anemic growth, that the product simply doesn't have any aha magic when, in fact, certain users might already be wildly enthusiastic about it. So a vital step in determining whether your product has the aha potential is to seek out truly avid fans by mining user data and feedback, and then to search for any similarities in the ways these people use the product for hints about what value they get from your product that less enthused users perhaps aren't. Sometimes this will surface a pattern such as the 30 people being followed on Twitter, but at other times your discoveries will point the way to further product development or even a substantial product pivot or rebuild.

The good news is that while discovering *how* to make a product deliver an aha moment can be very difficult, determining *whether* or not your product meets the baseline requirement generally doesn't require elaborate diagnostics. We advise a simple two-part assessment.

THE MUST-HAVE SURVEY

The first step is a simple survey Sean designed, one that he has found again and again throughout his career in Silicon Valley to be a remarkably reliable means of measuring whether customers love a product or not. This Must-Have Survey begins with the question:

How disappointed would you be if this product no longer existed tomorrow?

a) Very disappointed
b) Somewhat disappointed
c) Not disappointed (it really isn't that useful)
d) N/A—I no longer use it

Interpreting the results is simple enough; if 40 percent or more of responses are "very disappointed," then the product has achieved sufficient must-have status, which means the green light to move full speed ahead gunning for growth.

Many products won't hit the 40 percent threshold, however, and in that event, the growth team's first efforts must be focused on determining *why* the product isn't getting a better response. If 25 to 40 percent of respondents answer "very disappointed," then often what's needed are tweaks either to the product or to the language used to describe the product and how to use it. If less than 25 percent answer "very disappointed," it's likely that either the audience you've attracted is the wrong fit for your product, or the product itself needs more substantial development before it's ready for a growth push.

In these cases, a set of additional questions on the Must-Have Survey will help to point you toward your next steps:

What would you likely use as an alternative to [name of product] if it were no longer available?
I probably wouldn't use an alternative
I would use:

What is the primary benefit that you have received from [name of product]?

Have you recommended [name of product] to anyone?
No
Yes (Please explain how you described it)

What type of person do you think would benefit most from [name of product]?

How can we improve [name of product] to better meet your needs?

Would it be okay if we followed up by email to request a clarification to one or more of your responses?

The question about alternative products can help identify your chief competition for customers, and often point to features or aspects of the experience those products are offering that lead those customers to prefer them over others. This feedback can be used to determine the features that you should be adding, refining, touting more assertively, or making more prominent in order to win over those customers. Answers about the primary benefit may help uncover features that you might add to deliver this benefit; or if you already do, it could point you toward experimenting with new marketing messages that might better communicate it. From the responses to the question about whether users have recommended the product, teams can gauge whether the product has word-of-mouth marketing potential, and if so, what you can do to make the most of it. More important, the language they use to describe the product to their friends can unearth benefits, features, and language to use in your own product promotion.

The question about which type of person users think can benefit the most from the product can help the team focus on a better-defined customer niche and thus target those potential users more effectively. For example, at Inman, where Morgan works, they asked the question of users of a training product for real estate professionals that the company had recently launched, and the answers pointed to it being particularly well suited for new agents. Morgan's team used this feedback to improve the marketing and advertising targeting to focus on this group of potential customers.

The product improvement question can identify both glaring issues with the product that make it a nonstarter for broad adoption and opportunities to enhance the product that the company might not have thought of on its own.

WHOM TO SURVEY?

Clearly, the larger the user base when you conduct the survey, the more reliable and informative the information will be. You're looking to get at least a few hundred responses to the first question to be a reliable guide for this kind of survey.

If you don't have a large enough base of beta users to get about that number, you should be relying more on customer interviews instead, as having just a handful of survey responses can lead to false signals.

Somewhat ironically, it's best if you target the survey at active users rather than those who have gone dormant. This is because the answers you'll get from those who aren't using the product will generally not be particularly informative, likely just saying they haven't benefited and haven't recommended the product, for example, if they respond at all. Active users, by contrast, will be much more familiar with the product or service and as a result will often have much more specific and detailed responses.

One caveat: the Must-Have Survey isn't recommended much beyond the stage of determining whether you've achieved core product value. For one thing, once your growth has taken off, it's not a good idea to even suggest to your customer base that the product might be discontinued by asking them how they'd feel if it were no longer available. Can you imagine the panic if Facebook sent its users a survey suggesting it might go away? Moreover, once you have moved past this early diagnostic stage, your surveying and testing of the quality of the customer experience can and should become progressively more refined and your assessments more quantitative in nature, because you'll have more data to work with. You'll dive into more specific aspects of the user experience that people love and don't love, based on the data you'll accumulate about how people are using the product, in order to determine how you can continue to test improvements.

MEASURING RETENTION

The second measure to use in assessing whether or not you've achieved must-have status is your product's *retention rate*, which is simply the number of people who continue to use your product over a given time. More details of how to use the analysis of retention rates to guide growth experimentation are covered later in the book, but the general rule of thumb for making this determination is that you want to achieve a comparatively high rate vis-à-vis your competitors and for that rate to be stable over time. In order to evaluate whether you're achieving a stable rate, the team should be frequently tracking the number of users who churn, usually on either a weekly or monthly basis. Frequent monitoring provides early warning about defections, which can otherwise be hard to detect, especially if new user acquisition is strong. A company can be acquiring lots of new users but also be starting to lose some of its earlier adopters all at the same time, and those defections can be masked by the new user growth. Achieving stable retention should not be viewed as a benchmark that once passed can be assumed has been accomplished and that the team is done with; teams must expect to continue to work on sustaining retention. And, in fact, they should keep working to improve the retention rate. This is one of the most effective means of supercharging growth, and we'll be introducing a powerful set of methods for doing so. But what's critical at this early stage is that you have at least seen the retention rate stabilize, which indicates that you have a set of users who sees the product as worthy of continuous use.

The retention rate is simply calculated as the percentage of users who continue to use or pay for your product, generally tracked month to month. For products that are designed to be used very frequently, such as mobile apps and social networks and even visits to fast-food restaurants and convenience stores, teams may want to measure retention on a weekly, or even a daily, basis as well. The shorter time horizon helps you deduce how many users are making the use of the product a habit, making it a regular part of their lives, versus how many are only sporadically checking in.

Different types of businesses or products have different retention rates, so it's best to see if you can find benchmarks in your industry for successful products that are fairly comparable and, if possible, come up with an average rate in order to determine if you're doing better or worse. According to data published by mobile intelligence company Quettra, most mobile apps, for example, retain just 10 percent of their audience after one month, while the best mobile apps retain more than 60 percent of their users one month after installation.[12]

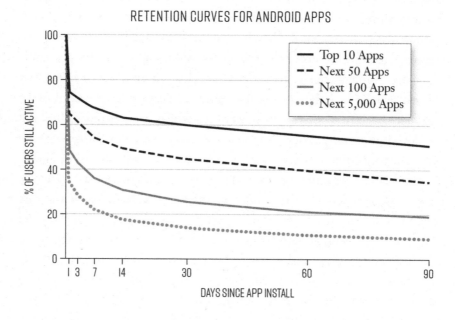

User retention for Android apps from Quettra

Business products, such as software as a service, fare much better, with annual retention rates north of 90 percent, according to a study of private SaaS companies done by Pacific Crest in 2013.[13] And fast-food restaurant chains see month-over-month retention of customers ranging from 50 to 80 percent. For example, McDonald's saw 78 percent of their customers come in every month to their restaurants in 2012.[14] A 2013 study concluded that credit card companies in the US see annual churn rates of roughly 20 percent, while European cellphone carriers see churn of anywhere between 20 and 40 percent.[15]

GETTING TO MUST-HAVE

If your product passes these tests, providing a clear indication that a significant number of customers have experienced the aha moment, it's time to move into high-tempo experimentation for growth. If you've determined the product *hasn't* made the grade, the first thing to do is to stop yourself from doing something that feels all too natural: guessing at what the elusive feature might be that may make your product more appealing to your customers. Sitting in an office with your smartest lieutenants and a whiteboard to hash out ideas for improvements may feel like exactly the right way to solve the problem, but trust us, that instinct is a head fake. It's essential that you instead talk to users (on a deeper level than achieved through the aforementioned survey) to understand what the true objections and barriers are to your product's success. If you don't, you run the risk of investing your very limited resources and time in a costly false start, such as shipping a feature that doesn't move the needle at all. In fact, while the addition of features seems the most obvious solution to improving a product, all product developers must be keenly aware of the danger of *feature creep*; that is, adding more and more features that do not truly create core value and that often make products cumbersome and confusing to use. In many cases, improvement comes from what you remove, not what you add on, as was true for Yelp, which pared down to focus on reviews.

So it's vital to take an analytical approach to finding out why that aha moment hasn't been achieved—and how to achieve it—rather than relying on conjecture. For this there are three key methods, all of which should be employed in concert.

- Additional customer surveying, including interviews and getting out in the marketplace to talk to customers and prospective customers;
- Efficient experimental testing of product changes and messaging;
- A deep plunge into analysis of your user data.

The team should divide up responsibilities according to the specialized talents of each member of the growth team to conduct these diagnostics: The marketing and product design specialists on the team have the necessary expertise in conducting interviews and surveys; engineers know how to implement product changes and to set up experimental tests within the product; and data analysts know how to dig deeper into user behavior, providing insights beyond those offered by basic metrics that off-the-shelf programs track. Let's look at how to go about each of these discovery processes.

GETTING OUT AND ABOUT IN THE ANALOG WORLD

As Steve Blank, one of the leading innovators in the field of customer development, stresses, no matter what business you're in, you need to get out of the building to find out what your customers really want from you and your product. Many resources for conducting customer interviews are available online. Whichever you choose, the most important principle to remember when conducting them is to be dispassionate about your product. The feedback will be worthless if you've spent the whole time selling. You've got to be listening and observing, not pitching.

Also important is the principle that actions speak louder than words. The best practice is to take the product, or a prototype, out into "the wild" so that you can actually *see* exactly how prospective users respond to it. This may reveal that features you *think* you've designed to be a breeze are actually too complicated or just of no interest, or make you aware of a problem users need solved that you hadn't at all anticipated. Users may even point to invaluable ideas for changes to the product you and your team would never think of.[16]

Such was the case for the online marketplace Etsy. Now that the company has had a successful IPO, in which it raised more than $287 million, and is valued at more than $1 billion, the founders' idea to create a site for the buying and selling of handcrafted products by individuals or small, artisanal firms seems to have filled an obvious need. But that need wasn't always so apparent. In fact, the early growth of the company was fueled largely by a great deal of legwork. As Danielle Maveal, who is Etsy's brand and community hacker, explains, Etsy "did something that works and is often overlooked. We got off the Internet."[17]

By sending a team of people out to attend craft fairs all around the country and meet with prospective sellers to bring onto the site and with their customers, Etsy discovered the network power of "Stitch 'n Bitch" groups, comprised of feminist crafters who were a key force in the growth of the craft movement. Etsy smartly singled out influential artists, crafters, and vintage collectors and actually took them to lunch to understand their motivations, i.e., what aspect of the selling experience they considered most important, and what kind of aha moment it would require to convince them to shift that experience to Etsy. Not only did Etsy convince many of these crafters to open stores on the site, but it facilitated the creation of community that those same influencers had expressed as being of critical importance. Upon learning that many groups of crafters had coalesced around publications, like the feminist magazine *Bust*, as well as a host of blogs, Etsy decided to host online message boards that contributed to community building. Etsy's community forums not only acted as a place for sellers to get tips on how to improve sales, they acted as recruiting boards for new sellers and as hubs of discourse around the feminist crafting movement.

This early "boots on the ground" market development not only was vital to Etsy in discovering how to become must-have, it also led the way to the strategies they would subsequently use to fuel growth, which was driven primarily by promoting organic, word-of-mouth and online community building, rather than big traditional (i.e., expensive) marketing campaigns. Guided by this *early adopter feedback*, the team spent their time building tools and resources to make sellers successful, such as the aforementioned forums, the *Seller Handbook* blog, and developing tools and partnerships to help sellers with customer communication, order management, and more. They also ensured that their seller stores and item pages were laden with social sharing hooks to make it easy for the sellers and potential customers to share their bespoke wares on their Facebook pages, blogs, and Pinterest boards.

The result was that, as one analyst wrote, the company spent "next to nothing" on customer acquisition to achieve the growth that brought it to its IPO, and that even in recent years, organic channels, such as social media, email marketing, and organic search traffic, have represented 87 to 91 percent of Etsy's traffic, while paid ads have been responsible for between just 2 and 7 percent of traffic.[18] All of this "getting out of the building" worked: at the end of 2014, just prior to their IPO, Etsy had grown to over 54 million members and $1.93 billion in sales.[19]

Another product group that smartly harnessed the growth power of a preexisting network by actually going out to meet with those target users in the real world is dating app Tinder, which, despite stiff competition from many other popular dating sites, managed to skyrocket to 24 million monthly active users in just 30 months.[20]

Yet Tinder faced a unique challenge in gaining early adopters that wasn't an issue for Etsy—people are only interested in finding dating prospects who are fairly close by, whereas crafters and their customers can do business over great distance, even all around the globe. If Tinder's users were localized then, so, its team smartly decided, would be its initial growth push. The Tinder team decided to focus on college fraternities and sororities because they are tightly networked with one another, which would speed word of mouth, and also because their members are social influencers; they would make not only instructive research subjects but also appealing early adopters who could help to establish the brand as *the* place for hot dating prospects. Whitney Wolfe, an earlier team member, did the legwork to actually go out and visit college campuses, making presentations to sororities, getting members onboard, and getting instant, face-to-face feedback about the app from real live users. When Wolfe would then walk across the street to neighboring fraternities and show their members all the new sorority members recently added, it wasn't, as you can much imagine, particularly difficult to get them signed on as well, quickly building the local dating pool in the process.[21]

Adoption was strong, and then, as founder Sean Rad recalls, growth broke out of this initial market organically. "It happened around January. We had been picking up on college campuses, then everyone went home and told their cousins and older brothers and friends about it, and all of a sudden Tinder started growing like a virus."[22] The company did not have to spend heavily on advertising or acquisition of email lists, and by focusing on a core group of users, it was able to deftly fine-tune the product with many ongoing improvements that its users loved. But it couldn't have happened had they not gone out into the world to gain a deep understanding of a core initial market.

FINDING A COMMUNITY TO SURVEY

Preexisting communities to target for insight into how to achieve the aha moment can also, of course, be identified digitally. This was the case with PayPal and eBay, as just one prominent example. When PayPal first launched, the team noticed that some of its earliest regular adopters were people who bought and sold items on eBay and decided to set out to understand how exactly they were using PayPal and how to get it into the hands of more of these avid users. A request from a seller for permission to use the PayPal logo on their auction listing piqued the PayPal team's interest, and they began to investigate how people were using PayPal on eBay. At the time, eBay sellers couldn't accept credit cards for payment, and because they understandably much preferred receiving funds instantly instead of waiting for a check or money order, they were more than happy to promote PayPal as the preferred method of purchase to potential buyers. The PayPal team scoured eBay auctions to understand how sellers were using PayPal, including how they displayed and spoke about it in their listings. They also pored over feedback from sellers in the eBay discussion forums, who shared feedback and insights the team used to better understand their needs. As a result, the PayPal team built AutoLink, the tool we mentioned earlier, to add the PayPal logo and a small snippet of text encouraging buyers to sign up and pay with PayPal to all of their auctions.[23] It turned out to be so effective that eBay, acknowledging how valuable PayPal was for its own growth, ultimately purchased the company.[24]

These days, the variety of online platforms with which to find the core audience for your product is almost limitless, from the large social networks like Facebook and Instagram, to the Apple and Google app stores, to WordPress and Meetup groups of all shapes and sizes. Tapping into these targeted platforms can help you find early adopters who are likely to have the problem your product solves and can give feedback into whether what you've built for them delivers an aha experience.

Conducting surveys and interviews may seem prohibitively time consuming but, in fact, crystal clear insights can often be gained with quite moderate numbers of survey responses and very few interviews. Nor do you necessarily need to ask an elaborate set of questions. Often just a few basic questions are all you need. Josh Elman, for example, highlighted just four questions that the Twitter team asked users who had gone dormant and subsequently returned: (1) Can you tell us why you signed up in the first place?; (2) What didn't work for you? Why'd you bail?; (3) What caused you to come back and try it again?; and (4) What worked this time?

And while it's true that research has shown the costly process of conducting focus groups to be largely ineffective and time consuming, simple user surveys of the kind Sean made use of to discover that users didn't believe LogMeIn was really a free service can be deployed very rapidly and easily, with no technical know-how required. And in most cases just a couple hundred survey responses are needed in order to get a good bead on the underlying motivations behind the behaviors you uncovered in your data dive, revealing deep insight into what your true growth opportunities are, and in turn where you should begin to focus your growth experimentation efforts.

EFFICIENT EXPERIMENTATION

The growth of low-cost and easy-to-use data analytics and online marketing technology has made it incredibly easy to experiment with both product and messaging to find the right combination of customer base and feature set you need to pass the must-have threshold. Some testing is remarkably easy and quick to do, requiring little to no technical ability and involving little or no cost, while more substantial experiments can involve considerable time and money, particularly if they require engineering staff to build a new feature or implement a substantial redesign. Decisions about what experiments to run must be made rigorously, and most growth teams have adopted the practice of a *minimum viable test (MVT)*, the least costly experiment that can be run to adequately vet an idea. If the MVT is successful, the team will invest in a more robust follow-on test or more polished implementation of the concept.[25]

In order to keep the experiment velocity high—which is always a mandate in growth hacking—the team should run a mix: tests of the more complicated product changes they want to try with the much-easier-to-run testing of the messaging and marketing. In the next two sections we'll look at each type of test in more detail.

IS IT BETTER THIS WAY OR THAT?

As Sean discovered in working to help grow LogMeIn, sometimes what's holding you back from achieving growth is not a matter of lack of value in the product or service itself, but rather of how you are communicating that value to existing and potential customers. Luckily, the rise of online marketing has made honing messaging a readily adopted science, enabling growth teams to alter and test messaging—even for non-Web-based products—extremely rapidly and at low to no cost.

One particularly powerful and typically inexpensive method is *A/B testing*, by which two different messages—say, two different headlines in an online newsletter, or two different designs of a landing page, are tested on two or more randomly targeted groups of people to determine which elicits the better response. Sometimes these tests can reveal that the simplest of tweaks, such as using a different subject line on an email, altering the copy on a button, or changing the wording on an online form, can lead to huge gains. Take the case of Highrise, a customer relationship management product that the firm Basecamp launched to complement its popular project management software, for whom an A/B test of the copy on the sign-up page revealed that simply changing the language from "Sign Up for Free Trial" to "See Plans and Pricing" netted 200 percent more sign-ups.[26] That might seem like a rare case, but it's not; in the companies we've worked with we've seen hundreds of examples of other equally simple changes—revealed through A/B testing—that have led customers to the aha moment and in turn driven massive increases in adoption.

As the value of this type of experimentation has become more apparent, software companies such as Optimizely and Visual Website Optimizer have built tools that make it easier and cheaper than ever for companies to set up experiments on their websites without much help from the engineering team. These products empower any team member who manages parts of a website to run rapid sequential A/B tests on headlines, taglines, images, videos, buttons, and more—which enables them to be swifter and more nimble in their testing while also freeing up the engineers to work on building more substantial tests.

One caution about A/B testing tools is that for all their ease of implementation, the data they provide is somewhat limited, because these tools rely on surface-level metrics, such as which button gets more clicks, rather than whether the people clicking the button ultimately become lasting users. Anyone who has clicked on an irresistible news headline only to be disappointed by the article can understand how a "click" is a poor indicator of long-term customer loyalty. In order to solve this problem, it's essential that your data analytics can track the participants in any given A/B test from click-through to long-term use.

A/B testing should also go far beyond the language and design of landing pages and marketing promotions. Remember that a core tenet of growth hacking is experimentation all through the customer experience funnel: not just customer awareness and acquisition but also activation, retention, revenue, and referral. At Inman News, for example, when Morgan's team A/B tested the pricing and length of their paid news subscription, they were able to significantly improve retention rates by replacing a month-by-month plan with a new three-month subscription.

Engineers can be powerful sources of ideas for additional kinds of test opportunities farther down the funnel, which tend to be more technically complicated and can often be beyond the vision of the nontechnical team members. Recall from the last chapter, for example, how the engineers on the Pinterest engagement growth team built the Copytune machine learning program in order to supercharge speed of experimentation with copy in 30 languages in numerous emails used to retain existing Pinterest users. This is an example of what's called a *multivariate test*, which goes beyond comparing two alternatives to comparing every possible combination of each element of a message to find the highest-performing permutation. Or, take what's called *multi-armed bandit*, a more sophisticated testing scheme used by companies to find winning results faster. We'll introduce more types of tests that can be run and explain them in more detail later in the book.

EXPERIMENTS WITHIN THE PRODUCT

The more complicated tests that require significant engineering time are usually those that are changes to the products themselves. While this type of experimentation is common in Web and software products, it's equally applicable to physical products as well. Building the simplest possible prototype and asking users to test it, or creating video or computer demos showing how a new feature would work and seeing how customers respond, are just two ways teams working on physical products can take advantage of experimental learning.

Adjustments that have historically proven to improve results and enhance the user experience should be prioritized, such as speeding up the response time of a Web shopping cart or improving the sign-up process. But other, less-battle-tested changes such as substantial redesigns or building of new product features should be done only on the basis of a strong hypothesis, formed through the analysis of user research and data. In other words, for tests that are time- and labor-intensive, teams should minimize the risk of this investment of effort with sound reasoning first, and mix bigger, riskier initiatives in with more sure things. In doing so the team will ensure that it strikes the right balance between big, moonshot bets and incremental improvements that lead to consistent growth.

TAKING A DATA DIVE

There is more data available to growth teams than ever before, but all this data is essentially useless without the ability to parse it for useful insights. What that means is that it's not about simply reviewing data provided by the various tools and dashboards out there; to uncover what makes (or will make) your product a must-have, you need to collect the right data for your business, and build the connective tissue between various sources, such as your email marketing database and your point of sale system, so you can create a complete data picture. Then you need a data analyst who can mine those sources of data for patterns and rich insights that can lead to growth ideas to experiment with. These days most companies, even the most nascent, shoestring start-ups, are keeping close track of basic analytics for their websites and products, such as those captured by Google Analytics. But while metrics like page views, visits, and bounce rates are important to collect, they barely begin to tell the whole story about how customers interact with your product. That's because these are very surface level metrics that don't tend to reveal deeper insights into what customers truly value about what you are selling and whether you have achieved product/market fit.

It's essential that your team have data on each piece of the customer experience—well beyond just how often they visit your website and how long they stay there—so that it can be analyzed at a granular level to identify how people are actually using your product versus how you have planned for them to use it. What this means is that the marketers, data scientists, and engineers must work together to add the proper tracking to websites, mobile apps, point of sale systems, email marketing, and customer databases. Once the proper tracking is in place, the multiple sources of user information must be stitched together to give you a detailed and robust picture of user behavior that your data team can analyze.

What you want to create is what's often called a *data lake* or *data warehouse*: a single location where all customer information is stored and where you can really dive in and uncover distinctive groupings of users who may be using the product differently from other groups. This also empowers you to explore product use at the individual user, or "atomic," level, examining, for example, how, say, an extraordinarily active user is spending her time on your website or with your app, or what a user who was about to make a substantial purchase but then didn't follow through to hit the Buy button did instead. Maybe you see that she got lured away by a special promotion feature for an item that popped up just as she was about to finalize the purchase; though this information is anecdotal for one user, it can steer you toward areas ripe for additional analysis and growth experimentation. When the data is properly collected, it will also make it that much easier for data analysts to share the results of the rapid-fire experiments you run as part of your growth push.

WHAT ARE ACTIVE USERS DOING?

The first step in collecting the data to then pan for nuggets of insight is to track the key actions of your users or customers. This is done through the process of event tracking. Most analytics platforms allow you to identify key events within your system such as when a user clicks a button, watches a video, downloads a document, fills out a form, plays a song, adds a friend, shares a file, and more. Again, growth teams must set up event tracking for the activities customers are engaging in all the way through the customer experience, as they go from a visitor to a new customer and from a new customer to a regular, loyal one. Can you track the complete path of what a customer does starting when they first visit your physical store or website all the way up through making their first purchase and then subsequent ones? If there are gaps there, those are the events worth tracking first.

The key mission at this stage is to look for the behaviors that differentiate those customers who find your product must-have—that is, those who use or buy repeatedly—from those who don't. Specifically, analysts should be looking for features that are most used by the most avid users and any other distinctive aspects of their behavior in interacting with the product. By dividing your customer data up by many different customer attributes, such as demographic info including location, age, or gender, and additional attributes such as their job title, industry, or mobile device they use, as well as by the ways in which they are using your product, such as whether they are power users or only intermittently use it, and examining the choices they are making, including which products they are shopping for or the services they are availing themselves of, you will discover correlations between those attributes and behavior and greater levels of purchasing, higher engagement, and longer-term use. For example, at Netflix, by examining the movies and shows that customers were watching, the company found that Kevin Spacey films and political drama series were both hugely popular with their customers. That insight gave the company confidence to green-light the development of *House of Cards*, which became not only a huge hit, but also a must-have experience for many subscribers.[27]

Similarly, at RJMetrics, a business intelligence company, the team found that users who edited a chart in the software during their free trial period were twice as likely to convert to paying customers as those who didn't and that that number went up even higher when a trial user edited two charts. So what did RJMetrics do? They made the editing of a chart a key step in their new user orientation.[28]

PIVOTING TO THE UNEXPECTED

These distinctive behaviors and preferences can be hard to uncover, in part because sometimes they are so unexpected; paradoxically, you often don't know what you're looking for until you find it. Take how Yelp discovered that its most avid users were drawn to the site because it allowed them to write reviews: they didn't know they were looking to tie review activity to repeat use; it was an insight that emerged by sifting through reams of website data. Such unexpected discoveries are the rationale for investing in data collection up front and the rapid and relentless experimenting growth hacking calls for; the more you test, the more data you have to analyze, and the more data you analyze, the more patterns are bound to emerge.

Instagram is another instructive case. The popular photo-sharing app originated as Burbn, which was meant to be a location-based social network, named after founder Kevin Systrom's favorite alcoholic beverage (short a few vowels). But Systrom admits that even he knew the product itself was initially too complicated, or as Keith Sawyer notes in his book *Zig Zag: The Surprising Path to Greater Creativity*, "a jumble of features that made it confusing." But Systrom kept poring over the data to understand how users were using the product. And what he found was that people weren't using many of the product features at all, except for one: the photos. Systrom and cofounder Mike Krieger realized that taking and sharing photos was the aha experience they should redesign around. As Sawyer writes, "Mike and Kevin saw an opportunity to slip in between Hipstamatic [a popular photo-editing app] and Facebook, by developing an easy-to-use app that made social photo-sharing simple. They chopped everything out of Burbn except the photo, comment, and like features." After refining the product down to that essence, they relaunched the service with the name Instagram, and 400 million users and a $1 billion sale to Facebook later, the company is still growing strongly, doing more than $1 billion per year in advertising revenue as of Q1 2016.[29]

Instagram isn't the only successful company that made a virtual 180 in its early days, based on close analysis of the data that revealed its aha moment. Pinterest, which in its original incarnation was Tote, a mobile commerce app, pivoted to relaunch as a discovery and sharing site when

Ben Silbermann saw that Tote users weren't making purchases as intended, but instead were stockpiling massive collections of things they coveted on the app. With this knowledge, Silbermann changed course to design a product that made it easy to display these valued collections on the Web. Brian Cohen, Silbermann's first investor, said the pivot was the "direct outgrowth of what he learned from the first business,"[30] made possible by examining the behavior of how active users were deriving value from the product.

The early iteration of Groupon, too, was on the brink of extinction when a close analysis of user behavior pointed founder Andrew Mason to a crucial pivot. Initially conceived as a fundraising site for causes and groups of all kinds called The Point, where people could fund campaigns that would only unlock when enough people joined in, the service was doing so poorly that Mason nearly gave his investors all their money back. That is, until in looking at their data, the company found that the campaigns that gave a group of users buying power to get a better deal were the ones having the most success, and so the team jumped on this promising insight to set up daily deals, for which he coined the phrase "Get Your Groupon.com."[31] The company took off from there.

Similarly, though it is hard to believe today, YouTube started as a video dating site, pivoting to be the home for all video online only once the founders saw that users weren't only uploading video profiles to find dates, but rather sharing videos of all types. Cofounder Jawed Karim said, "Our users were one step ahead of us. They began using YouTube to share videos of all kinds. Their dogs, vacations, anything. We found this very interesting. We said, 'Why not let the users define what YouTube is all about?' By June, we had completely revamped the website, making it more open and general. It worked."[32]

All of these pivots speak to the importance of collecting and analyzing both qualitative and quantitative data about customers' use of your product and their thoughts about its strengths and weaknesses before investing extensive time and resources in pushing for growth. Had these companies pushed to drive adoption before making their pivots, it's likely that we would've never heard of any of them. Instead of finding breakout success, they would have wasted precious cash and time on trying to sell products that simply were not yet a must-have.

Of course, deep data analysis into customer behavior may also provide confirmation that it's not the product or service, or even the messaging, that's the problem—but rather how the product is being introduced
to its target market. Such was the case for HubSpot, which sells enterprise level customer relationship management and marketing software.
By rigorously analyzing user data, it discovered that customers who
went through up-front product training were retained much longer than
those who didn't. So the company changed its sales policy to make paid
product training a mandatory part of the new customer experience.

The idea that customers should be asked to pay an additional sum
for training for software they'd already purchased ran counter to what
was considered best practice at the time. Companies feared that adding
that much overhead to the software cost would be a barrier to entry to
price-conscious customers. But the HubSpot team trusted the data and
enforced up-front training.[33] This is a great example of what Chamath
Palihapitiya means when he says that a growth team's responsibility is
to "invalidate lore" about products and markets and pursue growth efforts backed by empirical evidence. The result for HubSpot was a rapidly
growing customer base that powered the company to a successful IPO
in 2014.

DRIVING TO THE AHA

Remember that all of this experimentation and analysis should be focused on discovering the aha moment you are offering, or can offer, customers. Once the conditions that create that magical experience have
been identified, the growth team should turn its attention to getting
more customers to experience that moment as fast as possible. Recall
that at Facebook, once the growth team realized that the aha moment
for their users was the thrill they got from connecting with more and
more friends in their network (based on data revealing that people who
added at least seven friends within their first ten days of joining were
most likely to stay active users), all of its efforts were directed at tweaking the site in order to motivate people to friend more people. One of
the most important changes they made was updating the *new user experience (NUX)* to focus heavily on helping users find friends; whereas in

the original version of the NUX, the find-friends step was just one part of the overall orientation to how to use Facebook, now it was made the primary one. The growth team ran numerous experiments that stripped away more and more extraneous information from the new user starting pages and focused their attention on ways to help that new member quickly build his or her network, such as importing one's email contacts to find friends already using the service and by stripping away other information that only distracted new users from finding friends. The team also leveraged ad space on Facebook to get users to find and connect with new friends by using that space for messages suggesting people whom they were likely to want to connect with.

Twitter boosted its initial growth by using a similar tactic to get users to experience what they had determined to be the core value of the service. When the data revealed that the aha moment for Twitter users was discovering news from friends and people they respected, such as celebrities and politicians, Josh Elman and the team designed a whole new first-time-user experience aimed at getting people to follow 30 Twitter users as quickly as possible. They implemented a feature that made suggestions of people to follow a primary part of the sign up process, making recommendations of specific accounts based on the interests that users chose while signing up, such as recommendations about celebrities and athletes they might be interested in. Similarly, at Qualaroo, having discovered that people who received at least 50 responses to the surveys they set up were more likely to become active, paying users, we began suggesting survey types and placements to trial users that had a higher likelihood of reaching that 50-response threshold.

Companies deploy many additional tactics to drive users to the aha, such as product tours, email communication, special offers, and more, and we'll cover when and how to implement each type more fully in the later chapters.

Because getting users to the aha moment is so critical to building up a strong foundation for all further growth, companies often invest a massive amount of time and effort to get this right. James Currier, a successful entrepreneur and growth expert turned venture capitalist, suggests that one-third of a company's engineering time goes to getting the new user experience down just right. Facebook, Twitter, and Pinterest even treat these new user experiences as different products from their main product offering, and have dedicated teams of designers, product managers, engineers, and growth leads just to perfect this one user experience.

Once you have discovered a market of avid users and your aha moment—i.e., once product/market fit has been achieved—then you can begin to build systematically on that foundation to create a high-powered, high-tempo growth machine. The rest of the book will offer specific hacks and strategies for doing just that.

CHAPTER THREE

IDENTIFYING YOUR GROWTH LEVERS

Making a product compelling enough to pass the must-have test is the prerequisite for fast and sustainable growth, but in itself it's not sufficient. Even truly great products that are loved by a core group of early adopters will almost surely fail without a well-focused effort to vigorously drive growth. So much media coverage of failed products is devoted to ones that professed to be "the next big thing" but that, with hindsight, clearly failed to offer a compelling core product value to a large enough market beyond their early adopters, like the aforementioned Google Glass or the much-hyped Segway scooter. There is less coverage about the more perplexing failures: those of products that *do* offer a very appealing core value and for which there is a large potential market that isn't yet dominated by incumbents. Here the problem is often the lack of a well-designed and -executed strategy for driving growth.

Take the case of Everpix, which was one of the most highly regarded photo apps in recent memory. Designed for users who were tired of the hassles involved with managing large collections of photos on their devices, the service made the process effortless. Brilliantly designed, and praised by critics, the app was a snap to get the hang of and also boasted an average 4.5-star user rating. TechCrunch raved, "The best part about Everpix may be its 'set it and forget it' nature. After the onetime installation and configuration, there's nothing else you have to do."[1] The product's initial base of 55,000 users were also highly active; about half of them returned to the app at least once a week. The founders chose a freemium business model—the basic version of the app was free, with the option to upgrade to a paid pro version for a $49 annual subscription, and the conversion rate to the paid version was an extraordinary 12.4 percent, far above most freemium product conversion rates, which hover around 1 percent.[2] The founders did so much right. But they made one fatal mistake: they failed to focus on finding a way to leverage the enthusiasm of their early adopters in order to drive much faster growth.

Though the enthusiasm for the product and the high rate of conversion might have seemed sure indicators that Everpix was on its way to great success, the start-up was in fact a ticking time bomb. The founders needed to dramatically ramp up the number of paid subscribers, and they needed to do it fast. A year and a half after launch, the company's operating expenses totaled $480,674 while the revenue coming in from subscriptions totaled only just over $250,000. And the founders had spent almost all of the $1.8 million in seed capital they had raised on building the product features. The coffers had run dry, and with a bill estimated at $35,000 soon to come in from Amazon Web Services, the founders had no time left to do anything but try to raise more cash—and, when that failed, close up shop.

They had considered employing several growth hacks to drive more adoption. For example, they thought about requiring people to whom users sent photos to also sign up for the app in order to download the photos. But they decided against that because they were afraid it would annoy people. But remember that growth hacking involves more than picking from a menu of hacks; it is, rather, a process of continuous experimentation to ensure that those hacks are achieving the desired results. If they were truly practicing growth hacking, they would have run a test to determine whether or not their assumption was true. Instead they kept focusing on improving the product; for example, by offering a feature that sent users an email with photos they'd taken on the same day the prior year. That greatly increased the number of users who started to visit the app daily. But with their goal to generate more income, increasing daily active use wasn't the metric they needed to be focusing on. Their urgent requirement was to increase the number of *subscribing* users, not to make the users they already had more active.

They had hoped to get out of their cash crunch by raising more capital. But without stronger growth metrics, pitch after pitch fell short. When they were finally able to secure a $500,000 loan, they hired a traditional marketing specialist who crafted a new tagline, "Solving the Photo Mess," hoping that would ignite growth, but it didn't do the trick.[3]

The Everpix tragedy demonstrates the importance of focusing not just on growth but on the *right levers of growth* at the right time. The conversion rate and positive feedback were clear indicators that they already had a great product and a solid base of active users; what the Everpix founders needed to do was shift attention from making the product pleasing to making it more profitable—i.e., channel their considerable design and engineering talent toward the mission of turning more customers into paying ones. Had they done so, it may well have become a lucrative business.

HACKING YOUR GROWTH STRATEGY

Creating an aha moment and driving more people to it is the starting point for hacking growth. The next step is to determine your growth strategy. You have to understand exactly how you're going to drive growth—what your growth levers are and whether they are the right ones to achieve desired results—before you move into high-tempo testing of growth ideas. Doing so will make the difference between strong sustained growth that is of real, revenue-generating value and illusory growth that sputters out.

You must be rigorously scientific in identifying the kind of growth you need and the levers that will drive it. Especially in the early phase of growth, you must set a highly disciplined course for experimentation that focuses intensely on the most important levers to achieve your goals. Speed of testing alone isn't the goal; scattershot experimentation is a sure way to waste time and effort, and that's true even if you're testing at high tempo. Growth hacking is not about throwing ideas against the wall as fast as you can to see what sticks, it's about applying rapid experimentation to find and then optimize the most promising areas of opportunity.

In the early phase of growth, you want to craft a strategy for running the experiments that will have the greatest impact on growth in the least amount of time. The more focused efforts are at the start, the more intentional your experiments will be, and the more impact you'll achieve. While large companies can afford to deploy test after test to tiny slivers of their massive audiences, for smaller companies, each experiment has a significant opportunity cost, and so you must be aiming for high impact per test. Of course you can't know ahead of time whether you'll achieve that impact, but you should have a strong rationale for why a proposed experiment is the best one to run next.

In addition to the potential for bigger wins, high-impact tests will also produce definitive results faster. This can be a little tricky to appreciate. Andy Johns, former growth team member at Facebook and Twitter, created the example below to illustrate the point. He lists the results for three different experiments all aimed at improving the conversion rate of new visitors to a product into users, starting at a rate of 3 percent.[4]

EXPERIMENT IMPACT AFFECTS SPEED

	BASE CONVERSION RATE	% CHANGE VS. CONTROL	REQUIRED SAMPLE SIZE/ VARIANT	TEST DAYS REQUIRED
EXAMPLE A	3%	5%	72,300	72
EXAMPLE B	3%	10%	18,500	18
EXAMPLE C	3%	30%	2,250	2

Let's say experiment A is testing a small change, such as the color of the sign-up button. As results start coming in, it becomes clear that the increase in the number of new visitors signing up is very small—garnering just 5 percent more sign-ups than the original button color. Besides the obvious assumption that changing the color of the sign-up button may not be the key factor holding back new users from signing up, it's also an indication that you'll have to let the experiment run quite a long time in order to have enough data to make a solid conclusion. As you can see from the chart above, to reach statistically significant results for this test, you'd need a whopping 72,300 visitors *per variant*—or, in other words, you'd have to wait 72 days to get conclusive results. As Johns put it in an interview with *First Round Review*, "That's a lifetime when you're a start-up!" In a case like this what a start-up really ought to do is abandon the experiment quickly and move on to a next, potentially higher-impact, one.

Running lots and lots of tests of small changes, like button colors, isn't the way to start practicing the growth hacking process. Instead, small teams must focus on those tests that promise to have the highest potential for impact first. Johns is emphatic on this point: "Seriously. Be dramatic. Don't just move a button on a page. You may run that experiment, given that you have small traffic sizes, and because of the small lift, you may run that test for months or years. Produce dramatic lifts if you're a young start-up."[5] Then, as your user or customer base grows you can afford to experiment in more niche areas at once. As the number of customers grows, shifting toward a higher volume of tests of even the smallest changes can create big wins.

So how do you figure out how to strategically focus your efforts on the experiments likely to have the greatest impact? That is precisely what we'll address in this chapter.

THE METRICS THAT MATTER

The first step in determining your growth strategy and figuring out where to focus is to understand which *metrics* matter most for your product's growth. The best way to do this is to craft what Johns dubbed a company's *fundamental growth equation*. This is a simple formula that represents all of the key factors that will combine to drive your growth; in other words, your core set of growth levers. This equation is different for every product or business. Here's an example for the company Morgan runs, Inman News, which is a subscription business:

(WEBSITE TRAFFIC × EMAIL CONVERSION RATE × ACTIVE USER RATE × CONVERSION TO PAID SUBSCRIBER) + RETAINED SUBSCRIBERS + RESURRECTED SUBSCRIBERS = SUBSCRIBER REVENUE GROWTH

For eBay the formula is:

NUMBER OF SELLERS LISTING ITEMS × NUMBER OF LISTED ITEMS × NUMBER OF
BUYERS × NUMBER OF SUCCESSFUL TRANSACTIONS = GROSS MERCHANDISE
VOLUME GROWTH

Johns even created this equation for Amazon to illustrate the value of these formulas:[6]

VERTICAL EXPANSION × PRODUCT INVENTORY PER VERTICAL × TRAFFIC PER
PRODUCT PAGE × CONVERSION TO PURCHASE × AVERAGE PURCHASE VALUE ×
REPEAT PURCHASE BEHAVIOR = REVENUE GROWTH

While all products will share common drivers of growth, such as new user acquisition, higher activation, and better retention, each product or business has a more specific combination of factors that are uniquely its own. For Uber, for example, one crucial factor is the number of drivers, because there must be enough of them in any given location to ensure the aha moment of a ride showing up quickly. The number of riders is also crucial, not only for generating revenue, but for assuring that there's enough demand for drivers so that those who do sign on keep driving. This is why the growth team at Uber is tasked specifically with improving these two core metrics. For Yelp, core factors are the numbers of businesses reviewed and the number of reviews for each. For Facebook, the amount of items being shared by users and the time spent looking through the News Feed are key factors because newly shared content populates the News Feed, and results in more time spent browsing it, which in turn is vital to attracting advertisers and charging them a lucrative premium. So while the basic metrics that are tracked through traditional marketing and prepackaged data dashboards—such as the number of Web visitors, page views, the count of new and returning users, the number of new people signing up, and the time they spend on your website—are valuable, it's of greater importance to identify the specific metrics unique to the product or business you are attempting to grow.

The way to determine your essential metrics is to identify the actions that correlate most directly to users experiencing the core value of your product, such as, for Facebook, how many people users invite to join their friend circle, how frequently they visit the site, how many posts and comments they make, and how much time they spend on the site. You want to track, at a minimum, the metrics for each of the steps users must take to reach the aha moment and how often they are taking those steps. Take Uber, whose essential metric for riders is rides completed. So in addition to the number of new people downloading the app, the company would want to track in the number of rides being booked, the number of riders who return and rebook, and the frequency with which they are booking new rides.

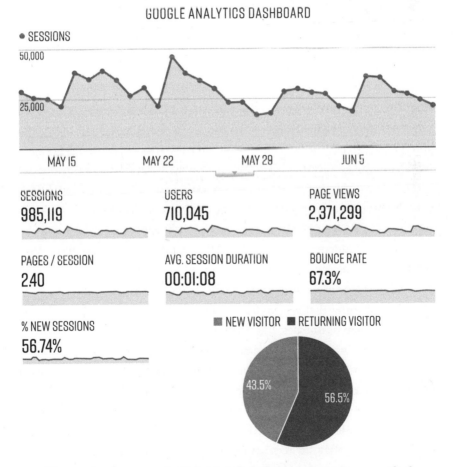

The metrics that appear in Google's default dashboards aren't necessarily the most important for your growth.

The equations above may seem overly simplistic. Clearly many more factors go into making a business work, such as R&D investment, cost of materials, shipping expenses, inventory management, and more. But the stark simplicity of the growth equation is the point. The sheer volume of data that is now available about customer behavior, even using the most basic analytics program, is daunting, with screen after screen of extraordinary detail. Google Analytics, for example, provides hundreds of charts and data points, which, while robust, can create confusion if it isn't used in service of tracking the most important metrics specifically for your growth. Reducing the complexity of your business operations down to a basic formula is immensely helpful in allowing the growth team to focus on the *right* signals in this vast sea of data noise.

Doing this can be tricky. Sometimes metrics that would intuitively seem to be crucial levers for you, including some of those that become the "it" metric for a period of time, such as daily active users, can in fact have very little impact on real sustained growth. Josh Elman explains that if you're a travel service, like Airbnb, for example, then daily active users—though it may look good on paper—is nonsensical as a metric for you. Why? No matter how much they love the service, no one is going to search and make vacation bookings every day. Even Airbnb's most active users are probably going to book a stay only maybe three or four times a year. Even for a review site, like Yelp, daily use is also unlikely. Searching the site perhaps once or twice a week might represent strong, regular use. These products simply have a built-in ceiling when it comes to how often a single customer needs their services. Whether you sell mattresses or mortgages, or offer fine dining or business services, regular use has a different meaning that is specific to your product.

Yet for some businesses, like Facebook, for example, daily active users is a hugely important metric because (a) as you may know from experience there is virtually no (or at least an alarmingly high) limit to the number of times one can visit Facebook in a single day; and (b) its advertising-based revenue model is premised on having lots of users who spend considerable time on the site. A metric that means nothing for one company, in other words, may be another's core growth lever. For example, Josh Elman also worked at LinkedIn in its early days; he highlights that total sign-ups was a crucial metric for the professional networking site. For many companies, total sign-ups can be misleading, because if those who sign up aren't really active, they're of no real value. But for LinkedIn, the large pool of people who have simply filled in their work profiles, even if they hardly ever visit the site, is the fundamental basis of the site's value. That's because LinkedIn's revenue was derived from job postings and premium subscriptions paid for by recruiters who wanted upgraded features to find and connect with potential job seekers, and the best way of hooking more recruiters—and thus creating more revenue growth—was making sure that enough people had posted their digital résumés. In addition, the more profiles on the site also resulted in more traffic coming from Google for people searching for professional contacts, driving even more people to the aha moment of making an important connection or finding a potential hire.[7]

By contrast, for eBay, one of the metrics that matters most is not daily users *or* new users but the number of items listed for sale. This is because the more items on the site, the more potential buyers will experience the aha moment of seeing exactly what they want to bid for; and in turn, the more sellers will experience the aha of making a sale. The more of each of those moments the site delivers to people, the more regularly users are likely to return, and the more merchandise will be sold. So while eBay clearly wants to increase the number of potential buyers who come to its site, getting sellers to list lots of items is arguably at least as, if not more, important, and thus should be where the bulk of their growth experiments are focused. And indeed, eBay determined that number of items sold is such an important metric for its growth that it designated *gross merchandise volume (GMV)* as the most important one to follow,[8] or what's commonly called in the growth hacking community *the North Star metric.*

CHOOSING A NORTH STAR

To hone your growth equation and narrow your focus, it's best to choose one, key metric of ultimate success that all growth activity is geared toward. This is hugely helpful in keeping teams focused on the most productive use of their time and avoiding the wasting of resources that generally results from haphazard, scattershot approaches to growth experiments.

Some in the growth community refer to this one key metric as the

One Metric That Matters, while others call it the North Star. We prefer the latter because it emphasizes that this metric becomes a guiding light to keep the team's eyes on the ultimate goal of the growth hacking process, rather than becoming too fixated on a short-term growth hack they're overly enamored of; one that may be wonderfully clever, or even create a temporary or illusory growth boost, but doesn't actually contribute to long-term sustainable growth.

The North Star should be the metric that most accurately captures the core value you create for your customers. To determine what that is you must ask yourself: Which of the variables in your growth equation best represents the delivery of that must-have experience you identified for your product? To consider eBay again, the gross merchandise volume is a great bellwether of customer satisfaction, for both buyers and sellers. The more items that are sold, the more buyers have had the aha of finding something they want to bid for, and the more sellers have found buyers for their goods.

Let's consider some other cases. For WhatsApp, the aha moment is the ability to send unlimited messages to friends and family no matter where they are in the world without worrying at all about the cost. WhatsApp's North Star was therefore the number of messages sent, rather than, say, daily active users, because even if a user is active with the app every day, but is only sending one message, it's unlikely that WhatsApp is their preferred choice for communicating with their network. Daily active users, therefore, doesn't represent the delivery of the core value to customers. For Airbnb, the North Star was nights booked. No matter what the team did, from getting more email subscribers or registering more users, if it didn't improve the number of nights actually booked, it wasn't increasing the number of aha moments users experienced, which for guests was staying in a place they were happy with, and for property listers was making money from their home.

SETTING NEW SIGHTS

The North Star may change over time as the company grows and initial goals are achieved. As Facebook learned how to engage users more actively, their initial metric of monthly active users became obsolete and daily active users became the better yardstick. At Zillow the Play is its North Star, and a new one is selected for each year, according to the shifting needs of the business.

As companies grow, they also create more product and growth teams, which have their own North Stars, even while the company may still have its one overridingly important metric. Recall that LinkedIn now focuses on initiatives in five areas: network growth; search engine optimization/ search engine marketing; onboarding; international growth; and engagement, with a team dedicated to each. For Facebook, while the initial strategy was to focus all effort on getting new users to quickly friend at least seven friends in ten days, it evolved as the company grew and priorities shifted, including building the number of advertisers using the site and the international user base through initiatives like the translation engine and Facebook Lite.

ILLUMINATING THE BEST BETS

In the movie *An American Werewolf in London*, two young Americans backpacking through the English countryside are warned by a man they meet in a local pub (colorfully named The Slaughtered Lamb) to "keep to the road, stay clear of the moors, and beware the full moon." Not long after setting off down the road, the two friends are so engaged in conversation that they veer off onto the moor (ragged grassland) on the night of a full moon and, of course, one of the two is soon attacked by a werewolf. In the movie, hilarity (albeit of somewhat ghoulish flavor) ensues. In launching products, the result of veering off course is far from amusing.

When you're gunning for growth, it's easy to find yourself in the moors, working madly on improving a metric that ultimately doesn't matter. Picking the right North Star helps to reorient growth efforts to more optimal solutions, because it helps illuminate when the focus of your experiments isn't producing the results you need.

Deciding to abandon a course of action or an experiment can be very difficult, especially if team members have become quite committed to a direction they've championed. When you're committed to an idea, pressure and emotions can all too easily bias judgment. As Facebook's original growth team lead, Chamath Palihapitiya, wisely cautioned in one talk, "If you can't be extremely clinical and extremely unemotionally detached from the thing that you're building, you will make these massive mistakes and things won't grow because you don't understand what's happened."[9]

To clarify how dedication to improving a North Star metric helps make difficult decisions about how to spend time and resources, let's look at how the Airbnb founders decided to conduct an experiment they thought might generate more nights booked—their North Star.

To begin, they looked at their data to identify markets where bookings were lagging and, to their surprise, discovered that New York City was underachieving. Clearly, New York is a major tourist destination, so they dug in, with early investor Paul Graham of Y Combinator, to analyze why bookings weren't stronger. Reviewing the apartment listings for the city, cofounder Joe Gebbia recalls that "the photos were really bad. People were using camera phones and taking Craigslist-quality pictures. Surprise! No one was booking because you couldn't see what you were paying for." Graham recommended that the two experiment with a hack to improve bookings that was low tech and high effort—but it was fast to execute on and wound up incredibly effective. The cofounders and Graham wrapped up the meeting and booked a flight to New York. Gebbia and his cofounder Brian Chesky rented a $5,000 camera and went door to door, taking professional pictures of as many listings in the city as possible. Then they compared the number of bookings for the listings with the improved photos versus the rest of the New York listings, and found that the new photos led to between two and three times more bookings, instantly doubling the revenue they were seeing from New York.[10]

With their hypothesis that photo quality impacted bookings proven, they quickly extended higher-quality photography efforts to other major cities that were also underperforming: Paris, London, Vancouver, and Miami. The uptick remained consistent, and so to ensure the highest number of bookings Airbnb decided to create a photography program that allowed hosts to schedule a professional photographer to come and photograph their listing.[11] Launching in the summer of 2010 with 20 photographers, it grew to include more than 2,000 freelance photographers, taking photos of 13,000 listings on 6 continents by 2012. Was it cheap? No, but the improved listings led to a two-and-a-half-times-better booking rate that held up all around the world.

Gebbia and Chesky could have tried to ramp up bookings by instead focusing on greatly driving up the number of people searching for listings in New York. They might have sent more promotional emails featuring popular New York destinations, or paid for search ads to appear when people Googled destinations. Maybe that would have increased traffic to the site somewhat, but the number of bookings would still have been limited by the lack of the appeal of the photos. By keeping their focus on improving the ultimate goal of increasing the number of nights booked, they not only improved the rate at which people booked, but also made any future increase in traffic they drove to the site more lucrative.

Just as it's easy to lose your North Star and find yourself veering onto the moors in pursuit of vanity or irrelevant growth metrics, it's equally easy to get lost in the weeds of data analysis and lose the sense of urgency to start experimenting with ways to actually drive growth. Alex Schultz notes that the team at Facebook's early charge to improve one key metric, which Mark Zuckerberg decided was monthly active users, helped the growth team break out of "analysis paralysis." Doing more and more data analysis can be an especially alluring trap; because delving into data is scientific, we can convince ourselves that we're just being rigorous and don't want to experiment without sufficient evidence of likely success. One of Schultz's favorite quotes when he talks about the growth process is of US World War II commander General George Patton, who said, "A good plan violently executed now is better than a perfect plan tomorrow."[12] The clarity of the North Star goal helps to keep data analysis tightly focused so you can get your high-impact experiment off the ground as quickly as possible.

THE DATA IMPERATIVE

In order to determine your growth equation and establish your North Star metric, of course the prerequisite is the ability to both gather data on customer behavior and measure product performance and the results of experiments. Only then can you know if your assumptions about both map to the reality of how people are using your product. Jack Dorsey, founder of Twitter, refers to getting your data tracking set up to be able to do so as "instrumentation." Much as an airplane can't fly without instruments providing information about altitude, air pressure, and wind speed constantly being monitored, without the right data at your fingertips, your growth team will be flying blind.[13]

Just as you have to determine the specific set of metrics that matters most to your growth based on your particular growth equation, you should take the time to pool your data resources and tailor your analytics capability so that you can do more refined analysis of customer/user information and behavior. Again, this often involves more than what the standard, off-the-shelf data apps like Google Analytics allow you to do. While those tools serve their purpose, when you're starting to make your aggressive growth push, it's important to be able to track every user from first visit all the way through all of that person's interactions with the product, from how they discover it, to experiencing the aha moment, to when they stop using it. Most start-ups and established firms alike use multiple software programs to collect, store, and analyze customer data. They'll have a Web analytics program to track user behavior on their website and within the product (if it's Web-based) as well as a customer relationship management program to measure engagement with emails and mobile notifications and a system to track payments, among others.

As discussed in Chapter Two, combining all of your data so that you can do detailed tracking of customers throughout the experience funnel is essential to learning how to make your product must-have. If you haven't pooled all your data at that stage, then it's imperative to take the time to do it now.

Having this unified data store not only helps point you toward areas in which to experiment, as discussed in Chapter Two, it also allows you to design better experiments specifically focused on improving what you have identified as your key growth levers. The best growth teams take the time to get their data collection and analysis right. The Facebook growth team decided that better data insights were so important that in January of 2009, they took the dramatic step of stopping all growth experiments and spending one full month on just the job of improving their data tracking, collection, and pooling. Naomi Gleit, the first product manager on Facebook's growth team, recalls that "in 2008 we were flying blind when it came to optimizing growth." After the project, the data picture was complete and they could see what each and every user on the site was doing; they gained a much more comprehensive view of how people used Facebook, and of where problems in the experience of the product were occurring. This enabled the growth team to come up with many more focused experiments for testing and driving growth.[14]

The good news is that while for a large company, as Facebook was by that time, or Walmart when it engaged in this process, the effort to combine all data is quite a chore, it can be done more easily in smaller companies or projects thanks to the availability of a host of tools and services that make it easier to collect data and combine it from multiple sources. In fact, marketing specialist Rob Sobers has outlined a simple method using off-the shelf tools that creates a data tracking system that (at time of writing) costs just $9 a month. (While we won't go into the details of how to do this here, you can find a link to it in the book's endnotes.)[15]

IT'S NOT ALL ABOUT THE NUMBERS

That said, user data does have limits, even remarkably detailed data. After all, even the most sophisticated analysis can really only tell you definitively *what* users are doing, not *why* they're behaving that way. Sometimes patterns of behavior allow you to easily conjecture a reason for user behavior. For example, if you see a significant number of people fleeing from your website when they try to use a certain feature—say, a video player—often you'll be able to readily identify a glitch in how it's working: what product designers refer to as a usability problem. Maybe in the case of the video player, when you dive into the data, you discover that this happens more frequently for users who are coming to the product via an Android phone, and realize that problems in how the video player functions on Android devices are leading to videos taking a long time to load. Such usability problems are low-hanging fruit. Other issues that are holding people back from avidly using your product can be much more difficult to understand, and figuring out the why behind what's going on requires conducting some user surveys or interviews, or both.

While the practice of talking to users in the early development stage of testing a prototype has become widespread, at far too many start-ups and established companies, it falls by the wayside once the product has been launched. Continuing to tap this vital resource as you move into the high-tempo experimentation process is extremely important, as the feedback garnered leads the way to many of the most powerful experiments you can run. Much of the quantitative analysis you do, in other words, should be complemented with this qualitative probing.

DESIGN ACCESSIBLE REPORTING

One last point on data: the critical importance of reporting the results of your data discovery (and then from the experiments you'll be running) in the most simple and accessible way possible. After all, even if you've looked at all the right metrics and crunched all the right numbers, if no one on the team (outside of the data analysts) can understand your findings, they are unlikely to result in meaningful action. Massive spreadsheets of user data, database queries, and highly technical displays, which can be enormously valuable for data analytics professionals, may be daunting if not downright paralyzing to other team members. That's why it's so valuable to take the time to create reports that vividly illustrate your progress as it relates to your growth levers and your North Star metric—using what are generally referred to as *dashboards*.

We are huge fans of dashboards because (a) they help focus team members' attention on key trends or metrics; and (b) they allow you to share findings with the whole company, which encourages more participation in the growth effort. When Sean invited everyone in the company at GrowthHackers (and also trusted advisers and board members) to participate in the process of generating ideas for how to grow the community, we received a flood of great new ideas, many of which worked out to boost growth nicely.

By making the data more accessible across the organization you also keep the North Star and other important metrics top of mind with the entire company and encourage more data-driven behavior in all teams, not just the growth team. When Willix Halim, the former senior vice president of growth at Freelancer.com, actually tested how displaying dashboards in work areas impacts the performance of their teams, he discovered that constant visibility to the numbers the team is responsible for increases their ability to positively impact the metrics they're responsible for significantly.[16]

To get a good sense of how valuable accessible reports can be, take a look at how complex the spreadsheets that growth teams typically create to track the metrics that matter can get. The figure below was shared by Dan Wolchonok, a senior product manager at HubSpot. It's a trove of invaluable information, but it can be daunting for those not schooled in reading such reports to parse and take action with this kind of data presentation.

TYPICAL GROWTH TRACKING REPORT

Now consider how easy it is to spot significant trends in the following graphs created by Pinterest, presented by Pinterest growth engineer John Egan in a post on his eponymous blog about the 27 key metrics that Pinterest tracks.

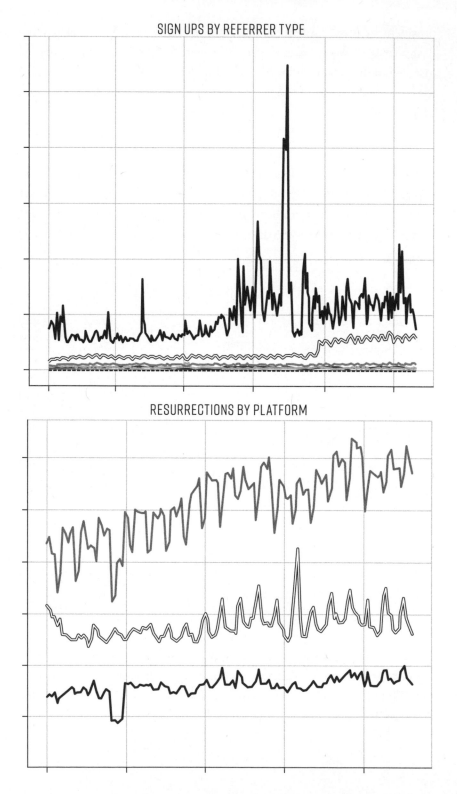

RESURRECTIONS BY REFERRER

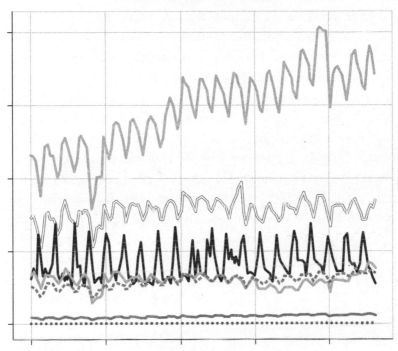

Pinterest Growth Dashboards[17]

Clear trends are immediately discernible in each, though we can't know precisely what they are because Egan has, for reasons of confidentiality, withheld the specifics in the versions you see here. Sharing data must be done judiciously, for sure, and you'll want to be careful about which reports you send out beyond the confines of the growth team, and certainly which you share outside the company.

Creating such simple dashboards is not, pardon the phrase, rocket science. There exist numerous tools to create sharp data visualizations, from simple tools designed for small start-ups such as Geckoboard and Klipfolio, to enterprise solutions such as Tableau and Qlik Sense and dozens more. Whichever you choose, your reports should be insightful and actionable. Too many reports are nothing more than "data puking," as Google Analytics expert Avinash Kaushik calls it.[18] Just disseminating metrics helter-skelter does little more than create confusion. The goal instead is to bring clarity to the metrics that matter most. To do so, dashboards should report only on the most important metrics that map to your growth levers. After narrowing the reporting to what really matters, the next step is to present information in a way that is actionable. For one, metrics should be presented as ratios rather than static numbers. For example, reporting on the total number of users acquired is static and tells you little, but new users acquired per day or week is much better, because it can be compared with previous time periods to see if the rate is rising or falling. Numbers also need to be accompanied by an indicator if they are above trend, below, or on par with past performance. This can be done by showing the percentage change over the previous period or using an indicator such as color to let the team know when a number is ahead or behind of where it typically should be.

Numbers can also be compared with a goal. For example, at Inman the team measures their subscriber growth metrics against the targets outlined in their quarterly goals to see if they are ahead of or behind pace. Dashboards should help team members grasp the health of the business growth, and answer questions quickly and clearly with the information they provide. While data visualization design is an intricate skill, a talented data analyst working with the growth lead can create a set of insightful and actionable dashboards for the team to keep track of the metrics that matter most.

PUTTING IT ALL TOGETHER

To illustrate how identifying growth levers, conducting in-depth analysis and reporting, and supplementing it with customer queries can be used to unlock and then optimize an opportunity for growth, let's look more closely at the way Josh Elman and the growth team at Twitter discovered that people who were following at least 30 other users became avid, long-term fans. Elman made an initial discovery by doing what's called *cohort analysis*, which is dividing your customers or users into distinctive groups by a common trait. For Twitter, a basic division of users might be by the month they joined the service. This can be determined fairly effortlessly, but with a large and detailed data cache, you'd be able to create much more refined cohorts, such as people who look at Twitter

up to five times a day but never tweet, people who tweet only on weekends, people who add ten or more new followers a week, and so forth.

At the time Twitter's problem was retention of users; lots of people
were signing up but then leaving, while at the same time a much smaller
group were becoming quite active. So Elman and the team started by
dividing up users into cohorts based on the number of days they visited Twitter in a month. Then they compared the number of visits made
by those same users for the next month. They made a striking discovery:
those who visited at least seven times in one month were retained in the
next month at a very high rate, between 90 and 100 percent.

RETENTION RATE BASED ON TIMES USED IN MONTH ONE

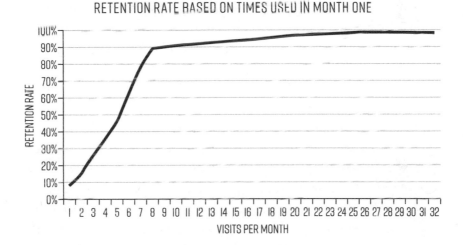

He then divided users up into three cohorts: core users, who visited
at least seven times a month; casual users, who visited less often; and cold
users, who never came back after a first visit. That allowed the team to
determine that only 20 percent of those who visited became core users.
So the team dove into the data further, conducting a correlation analysis,
which looks for any similarities of behavior within one group of users
that are not found in other groups. The analysis of the highly retained
users who came back at least seven times a month revealed that these
people were generally following a number of other users that hovered
around 30; some were following many more, but 30 seemed to be a "tipping point" number that hooked people to coming back for more.

But Elman and the team didn't stop there. They knew that, as the mantra in statistical testing goes, correlation does not equal causation. Now, at that point they might have started just trying to boost the number of people that users were following and left it at that. And indeed that might have produced appreciable results. But what if the sheer desire to follow a significant number of people wasn't the underlying reason that following 30 people made the product sticky? So the growth team dug further into the data and soon found another correlation. Whether or not people became active users also had to do with how many of those 30 or more people they were following were following them back. But contrary to what you might expect, it wasn't that the more people followed a user back, the more likely they were to stick with Twitter; rather, those who were being followed by just a third of those they followed were the ones who became loyal users. But why? Here's where collecting insights by interviewing Twitter users came in. By calling users and interviewing them the team discovered that if much more than a third of those you were following were following you back, then Twitter seemed pretty much like just another social network. The distinctive value of the product wasn't clear. If *less* than a third of the people you were following were following you back then Twitter seemed more like a news site, of which there were already a plethora of other options. The unique product value of Twitter as a place for people to find out what's happening in their world became clear to people when they had the one-third to two-thirds ratio.

The team also used interviews to learn about the behavior of another distinctive cohort of users: those who had gone "comatose," disappearing for a time, and who then suddenly returned and became active. By actually picking up the phone and calling these people, the team learned exactly what was going on: when these people had first started using Twitter, they had thought of it as mainly about sending tweets, as a form of broadcasting, especially for promotional purposes. They didn't have an interest in that, and so they checked out. But then someone they knew had told them about someone they were following, maybe a celebrity or someone they respected in their career or community, and these Twitter refugees realized the value of the site as a tool for connecting with and learning from others. The conclusion was clear: the number of people following and being followed by a user was the key lever they would need to focus on to drive growth. And they used this information to further refine their ways of suggesting people for users to follow.[19]

As the example from Twitter shows, identifying your growth equation and the key metrics to improve, along with establishing the proper instrumentation, data collection, and reporting that includes customer feedback, to discover and monitor your core growth levers, is an essential and powerful first step for successful growth hacking. Now you are ready to put your growth engine in motion. It's time to introduce the step-by-step process we've developed for: honing the best set of ideas to test; getting tests done as efficiently as possible; running a highly disciplined growth meeting; and continuing to learn from and building on your findings in order to kick your growth engine into high gear.

CHAPTER FOUR

TESTING AT HIGH TEMPO

I n 2007, the Baylor University football team placed last in the Big 12 South college football conference once again. The team hadn't gone to a bowl game in over a decade. Then Art Briles took over as head coach, and soon the Baylor Bears were averaging a remarkable 64 points a game and heading to bowl games every year as one of the top-ranked teams in the nation. Key to the turnaround was a new high-tempo, no-huddle offense that caught opponents off guard, leaving them breathlessly struggling to keep up with the pace of play. One sports journalist dubbed Baylor's offense an "unstoppable system." The speed of Baylor's offense not only allows the team to outhustle its opponents: each game teaches the team more about how to win.

By running plays faster and shortening the time between plays, Baylor was able to run about 13 more offensive plays per game than their competitors. Those 13 extra plays amount to a 20 percent increase over the average number of plays for college teams per game, which, over the course of a 10-game season, adds up to the equivalent of nearly 2 full extra games.[1] That translates into much more experiential learning, in the actual heat of battle, about which plays work best and in what circumstances.

Learning more by learning faster is also the goal—and the great benefit—of the high-tempo growth hacking process.

The companies that grow the fastest are the ones that learn the fastest. The more experiments you run, the more you learn. It's really that simple. The high volume is ideal, because most experiments fail to produce the results you're hoping for. Others produce some indication of success but are inconclusive, not producing results significant enough to support making the change tested. Some produce small but not earth-shattering wins. Only very few tests produce dramatic gains. Finding wins, both big and small, is, in other words, a numbers game.

Remember that, generally, big successes in growth hacking come from a series of small wins, compounded over time. Each bit of learning acquired leads to better performance and better ideas to test, which leads to more wins, ultimately turning small improvements into landslide competitive advantages.

To illustrate the power of small gains, Peep Laja, a renowned expert in conversion rate optimization—the science of getting more visitors to a website or app to become customers—loves to point out that a 5 percent improvement in conversion rate every month nets an 80 percent improvement in a year due to the compounding nature of wins. If you were generating visitors through search ads, that increase in conversions would cut your costs of advertising per customer just about in half. This same principle applies everywhere in a company. In fact, small increases in retention can be even more powerful. As a team of researchers from Bain & Company and Harvard Business School discovered, a 5 percent increase in retention leads to an increase in profits of between 25 and 95 percent, because just small gains in retention lead to compounding revenue growth the longer customers stick around.[2]

This chapter will discuss how to run the kinds of rapid-fire experiments that will produce these kinds of compounding wins.

TEMPO PICKS UP OVER TIME

The volume and tempo of experiments that growth teams can run vary greatly depending on the size of the company and the resources available to support testing. Many of the leading growth teams regularly run 20 to 30 experiments a week, and some run many more. Early stage start-ups might be able to launch only one or two tests per week and then steadily build up to a higher volume, while later stage start-ups and large, established firms might well be able to start out with a much higher number. Whatever the size of the company or team, in order to maximize the number of experiments you can run and the gains you achieve from them, it's essential to follow a highly disciplined process that allows you to create a pipeline of good ideas and efficiently prioritize them. This assures that you can maintain continuous testing at the highest possible speed you can manage without getting sloppy in your execution, collecting invalid test results, or getting bogged down in time-consuming brainstorming and debate about which ideas to try next.

We advise that teams start slow and build to a faster tempo after the team gets its footing with the new process; trying to launch too many experiments right off the bat can lead to poor test implementation, team confusion, and discouragement as targets are missed. Running careless or poorly designed tests can do more harm than good. Just as you shouldn't try to run a triathlon without proper training and warm-up, neither should you jump into the growth hacking process at breakneck speed. That is a sure recipe for failure.

We've developed a four-part cycle and a set of simple but powerful tools for making sure a growth team operates as a well-trained, finely tuned, fast-tempo experimenting machine, which we'll introduce in this chapter.

THE GROWTH HACKING CYCLE

Recall that the stages of the process are: data analysis and insight gathering, idea generation, experiment prioritization, running the experiments, and then returning to the analyze step to review results and decide next steps, in a continuous loop. No matter what your product or what aspect you are testing, each turn through this cycle should be completed on a consistent interval, preferably in one or two weeks (at GrowthHackers we use a one-week cycle). The cycle is managed by a one-hour weekly growth team meeting to review results and agree on the next week's set of experiments to implement.

THE GROWTH HACKING PROCESS

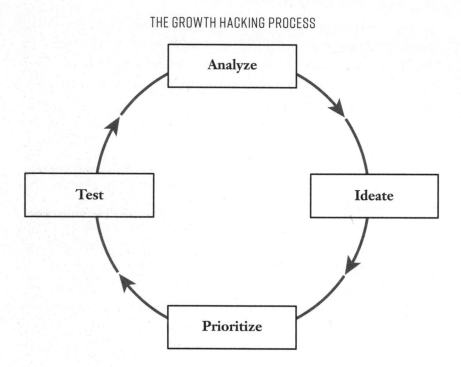

To illustrate how the process works from start to finish, we'll use a hypothetical case of a growth team that has just been created at a large brick-and-mortar grocery retail chain, but as we hope will soon become clear, this is a process that can work for any team or company—large or small—and for any product or project—anything from a new software tool, to an online retailer, to a media product, to a hardware business, and even to a blog or single ad or PR campaign. We'll describe what all of the members of the team should be doing in each of the stages, and we'll introduce a model agenda detailing exactly how the crucial growth meeting should be run.

PREPARING FOR LIFTOFF

Before you launch into the cycle, you'll want to hold an initial team meeting, to explain to everyone on the team how the process will work. Here the growth lead should clarify the role to be played by each team member and how they are expected to work both individually and collaboratively to support the team's work. The methods for generating and prioritizing ideas, which we will introduce later in the chapter, should be explained. The growth lead should then ask the data analyst to share the results of the initial analysis done, and the growth lead should present the key growth levers, the North Star metric, and the area of focus or objectives for the team. The team should then set the goal for the volume and tempo of experiments to launch each week; i.e., how many tests they think they can reasonably manage to design and implement. Generally, the data analysts and engineers will have the expertise to make an initial assessment, and adjustments will almost inevitably be made as the process proceeds.

Let's say the growth team of the hypothetical grocery chain has been assigned the task of driving more sales through the company's new mobile app. Launched with a big traditional marketing push several months ago, the app has attracted a good number of early adopters, with 100,000 people having downloaded it to their phones. But so far, sales coming from orders placed through the app have been sluggish. Rather than make another big acquisition push, the company has decided to try growth hacking.

The product team did a good job of building the app. They set it up with the proper analytics instrumentation to provide the most useful feedback on users' behavior as they move through the app. They also tested the app with likely users during the development phase, and the feedback indicated that it is well designed. It offers lots of appealing features, like item search, recommended items, stock levels and availability, healthy recipes and the option to purchase the ingredients for them with one click, as well as a calorie counter that lets shoppers get a quick read on the calorie count for any given item, and also for a whole meal. The product team also thought shoppers would appreciate a feature that offers the ability to search by gluten-free, kosher, and organic options only. All in all, the app is an impressive piece of work. So it's perplexing that it isn't generating more sales.

To get at the bottom of this puzzling problem, the company has brought in an experienced growth team leader. Her first step is to pull staff from the marketing, engineering, product, and data science groups to create a team. Next, the team will need to uncover what the aha moment is for people who are using the app, and what it is about them and their usage that differs from those who don't. Let's say the team's initial research shows that the aha moment is the convenience of ordering groceries on your phone and having them arrive at your door the next day. To prepare for the first growth team meeting, the growth lead works with the marketing and data team members to think through the app's growth equation, and they determine it is:

NUMBER OF INSTALLS × NUMBER OF MONTHLY ACTIVE USERS × NUMBER OF PURCHASERS × AVERAGE ORDER SIZE × REPEAT PURCHASE RATE = AMOUNT OF GROWTH

They determine that their North Star should be monthly revenue per shopper. This is because the end goal, after all, is to generate sales. They want not only to engage more people in using the app but to build a large base of highly active shoppers who make substantial purchases on a regular basis. With the aha moment in hand, the data tracking in place, the core metrics identified, and the team assembled, it's time to kick off the high-tempo growth hacking process.

In the very first growth meeting, you won't yet be making decisions about which tests to run. Rather, team members will take the next week to brainstorm and percolate ideas for what experiments to run in the first cycle; these will be discussed and selected from at the next week's growth meeting. We'll continue on with the grocery app team throughout the chapter to see what ideas they come up with and exactly how the testing process should be run.

STAGE I: ANALYZE

In this stage, the growth lead works with her data analyst to dive into the data available from the initial wave of users to identify distinctive groups, starting by separating the regular shoppers from those who have barely ever, or never, used the app after downloading it. To start probing for areas of growth opportunity, they formulate a set of questions to guide their analysis, as follows:

WHAT ARE MY BEST CUSTOMERS' BEHAVIORS?

- What features do they use?
- What screens in the app do they visit?
- How often do they open the app?
- What items do they buy?
- What is their average order size?
- What time of day do they shop and on which days?

WHAT ARE THE CHARACTERISTICS OF MY BEST CUSTOMERS?

- What sources were they acquired from? Was it an ad, a promotional email to the chain's customer base, or some other place?
- What devices do they use?
- What is their demographic background, including age, income, and more?
- Where do they live?
- How close are they to the store or other stores?
- What other apps do they use?

WHAT EVENTS CAUSE USERS TO ABANDON THE APP?

- What screens have the highest exit rates?
- Are there bugs that are preventing users from taking a particular action?
- How are the products priced relative to other services?
- What actions don't they take that users who purchase do?
- What is their path through the app, and how much time do they spend in the app before they abandon it?

While the data analyst works on crunching the numbers, the marketing expert on the team conducts a set of user surveys and a set of interviews. With one survey, the goal is to obtain a good set of demographic and psychographic information about users. In another, users are asked about their online and offline shopping habits. Lastly, users are asked about their favorite apps and mobile device usage.

All of the data analysis and responses from user surveys and interviews are summarized in a set of reports from the data analyst and marketing member and are sent to the team prior to the first growth meeting, which is scheduled for a week later. In preparation for that meeting, the growth lead writes a summary of the findings so far, in which she highlights several interesting shared characteristics of the regular shoppers versus those who have never shopped or have only made a purchase or two.

The first is that the group of avid shoppers have an average order of more than $50, which is just above the purchase threshold for free delivery. In addition, a large number of the regular shoppers purchase many of the same items each time, which are clearly staples for them. Finally, a large portion of the most active shoppers come to the app from the grocery store's mobile website.

The team has a good number of growth ideas already in mind based on the analysis, and is now prepared to come together for their first meeting, in which they will discuss the findings thus far, review the initial ideas to leverage those findings, and plot a course to begin experimenting with ways to drive increased revenue from the app's users from a first set of tests to run.

STAGE 2: IDEATE

Ideas are the rocket fuel of growth. And you need a pipeline of them delivering a steady flow. As Linus Pauling said, "The best way to have a good idea is to have lots of ideas." This is why unbridled ideation is key to the growth hacking process. This doesn't mean that you'll also engage in unbridled *testing* of them; your testing will be rigorously prioritized. But you want to encourage the growth team to tap into their creativity and not hold back in suggesting ideas. This ensures you'll generate the volume of ideas that you'll need to find the few diamonds in the rough.

Over the four days following the team meeting, all members should submit as many ideas as possible for hacks to try to improve the revenue from the app users. Self-censorship is discouraged, and nothing should be considered too crazy to put out there. The team members should be tasked with contributing ideas based on their specific expertise, though they shouldn't be limited to ideas in that domain. The user experience designer might, for example, propose changes to the design of certain screen displays, while the marketing member might focus on different ways to encourage users to make their first purchase, and the engineers might come up with ideas to enhance the product's speed of performance.

The growth lead should set up a project management system to coordinate the submission and management of ideas, as well as the tracking and reporting of results. Remember that cross-functional collaboration and the sharing of information are key tenets of growth hacking; that's why it's critical that everyone on the growth team have access to the growing bank of ideas, and be able to add to it at any time. At Growth-Hackers, we created our own software program, called Projects, which allows anyone who is given access to it to both submit ideas and track, comment, and review experiments and their results. Any number of project management software packages can be used to facilitate the management of experiments and communication among team members about the status of experiments.

Ideas should be submitted to an *idea pipeline*, following a templated format by which they should be submitted. It's important to standardize the format so that ideas can be quickly evaluated, without the team needing to ask lots of questions. Instead of vague suggestions like "Our sign-up form is too hard; we should make it easier to sign up," submissions must articulate exactly what change is to be tested, the reasoning behind why that change might improve results, and an explanation of how results should be measured.

To illustrate the proper style in which ideas should be submitted, let's return to the team working on the grocery mobile app. Ideas generated in that first week between the first and second growth meeting might be directed at any one of several methods of driving more buying. Some ideas might be aimed at enticing people who've downloaded the app but haven't purchased yet to take the plunge and make their first purchase. Other hacks might be aimed at people who've already made a purchase, whether by trying to get them to buy more frequently, or increase their average order value on subsequent purchases. Lastly, the team might try some efforts to drive even more new shoppers to the app from the company website, since their data showed that those who come from the site tend to be the best purchasers.

Let's say the product manager on the grocery app team comes up with the idea to build a "shopping list" feature that will store a list of shoppers' prior purchases so that they can easily reorder them. The idea should be submitted in this format:

IDEA NAME: We've found that giving each idea a brief name makes the discussion of them easier and more efficient. At GrowthHackers, to force brevity and clarity, we limit them to under 50 characters. For the purposes of this example, let's call this feature idea "Shopping List."

IDEA DESCRIPTION: The best way to think about what the idea description should look like is along the lines of an executive summary. It should address the who, what, where, when, why, and how of the idea. *Who* is being targeted? For example, all visitors, new users only, returning users, or users from a particular traffic source? *What* is going to be created, such as new marketing copy or a new feature? *Where* will the new copy or feature be implemented: Will it be on the app's home screen or elsewhere? *When* will it appear during the customer's use, such as on the landing page when a visitor first comes to the site? In addition, the description must include the *why*—the rationale behind the idea—and the *how*—a recommendation of the type of test to be done, such as an A/B test, or new feature to be built, or a new ad campaign to be launched.

For the shopping list, the product manager's description might look something like:

Making it easier to view and reorder previously purchased items will increase the number of people who make repeat purchases and potentially the rate at which they purchase. Improving the convenience of reordering should prompt more reordering. The shopping list feature, which should be added to the app's navigation and be available to every user, will make it easy for users to save and reorder their favorite items. This feature should be tested with a group of initial users before it is made widely available to all users.

HYPOTHESIS: Like in any other type of experiment, the hypothesis should be a simple proposition of expected cause and effect. Again, broad strokes and vague outcomes are not going to cut it here; the statement "Not enough people are coming back and making repeat purchases; we should incentivize them to do so" is simply a statement of a problem and general direction for making improvement. Instead, a hypothesis might be: "By making it easier for shoppers to view and reorder previously purchased items, the number of people who make repeat purchases will increase by 20 percent."

Some teams may elect to state an expected gain in their hypothesis while others will not. The pro of doing so is that it gives the team a clear idea of what success looks like. If they're expecting a 40 percent gain and the win is 5 percent, then they still have work to do. On the other hand, predicting the results of a test ahead of time is an inexact science at best, and so some teams forgo it. At GrowthHackers we state an expected lift, which is calculated from past, similar experiments, benchmark data available online, and rough estimations based on the amount of people who are likely to see the experiment and its expected impact on their current behavior.

METRICS TO BE MEASURED: The metrics that should be tracked in order to evaluate the outcome of the test must be specified. Most experiments should measure more than one metric because sometimes, improvements in one metric come at the expense of others. Say that you're testing a new sign-up form to your landing page. You may find that the new design increases the number of new people signing up, because you made it easier to do so, *but* that those sign-ups are less engaged than previous new users because they didn't understand exactly what they were signing up for. Ultimately, that might be a serious impediment to growth.

Identify metrics to be tracked by looking at the metrics "downstream" from the experiment that will be impacted. For example, for the shopping list, the metrics to be measured are the number of customers who use the shopping list feature, the number of items saved to each list, the number of repeat order purchases, the rate at which people reorder, and the average order size of each order. These metrics will help the growth team assess the experiment and its impact on the metrics that matter to them. The scope of measurement includes how many people use the new feature and also the feature's impact on their purchasing behavior, which gives the team insight into whether the experiment improved their key metric—namely, the revenue per shopper—and whether the experiment's hypothesis was correct or not, such as whether it increased the repeat order rate of those app users who used the feature.

A GROWTH IDEA IN "PROJECTS"

Shopping List
by **Morgan Brown**   Thu Oct 13 2016

4.7   4 Impact
8 Confidence
2 Ease

ABOUT THE IDEA

Making it easier to view and reorder previously purchased items will increase the number of people who make repeat purchases and potentially the rate at which they purchase. Improving the convenience of reordering should prompt more reordering. The shopping list feature, which should be added to the app's navigation and available to every user, will make it easy for users to save and reorder their favorite items. This feature should be tested with a group of initial users before it is made widely available to all users.

By making it easier for shoppers to view and reorder previously purchased items, the number of people who make repeat purchases will increase by 20%.

Filed in REVENUE

♡ Like?   O likes
⬇ Saves   O saves
☆ Nominate?
Ａ Test
⧉ Duplicate
🗀 Archive
⧉ Get Shareable Link
＋ Add to Roadmap

TAGS

You need some tags

＋ Add Tags

Test This Idea

Remember, the more ideas that go into your pipeline the better your chances of finding winners that spur growth. In the next phase of the cycle you'll implement a process for sifting through the (hopefully) massive volume of ideas being generated and prioritize which to test now, later, or not at all.

One final note. With the goal being to generate as many ideas as possible, you ultimately want ideas coming in not only from the members of the team, but from people all around the company. The sales team might have valuable insight about customer pain points, and the marketers may have learned about a new promotional platform to experiment with for customer acquisition. While your initial efforts should leverage the creativity of people within the company, over time you should consider opening the call for ideas to outside suppliers and partners. Outsiders can offer surprisingly helpful suggestions that help teams break out of preconceived notions about the types of things they should be trying. In particular, advisers who have worked with a similar business to yours may have knowledge about a tactic that had great effect elsewhere. Asking your customers to share ideas can also be enormously enlightening, especially your most passionate users. They're often thrilled to be asked and may have a good deal more experience with actually using your product than (sadly) your team does.

At GrowthHackers, we at first kept the ideation process to the members of our growth team. But we found ourselves getting stuck in a rut of similar tests. So we turned to our colleagues and asked for their ideas. At first, we made the mistake of not sharing the growth levers and target metrics with them, which resulted in lots of vague responses like "What do you guys need help with?" or "I'll let you know if I think of anything." But when we shared our focus, a wealth of great ideas flooded in. The result was so positive that we then opened up the ideation to our investors and advisers as well, and then ultimately also to trusted members of the growth hacking community.

We started off taking ideas via email and putting them into the right format ourselves for adding to our pipeline. Once we created our Projects software, we allowed all those we'd invited to submit ideas to log in and add their ideas themselves.

And indeed, some of the best ideas the team has ever tested came from outside the company. One of our most active community members, for example, recommended we do question-and-answer sessions on the site with well-known growth experts, which have since become important traffic and engagement drivers for the site. And after one of our advisers shared some search engine optimization tactics that worked well on his site, we found that when we deployed them they worked powerfully to drive our search rankings up on Google. These are just two of dozens of winning ideas that came from outside the team.

The final step before submitting an idea is to give it a numerical score to help the rest of the team prioritize it against other experiment ideas in stage 3. We'll go over the scoring system and how it's used to rank and choose hacks in this next stage.

STAGE 3: PRIORITIZE

Before an idea is ready to be considered by the team, it must be scored. This scoring helps the team rank ideas against one another to determine what to test and when. Ideas are scored by the individual submitting the idea, prior to the idea going into the pool of available hacks to consider for testing.

At GrowthHackers, Sean developed the *ICE score system*, with ICE standing for Impact, Confidence, and Ease, as a way to organize all the ideas generated in the ideation process of the cycle. Here's how it works.

THE ICE SCORE

When submitting ideas, the submitter should rate each idea on a ten-point scale, across each of the following three criteria: the idea's potential impact, the submitter's level of confidence in how effective it will be, and how easy it will be to implement. Then those ratings are averaged to provide an aggregate score for each idea. The entire bank of ideas are then ranked by their scores, and the team begins experimentation with the highest-scored ideas in the area of focus chosen by the growth team. For example, a highly rated customer acquisition idea will be passed on in favor of a lower-scored idea around retaining users if the growth team is currently focused on improving customer retention.

Here's an example of the style of ranking we create, listing the results for the grocery app team's ideas. This ranking can be done in a spreadsheet or in your project management software. You can see how the scoring has led to clarity about which two are the best ones to try first. Though the aggregate score of an idea may not always be the ultimate arbiter of which are selected in what order, because the team may decide after discussion in the team meeting that there are reasons to go with a lower-scoring option, you've got a great starting point.

IDEA	IMPACT	CONF	EASE	AVG
ADD SHOPPING LIST FEATURE TO IMPROVE REORDER RATE	4	8	2	4.67
$10 FIRST-TIME-SHOPPER PROMOTION	7	4	8	6.33
IMPROVE VISIBILITY OF FREE DELIVERY FOR $50 ORDERS	6	7	6	6.33
IMPROVE RECOMMENDATION ENGINE	4	6	3	4.33

It's true that scoring your own ideas can be challenging, as they do require relative subjectivity and some degree of trying to predict the future. But with experience and practice, you'll soon learn how to use data, previous experiment findings, and industry benchmarks to estimate your idea's value. In addition, your "feel" for the potential return of a given idea will improve the more ideas you see tested and observe the results they deliver. But it also helps to have a good handle on what exactly these three criteria are and how to evaluate them. So let's look at each a little more closely.

IMPACT: This is the expectation about the degree to which the ideas will improve the metric being focused on, which, in the case of the grocery app, is the revenue per user. You might think that only ideas that are very high impact are worthy of being submitted, but remember that a team should be selecting a mix of potentially high-impact experiments, which will generally require more work, and some that are easier to implement but also have a good, if not great, chance of producing meaningful results. The goal is to privilege as many high-impact tests as possible, but if some of them will take several weeks, or longer, to prepare for launch, then some easier tests should be slotted into the schedule—which is why ease of testing is also a component of the ICE score.

CONFIDENCE: This is a measure of how strongly the idea generator believes the idea will produce the expected impact. This rating should be based not just on conjecture, but on empirical evidence of some kind, whether from data analysis, review of industry benchmarks, published case studies, or knowledge of previous experiments.

Confidence should be higher if a test is an iteration of a previously successful test, which is a good practice and is commonly referred to in the growth hacking community as doubling down. Say, an email sign-up form offering a free product demonstration on a landing page promoted via a Facebook ad brought in a lot of new email addresses. You might next try promoting that same landing page through other sources, such as Google. Your confidence in the first experiment might have been relatively low, say, a score of 4, because you thought the sign-up form would deter people from wanting the demo. But for the next test, you might up the score to an 8 because of its success in the first experiment. A high confidence score might also come from knowledge that an experiment was successfully performed by another team, whether within your company or not.

EASE: Ease is the measure of the time and resources needed to run the experiment. Ideas such as substantially redesigning the new user experience or revamping the shopping cart in the checkout process might be high impact, but they are usually not easy undertakings, requiring weeks or months of work to launch. The ease score both provides the growth team a reality check about overly ambitious ideas and helps identify some "low-hanging-fruit" tests to run each time through the growth hacking process.

Before the team meeting, the initial scores should be reviewed by the growth lead, who might see issues that the submitter of the idea hadn't seen or appreciated. The growth lead may suggest modifications to the score based on her past experience and consultation with other team members. It's important that the team not get bogged down in trying to fine-tune the score too much. The score is to be used for relative prioritization and will not be perfect. A growth meeting can devolve quickly if team members squabble over a test's impact score, for example. It's better for the team to use the score as a valued guide, rather than the be-all and end-all for test prioritization. When there is uncertainty or concern about a score, the growth lead should use her best judgment and act decisively to keep the team moving.

This scoring system is clearly not fail-safe, and the results of tests will often defy expectations. Some of the lowest-rated experiments can—and have—turn out to be the biggest winners. At GrowthHackers, we once ran a simple experiment that involved moving the location of a sign-up form to receive our weekly "Top Posts" email newsletter. We had originally put the form at the bottom of our home page because we thought that users would want to evaluate the content on the site—i.e., scroll through the feed of trending posts that we feature on the home page—before they could decide whether they wanted to sign up to get the newsletter. Then Morgan had the humble idea to move the invite from the bottom to the top, giving it more visibility. Truth be told, he wasn't sold on the impact the change would have, assigning it a score of 4 out of 10. But we decided to test it nonetheless because he gave the experiment a 9 for ease based on feedback from the engineering team, who said it was relatively easy to implement, and on his confidence that it would improve email sign-ups to some degree by being more visible, giving it a confidence rating of 8 that it would do so. The results were staggering. Much to our surprise, we saw a 700 percent jump in sign-ups, far exceeding our humble assumptions about the experiment's potential impact on our growth.

We don't tell this story to boast about Morgan's ability to come up with good test ideas—he's recommended his share of duds—but rather to show that our own expectations for our ideas aren't foolproof, and to warn against tossing away all ideas that don't have high scores.

While we like to use the ICE system, many other scoring systems have been created by fellow growth hackers. Bryan Eisenberg, considered the godfather of conversion optimization, recommends his *TIR system*, which stands for Time, Impact, and Resources.[3] Another system is PIE, for Potential, Importance, and Ease.[4] Many teams also develop their own systems to suit their particular needs. Though the specifics may differ, all scoring methods achieve the same overarching goal—assessing ideas in a quantitative way that makes it easier to sift through the options and decide what to test next.

Even after going through the scoring process and narrowing down a list of experiments you know you want to try, you'll likely still end up with more ideas than you can test during the coming week. Some ideas will also require more preparation than can be done in one week, such as those that require extensive software development or design work. Those should be assigned a target future test date under the advisement of those who will be most involved in getting the experiment from idea to launch. So if the work involves software engineering, the engineer and product manager should give the growth team an estimate of the timeline, whereas if the experiment involves testing a new customer acquisition channel, the marketing team is responsible for advising the growth team on the schedule.

All ideas that can't be launched during the current week should be stored in the experiment pipeline. You may decide to slate some of them for the following week, and others you might wait to revisit farther down the line. What's key is that the team prioritize their efforts for the optimal use of their time and resources directed at the most pressing needs for the business in the area of focus identified by the growth lead.

To see how the selection process works, let's return to our grocery mobile app team, who you'll recall have a goal of increasing the revenue per user. Out of their set of ideas that follows, let's say they reach a consensus and select the first-time-shopper promotion and the improved visibility of the free delivery offer for testing due to their high scores for both impact and ease.

IDEA	IMPACT	CONF	EASE	AVG
ADD SHOPPING LIST FEATURE	4	8	2	4.67
$10 FIRST-TIME-SHOPPER PROMOTION	7	4	8	6.33
IMPROVE VISIBILITY OF FREE DELIVERY FOR $50 ORDERS	6	7	6	6.33
IMPROVE RECOMMENDATION ENGINE	4	6	3	4.33

The marketing team member is most likely to be put in charge of managing the first-time-shopper promotion and the product designer is charged with owning the free delivery test.

Say the team also decides that the shopping list experiment is worth a try, but because creating the feature will be fairly complex, the growth lead might task the product manager with consulting the product team about when they can slot the work into their schedule. The growth team will consider when to slate the experiment once that information is available.

We recommend making experiment selection a collaborative process. One day prior to the growth meeting, the growth lead should notify the team that it's time to review the idea pipeline and nominate the experiments they think are the most promising candidates (which might include not only the new set submitted but some already in the pipeline). These nominations will determine the set of ideas to be discussed in the growth meeting, where the team will come to a collective decision about which experiments to launch, and when. Nominations can be done either over email or, if the system you're using allows for this, by highlighting them in the pipeline. In GrowthHackers Projects, for example, team members "star" ideas, which then get pulled into a separate queue where the growth lead can view them all for review and debate in the upcoming meeting. To keep the number of ideas for discussion manageable, we limit each team member to a maximum of three test candidates for the week.

These "finalist" ideas will be presented and reviewed at the growth meeting, where the experiments to be run will be chosen by the growth team. The next section describes how.

STAGE 4: TEST

Once the experiments for the next week's testing cycle have been chosen, they are moved to what we call the Up Next queue (this can be as simple as a new spreadsheet if you're tracking manually, or if you're using project management software, these experiments can be moved to a special work queue or list within the system). Now it's time for those in charge of the experiments to work with the other members of the growth team, and/or with colleagues in the departments who must contribute work, to prepare and deploy the experiments.

This is where the cross-functional collaboration really comes into play. Using our trusty example of the shopping app, the marketing team member might work with the graphic design and email teams to create the first-time-shopper-promotion graphics and marketing copy. She'll also collaborate with the data analyst to identify both the control group—the group of users who won't be exposed to the experiment—and the experiment group, and to ensure that results can be tracked properly.

Once the experiments are ready to go, the growth lead will send a notification around the company that they are being launched so that there are no surprises for other teams also working on the product. If roadblocks to launching certain experiments are encountered (e.g., the engineers are working on another big initiative and won't have time to code the growth hack for another number of weeks), the team member in charge must inform the growth lead right away so that other experiments in their Up Next queue can be considered for deployment in their place.

TESTING RULES OF THE ROAD

Each experiment run comes at the expense of another candidate. Therefore it's important that care is taken in the selection of the idea and the way the idea is tested. A poor test is one less opportunity to learn, slowing the team down, and bad data can send the team down a very wrong path. That's why it's critical that every experiment be designed to produce statistically valid results. Guidelines for ensuring reliable results should be well established, and the data analyst on the team should be responsible for applying these rules to experiments being run. The details of test design are outside the scope of this book, but we'd like to offer two rules of thumb for testing that we've found particularly helpful.

USE A 99 PERCENT STATISTICAL CONFIDENCE LEVEL: Many tools automatically set, or let you set for yourself, the confidence levels for tests. Common levels are 95 percent and 99 percent. While the difference of four percentage points may not seem like much, it is actually quite significant from a statistical point of view. A 95 percent confidence level means that a "winning" test can still be wrong 5 percent of the time. That means that 1 out of 20 tests that come back as winners could actually be losers. At 99 percent confidence, however, that number of false-positive tests drops to 1 out of 100: a much more valid result. Therefore, when in doubt, go with 99 percent confidence to greatly reduce the risk of mistakenly choosing a winning experiment on the basis of a false-positive result.

CONTROL ALWAYS WINS: When an experiment clearly fails, it's usually easy for a team to look at the data and come to quick agreement about that fact. Reaching consensus is dicier when the results of a test are neither clearly positive nor negative, especially if running it involved a good deal of time and effort. No one likes to have wasted good work, and team members may want to let a test run much longer than is cost effective in the hopes that a larger sample size will change the current trend. While we understand why this is tempting, when results are inconclusive, the best course is to stick with the original, or control, version. That's because even though the results may be inconclusive, the new variant could actually be a loser in the long term, a potentially costly risk. Think of it this way: in case of a "tie," the "win" should go to the control.[5]

BACK TO STAGE 1: ANALYSIS AND LEARNING

The analysis of the test results should be conducted by either the analyst or the growth lead, if he or she has the expertise. The results should be written up in a test summary, and this document should include

- The name and description of the test including the variants used and the target customers (for example, was the test run in a marketing channel, only toward mobile users, or to paid subscribers, etc.?)
- The type of test run: was it a test of a product function, a change to marketing copy on a website page or screen in a mobile app, a creative test, or a new marketing tactic deployed?
- Features it impacted: this could include the screenshots of where the test was run on the site, or on the screen of a mobile app, or include a copy of the creative from a particular billboard ad, TV, or radio ad experiment
- Key metrics: what were the metrics that you were trying to improve with the test?
- Test timing, including start and end dates of the test including day of week
- The hypothesis of the test and the results, including the original ICE score, sample sizes, statistical confidence, and statistical power
- Potential confounding issues, such as the time of year the test was run, or if there were other promotions that may have skewed visitor behavior
- The conclusions drawn.

This summary should then be shared with the growth team via email along with a memo offering a brief synopsis of what's been learned. It should also be added to a database where you store all test summaries, which we call the *knowledge base*. That can be as simple as a special folder that is accessible to everyone on the team on a shared file server, or perhaps a page in the company wiki or intranet. In GrowthHackers Projects, the knowledge base is a special part of the software that has a feature to indicate whether the test was a winner, was a loser, or was inconclusive. No matter how the reports are stored, the essential requirement is that the results of all experiments are easily searchable so that teams can revisit them and consider variations, and also so that they can assure that they are not repeating tests, which is all too easy to do, especially when operating at high tempo.

In addition to creating a knowledge base, many teams send out regular communications far and wide within the company or, if more appropriate, the department to keep employees up to speed on the growth process. Your company culture and norms will determine what style of communication works best for you, but here are a few examples that you might want to try:

- Create a "Wins" email distribution list, so that recipients can get regular updates on which experiments have won, and the impact on the business. We've done this at Inman, and it goes to 20 people, all of whom have expressed interest in being kept informed. Some companies also send an email that lists *all* of the tests run, and shares the results for failed and inconclusive tests as well.
- For teams using instant messaging software (like Slack), you could consider creating a channel or chat room dedicated to the sharing of test results and discussion about them. We have a testing channel at Inman in our company Slack account that we use only for communicating new tests being launched and the results of recently concluded tests—both wins and losses.
- Publish test results to company dashboards. If the company doesn't use dashboards, then simply printing and posting test results in common areas around the office is an effective low-tech way to spread the word.

THE GROWTH MEETING

Since much of the process described above takes place around the cadence of the growth meeting, it's useful to have a template for how that meeting should be conducted. We advise holding a growth meeting once a week, but some teams might want to hold them once every two weeks, depending on the time they can devote to the process. The goal of the meeting is to focus rigorously on the set of nominated ideas and agree on the plan for experimentation. It's vital that this meeting not be used for brainstorming ideas; ideas should be brainstormed well before using the process described above. Teams may also want to hold additional brainstorming meetings, for example, perhaps once a month.

The following is the protocol for running the meeting that we developed at GrowthHackers that has proven highly effective. Feel free to tailor the specifics to your own team's needs, but the overarching process is designed to work for any team or company, large or small.

The growth meeting is held on Tuesdays, which provides the team with a day at the beginning of the week to finish some of the requisite prep work. On Monday, the members check in on experiments in progress to identify any that can be concluded, or to collect data to update the team on during the meeting. The growth team lead does a review of the activity from the prior week, including:

- look at the number of experiments successfully launched and compare it to the velocity goal of the team
- confer with the data analyst to update all of the key metrics they're following so that she can brief the team about them, perhaps distributing reports
- gather the data about any tests that were concluded
- conduct a high-level assessment of the previous week's activity and results, including a summary of findings about both the positive and negative effects on growth discovered from the experiments
- compile this information and include it with the meeting agenda, which acts as a living document and is shared with the team beforehand. Some teams keep this document as a file that lives in the cloud, such as in Google Docs or Dropbox, while others use an

internal wiki page in software such as Google Sites, Confluence, or the corporate intranet.

On the day of the meeting the growth team comes together for an hour and marches through the following standard agenda. Remember that the growth lead is responsible for keeping the team on track with this agenda as well as running the meeting more generally.

15 MINUTES: METRICS REVIEW AND UPDATE FOCUS AREA

The growth lead reviews the latest data for the North Star metric and the other key growth metrics, such as progress on short-term growth objectives in the team's area of focus. The grocery app team, for example, might review the week's average revenue per shopper, number of shoppers completing purchases, and so on. This helps get everyone clear on whether things are going well or not, what is working in the business, and what could be better.

Additionally, the growth lead will highlight the following set of information:

KEY POSITIVE FACTORS: Improvements in metrics resulting from experiments, or perhaps from other factors outside the scope of the team's work, such as improved reorder rates observed after implementing the shopping list idea in the grocery app or an influx of new app users brought in by an in-store promotion run by the marketing team.

KEY NEGATIVE FACTORS: Drop-offs in performance and a review of issues that are holding back growth, such as if the number of people using the grocery app dropped measurably, or if the purchase rate dipped, or if a planned marketing push for the app was underperforming or delayed.

GROWTH FOCUS AREA: What part of the user experience or growth lever is the team focused on? Are there any short-term objectives that the team needs to work toward? If the focus is staying the same, this is a simple confirmation. If it's changing: say, a shift from user acquisition to retention or monetization, a discussion of the new focus area and the reasoning behind the change should take place. Short-term objectives in service of these goals should also be noted, such as a short-term goal to get a certain percentage of app users saving items to their shopping lists.

10 MINUTES: REVIEW LAST WEEK'S TESTING ACTIVITY

A review of the results of efforts of the previous week, to include an assessment of the:

TEMPO: the number of experiments launched in the previous week as compared with the team's tempo goal.

HOW MANY TESTS "UP NEXT" WERE NOT LAUNCHED IN THE LAST WEEK: This discussion should explain about why tests were delayed.

15 MINUTES: KEY LESSONS LEARNED FROM ANALYZED EXPERIMENTS

The growth lead and data analyst, in conjunction with any specific experiment owners, such as the product manager leading the development of a new feature, go over the preliminary results from the tests launched, as well as the conclusive results of experiments for which full analysis has been conducted. They answer any questions, take suggestions for further analysis, and codify the team's assessment of the experiment and its implications for further action, or not.

15 MINUTES: SELECT GROWTH TESTS FOR CURRENT CYCLE

The team discusses the nominations for the next set of tests to launch. The growth lead asks each member to give a brief overview of the ideas they've nominated, which is followed by a brief discussion among the team about the merits of those experiments. The aim is to reach consensus, but if there is disagreement, the growth lead makes the final call. The experiments are then assigned to team members as "owners" of each experiment, responsible for getting the test launched. The growth lead will assign owners based on the expertise of the member who is best suited to manage the experiment. For example, a new product feature will be assigned to a product manager, while a new video ad campaign may be assigned to the marketing member, and so on. Any experiments that are deemed worthy of testing but will not feasibly be ready for next week's cycle are slated for a future date, pending information from the relevant teams on how long they will need to ready the test for launch.

5 MINUTES: CHECK GROWTH OF IDEA PIPELINE

The growth lead reports about the number of ideas waiting for consideration or tagged for future launch. If the ideation volume is down, the growth lead should spur the team to add more ideas in the coming week. Recognizing top contributors from the previous week is a great way to inspire the team to keep the flow of fresh ideas coming.

GROWTH WITHIN WEEKS

The speed with which the growth hacking process can produce significant improvements is astonishing. Sometimes a hack can go from germ of an idea to growth driver with just two weeks or so of work, including time spent on the preparatory data analysis and the first team meeting.

For example, the team working on the grocery mobile app might well get conclusive results from the two experiments selected for its first week of testing, one of which might support implementing a significant improvement to the app that can be designed and implemented almost immediately. Let's say that the number of visitors who were converted to first-time shoppers increased by about 15 percent due to the $10 special offer for making a first purchase. This strong result leads the growth team to make the $10 incentive a part of every new user's first experience in the app, and the 15 percent improvement in conversion holds up, leading to hundreds of thousands of dollars in new revenue from first-time app shoppers.

Through the success of this simple experiment, the team might also make a significant discovery that would lead to another good hack to test. Perhaps in closely reviewing the results, the team notes that the average order size for the new shoppers was smaller than the overall average for users. So the team might decide to try some experiments aimed at increasing the value of purchases made by these first-time buyers. For example, they add to the pipeline the idea of offering a scaling discount, which is larger the more the first-time shopper purchases.

One of the great things about growth hacking is that even failed experiments can lead to significant learning over an incredibly short time frame. Let's say the other experiment proves a failure: increasing the visibility of the $50 free delivery offer was found to lead to no increase in volume of merchandise purchased. The team might hypothesize that perhaps $50 is too high a threshold and decide to add a test to the pipeline to be run the next week of a free-delivery offer starting at orders of $40. Perhaps that doesn't drive an appreciable increase in order size either, but if they keep testing, they might discover in another week that a minimal order of $35 does the trick. Within just two more weeks, the team would have learned about a second powerful way to drive the growth of the app.

Now that you have the data puzzle solved, the team assembled, and the growth hacking process down, it's time to move into the playbook section of *Hacking Growth*. In Part II we'll devote a chapter to each major lever for growth—user acquisition, activation, retention, and monetization—and share with you the strategies and hacks that growth teams can use to unlock new growth in each area. Along the way we'll also share more stories from successful growth teams and how they discovered and solved for big wins in each area, as well as follow the progress of our grocery app team to take you step by step through applying the growth hacking process in each.

PART II:

THE GROWTH HACKING PLAYBOOK

CHAPTER FIVE

HACKING ACQUISITION

To be sure, gaining new customers is hugely important for any company. But if acquiring those customers is costing you more than you stand to make from them, well, we'd say you have a bit of a problem. Yet far too many companies fall into the trap of spending way too much to lure potential new customers. And it appears it's only going to get worse: spending on online ads in the US has doubled since 2010,[1] and what's more, in the US, Canada, and Western Europe at least, the growth of the Web audience is slowing, which essentially means companies are spending (and will continue to spend) more money to chase fewer potential customers.[2]

Before Sean and the team at Dropbox implemented the referral program, the company was spending nearly $400 to acquire each new user and the premium subscription price was just $99. Drew Houston smartly recognized that the expense-to-payoff ratio was unsustainable, but unfortunately, not every company comes to that realization in time. Take, for example, Fab, a flash-sale site for specialty designer goods. Once lauded as the "Amazon for design," and feted as the latest Silicon Valley unicorn, the company was growing its customer base at breakneck speeds; the only problem was, it was spending $40 million a year on advertising and customer acquisition costs to do so—more than 35 percent of its revenue.[3] Suffice it to say, excessive spending quickly caught up with them, leading to the start-up's dramatic implosion and sell-off at a fire-sale price.

This is not to say that spending lots of cash, even many millions of dollars, to stoke customer acquisition is always misguided. A business-to-business software company, for example, may have to invest a great deal up front in hiring a large salesforce in order to make any headway in lining up customers. Or a business in a "winner take all" situation, where it's likely that one firm will become overwhelmingly dominant (as is often true for network effect businesses such as LinkedIn or Whats-App), spending a great deal up front to make a land grab and try to lock in dominance may be a brilliant strategy. Or, if a company is running neck and neck with a strong competitor, as is the case with car-service providers Uber and Lyft, there may be no choice but to spend heavily on acquisition efforts. That's assuming, of course, that the company has the cash on hand to sustain that up-front spending and a solid plan to recoup it down the line.

The amount a company should spend on customer acquisition is not a matter of any preordained formula; it's a function of many variables specific to each company's business model, competitive situation, and stage of growth. Mature businesses with deep cash reserves, for example, can obviously afford to employ more expensive customer acquisition tactics like television and print advertising, while cash-strapped start-ups must utilize scrappier methods that may have more limited reach but cost next to nothing. All that said, making acquisition efforts as cost effective as possible is always good business, and all companies should always be striving to spark strong word of mouth in order to reduce the expense of acquiring new customers. The growth hacking process is designed to help discover the most cost-effective ways to acquire new customers— and then optimize those efforts to drive growth.

Once you've put together your growth team, determined your key growth levers, and done sufficient testing to establish that your product is a must-have, you're ready to start hacking the first stage of the growth funnel: acquiring customers. We advised earlier that you should not launch into a full-court press for large-scale customer acquisition until you've achieved product/market fit—i.e., until you've determined not only that you have a good product, but that your product is compelling to its target market. (Though for network effect businesses the push for user acquisition typically must go hand in hand with product development.)

The first phase of work in scaling up your acquisition of customers should be devoted to achieving two additional types of fit: *language/market fit*, which is how well the way you describe the benefits of your product resonates with your target audience, and *channel/product fit*, which describes how effective the marketing channels are that you've selected to reach your intended audience with your product, such as paid search advertising or viral, or content, marketing.

In this chapter we'll show you how to use the growth hacking process to find those fits by using rapid-fire testing to identify the more effective and cost-efficient methods to both reach and engage your target market. First we'll look at how to hone your marketing language to best communicate what is not just valuable, but special, about what you have to offer. Then we'll talk about how to identify a core channel or two to focus on, and ways to leverage that channel for optimal growth. Next we'll explore how to come up with clever hacks for acquiring customers through viral mechanisms, like referral programs, built into the product itself.

CRAFTING A COMPELLING MESSAGE

The term *language/market fit* was coined by James Currier (who we met in the introduction) to refer to how well the language you use to describe and market your product to potential users resonates with them and motivates them to give it a try. This includes the language used in all aspects of the marketing campaign—from emails, to mobile notifications, to print and online advertisements—as well as, in the case of Web- and mobile-based products, the messaging used within the product itself: not just the tagline and value proposition on the landing page, but also the text accompanying the product's every feature or screen or page. This is critical for customer acquisition for all businesses, not just Web-based ones, because today every product must have a Web presence and with users finding their way to yours through so many different routes, the first page they encounter might well not be the one you've specifically designed as a greeting for them.[4]

No matter how a potential customer discovers your product—whether via ads, articles and reviews, or word of mouth—the first text they see must send the right message fast; and in fact, it must do so a good deal faster today than just a few years ago. Research has shown that the average attention span (the amount of time we focus on a new piece of information online) of humans is now eight seconds, which is down from twelve seconds in 2000, and confers on us the dubious distinction of having an attention span shorter than that of goldfish.[5] With so little time to impress people, it is imperative that they understand almost immediately how your product can benefit them. This means that the language you use must *directly and persuasively* connect with a need or desire they have in order to hook them—in eight seconds or less!—into giving you a few more heartbeats to convince them of why they should come on board. In other words, you must craft language that very concisely communicates your product's core value—conveying the aha moment—and answers the simple question foremost in every consumer's mind: "How is this thing you're showing me going to improve my life?"

One of the best examples of an enormously compelling product description is the language Steve Jobs used to introduce the original iPod. When the product was unveiled in 2001, the market was full of MP3 players, and it would have been tempting for Jobs to fall back on messaging explaining why his version was different and better. Instead, he brilliantly chose not to resort to any of the language being used to describe MP3 players and their utility whatsoever. Instead he completely reframed how people thought about the appeal of portable music players with the simple and captivating phrase "1,000 Songs in Your Pocket." Rather than spend his time trying to differentiate his product from others on price or features, in other words, Jobs understood that the core value, the magical aha experience, was carrying your entire music library around with you anywhere, all the time, totally hassle free. Of course we're not all such brilliant marketing minds as Steve Jobs—but with the right testing strategies in place, we can come close!

For most of us mere mortals, crafting appealing language is extremely difficult. The human response to language is highly emotional, and largely subconscious. Words that resonate for some people may have no particular appeal to some, or even be off-putting to still others.

Marketers agonize endlessly trying to come up with brilliant taglines and advertising copy, and even so their messages often fall flat. This is what makes famous slogans like "It's the Real Thing" and "Just Do It" so impressive. Each of those phrases is so simple—there is nothing particularly poetic or even distinctive about the language—and yet they are both powerful and memorable. Why did they resonate so well? Advertising experts and business scholars could no doubt write long papers positing answers, but it's likely that no two of them would agree completely. Writing marketing copy is not an exact science. This is why growth hacking is designed to bring the rigor of scientific experimentation to the creative process. What this means is that you don't *need* to be a marketing savant like Jobs to get language/market fit right; the growth hacking process will get you there.

Another reason the up-tempo growth hacking process is so perfectly suited to this challenge is the fact that language is a breeze to run A/B tests on. Website copy can be swapped out and tested relatively easily with tools like Optimizely and Visual Website Optimizer, which install a small piece of code on your website or app that randomly displays different versions of copy to your visitors and then measures and compares their responses. Most email marketing systems, such as Salesforce Marketing Cloud and MailChimp, make it easy to test specific pieces of your email copy, such as the subject line or call to action. And online advertising platforms like Facebook and Google also let you test many different versions of ads. None of these services require technical expertise, though if you have the engineering talent at your disposal, you can even devise your own system, as Upworthy, the viral news publisher, did.

Now one of the largest media sites on the Web, Upworthy grew at a lightning-fast clip, thanks in large part to their dedication to seeking language/market fit for every story they publish—their genius is in repackaging content they find on the Web with headlines so catchy they often go immediately viral. But it's not that Upworthy's editors are necessarily the most naturally brilliant or creative; their brilliance is that they don't leave creativity up to chance. Instead, they hack it. The process of selecting headlines begins with a staffer writing at least 25 different possible headlines for each story. Out of these 25, a curator chooses a handful of favorites, and then the managing editor green-lights a set of those for testing. And their testing method couldn't be simpler. The only tools necessary are Facebook, Bitly (a free online site that generates trackable URLs for Web content), and an old-fashioned timer. Here's how they do it.

They pick two promising headlines for the same story and give each its own Bitly URL. Next, they segment their Facebook fans to find two cities with similar demographics and populations, such as one group of people in Minneapolis and another in Milwaukee, and they share one Bitly link with each group. Then they simply set a timer and wait, tallying the clicks and shares that roll in. When the time is up, the headline with the most clicks and reshares wins. And in addition to the viral boost this gives that specific article, all of their testing contributes to a growing body of knowledge about the most appealing words and phrasings that staffers can draw on for every subsequent headline they write. Given that, according to Eli Pariser, the site's founder, "a good headline can be the difference between 1,000 people and 1,000,000 people reading," this extra work is well worth it.[6]

Whether your product is a news article or a mobile app or a retail site, you can use this same method to optimize your messaging. And if you think you need a team of seasoned marketing minds who can generate dozens of potentially viral taglines out of thin air, think again; as your growth team works to craft copy for experiments, there are several sources you can tap to find words and phrases that have a good chance of resonating strongly. One is to adopt the language that your customers are using to describe your product and its benefits in social media posts and in online reviews. Another is to draw on comments from the customer surveys you hopefully conducted when determining if your product is a must-have. You can even pick up the phone and call customers directly; simply asking them how they describe your product and its value to their friends or colleagues will inevitably elicit some potentially powerful language or phrasings. Talking to customer support team members can also be very enlightening, as can reading the transcripts of customer support calls and scouring forums and online product reviews to get a sense of the kind of language your target customer is using.

START SMALL

Often it's the smallest changes in language that can have the most outsize impact on bringing in customers, which is why the most efficient experimentation process is one that lets you quickly test many different iterations. Consider how Tickle, a start-up James Currier founded in 1999, achieved two breakthroughs by experimenting with small changes to the language describing its social networking and photo-sharing products. When the response to the original webpage language that described the photo service as a way to "store your photos online" was "anemic," Currier hypothesized that users weren't spreading the word because they didn't see a storage vault of images as a particularly share-worthy product. So Currier and his team experimented with a small change in language, to "Share Your Photos Online." The test took almost no time to implement and the results were instant and staggering. The change of one word, from "store" to "share," completely altered users' perceptions of what the product was and how they should use it. Suddenly they were uploading and sharing photos like crazy, and in just 6 months, Tickle added 53 million users to the service.

Buoyed by this success, the team pulled off a similar feat shortly thereafter with a dating app. The original app featured the tagline "Find a Date," and once again, growth was sluggish. They thought that maybe they could once again ignite growth by positioning the app as a social product, not just for people to use simply to find a date, but as a hub for connecting singles to one another through their friends' networks. So they changed the tagline to "Help People Find a Date," and sure enough, users started sharing invites with their friends, even sending them to married people because, after all, they can help their single friends with finding dates, too. The service added 29 million users within 8 months of making the single change.[7]

So as you plan your first hacks to test, start with language, and then go from there.

LANGUAGE FIT HELPS HONE YOUR PRODUCT, NOT JUST YOUR BRANDING

Sometimes the changes in wording you arrive at will lead you to additional changes to make, not only in your copy, but in your overall branding and maybe even in the nature of your product itself—one of the reasons why growth hacking teams should consist of product developers and engineers as well as marketers, sharing data freely among them. Because while it's possible that tweaking a few words in an ad or one on a webpage will yield amazing results as they did for Tickle, it's equally possible that they won't have any impact—in which case it's time to dig deeper, and experiment with more substantial changes. It's entirely possible that during this process you'll find that a whole overhaul of your positioning is necessary. But don't worry; keep in mind that many great products have required such overhauls to take off. Procter & Gamble's Febreze, for example, was an honest-to-goodness breakthrough product: a chemical mixture that truly eliminates odors rather than just masking them with a pleasant scent. So when P&G launched it, they understandably touted this unique feature in their messaging, with the line "Febreze cleans bad smells out of fabrics for good."[8] Yet sales remained sluggish until P&G realized, through market research that included videotaping how avid buyers use the product, that the better positioning was as another product to use as part of your regular cleaning routine, in part to fill a freshly cleaned room with a pleasing scent.[9] So P&G added scent and then repositioned the product in a major ad campaign showing women loving the way it smelled, and using language such as "for freshness that surrounds you like never before."[10]

Sophia Amoruso, the founder of Nasty Gal, a women's fashion brand that soared to popularity among millennials in its early years, recounts how learning what language resonated with her target customer was crucial not just for bringing in new business, but for the development of her brand's whole identity. When she started her business by selling second-hand clothes on eBay, she would spend hours scouring the Web for the most enticing descriptions of similar items. To get ideas, she researched popular search terms to learn about current trends, which she then used for inspiration in defining her brand. As *New York* magazine reporter Molly Young recounted in a story about Amoruso's success, "[B]atwing, *lamé*, and *lumberjack* were big in 2007; *studded* and *architectural* and *origami* in 2008"; with this knowledge she scoured rag houses, with their stockpiles of secondhand clothes, to resell on eBay. She crafted a unique, always on-trend brand that resonated with millennial fashionistas.[11] Amoruso recalls in her book *#GIRLBOSS* that "[e]ach week I grew faster, smarter, and more aware of what women wanted." The words shoppers responded to best helped her realize that her brand should be about empowerment, about helping women enhance their personal image and sense of self-worth. That was what made the brand so distinctive and fueled extraordinary growth. Unfortunately, the company couldn't sustain the growth that Amoruso found early on and, after a series of poor business decisions, filed for bankruptcy in late 2016.

FINDING CHANNEL FIT IS NOT LIKE PORTFOLIO MANAGEMENT

In stock market investing, experts agree that it's best to spread your money across a wide swath of diverse types of businesses and sectors. But this is not the right strategy when it comes to finding the channels for marketing and distributing your product (which in Web business are often one and the same). Marketers commonly make the mistake of believing that diversifying efforts across a wide variety of channels is best for growth. As a result, they spread resources too thin and don't focus enough on optimizing one or a couple of the channels likely to be most effective. Most often it's better, as Google founder and CEO Larry Page has said, to put "more wood behind fewer arrows." Or as Peter Thiel, cofounder of PayPal, Palantir, and the first outside investor in Facebook, tells start-up founders, "It is very likely that one channel is optimal. Most businesses actually get zero distribution channels to work. Poor distribution—not product—is the number one cause of failure. If you can get even a single distribution channel to work, you have great business. If you try for several but don't nail one, you're finished."[12]

At the same time, too many companies get caught in the trap of following the herd, using the same channels as everyone else, such as Google paid ads or Facebook advertising, and not experimenting with options that might be more effective for their specific product, *and* less expensive. It's understandable; finding the right channels to focus on can be a truly daunting task not only because it is hard to know without extensive testing which channels will be the best ones for your particular business, but because there are so many different channels to choose from now, and new ones emerging all the time. Experimenting through the growth hacking process allows you to discover your optimal channel or two relatively quickly, ideally before your competition does.

NARROWING THE FIELD

There are two phases in which to home in on your best channels: *discovery* and *optimization*. In the discovery phase, the growth team should experiment with a range of options, and this does not mean trying all sorts of things haphazardly to see what sticks. Channels must be researched thoroughly, then prioritized down to a few to target for experimentation, and we'll introduce a simple but hugely helpful method for doing that in just a moment. Once you have found those one or two with the right fit, you can move to the second phase, optimization, in which you should be working to maximize both the cost-effectiveness and the reach of your channels as you keep scaling up. But first let's see how the prioritization process works.

To get started, you've first got to get a fix on all of the channels that might make sense for you to consider. Almost surely, some will be very obviously inappropriate for your product and can be quickly eliminated: if you are selling enterprise business development software, for example, advertising on popular entertainment sites won't make sense; rather you'll likely want to focus on channels directed to business professionals, such as business news periodicals. In order to impose some order on the ever-expanding set of options, growth experts like Justin Mares, Gabriel Weinberg, Andrew Chen, and James Currier have helpfully sorted leading channels into three basic categories: *viral/word-of-mouth*, *organic*, and *paid*. We've drawn on their categorizations to compile the following (representative, but not exhaustive) set of options.

THE THREE CATEGORIES OF CHANNELS

VIRAL/WORD OF MOUTH	ORGANIC	PAID
SOCIAL MEDIA (FACEBOOK, PINTEREST, SNAPCHAT)	SEARCH ENGINE OPTIMIZATION	OFFLINE ADS (TV, PRINT, BILLBOARDS)
EMBEDDABLE WIDGETS	PUBLIC RELATIONS AND SPEAKING	ONLINE ADS (GOOGLE ADWORDS, FACEBOOK, YOUTUBE)
FRIEND REFERRAL PROGRAMS	CONTENT MARKETING	AFFILIATE ADVERTISING
ONLINE VIDEO	APP STORE OPTIMIZATION	INFLUENCER CAMPAIGNS
COMMUNITY ENGAGEMENT	FREE TOOLS	RADIO
CONTESTS AND GIVEAWAYS	EMAIL MARKETING	RETARGETING
PLATFORM INTEGRATIONS	COMMUNITY BUILDING	AD NETWORKS
CROWDFUNDING	STRATEGIC PARTNERSHIPS	SPONSORSHIPS (BLOGS, PODCASTS)
GAMES, QUIZZES	CONTRIBUTED ARTICLES	NATIVE CONTENT ADS
	WEBSITE MERCHANDISING	

Of course, within each of these channels many specific tactical options are available. For content marketing, for example, GrowthHackers member Pushkar Gaikwad compiled this helpful list of just some of the types, which of course are always proliferating:

THE LEADING TYPES OF CONTENT MARKETING

CASE STUDIES	HOW-TO GUIDES	PRESS RELEASES
INFOGRAPHICS	SPECIAL REPORTS	ARTICLES
PDFS AND E-BOOKS	WEB FORUMS	REVIEWS
VIDEOS	POWERPOINT PRESENTATIONS	IMAGES AND PHOTOS
INTERVIEWS	LISTS	Q&A WEBSITES
PINTEREST	INSTAGRAM	FACEBOOK
SNAPCHAT	TUMBLR	LINKEDIN PULSE
TWITTER	LOCAL BUSINESS LISTINGS	PODCASTS
ASK ME ANYTHING SERIES	QUIZZES	FREE TOOLS
MEDIUM POSTS	BUZZFEED	TESTIMONIALS

Listing all of the specific options for each of the channels and discussing the ins and outs of each is beyond the scope of possibility here—that would require many books. But a wealth of detailed information about best practices for all of these options is available online, from the experts mentioned above and many others, and our point is that exploring them should be your first step in the prioritization process. Then you should focus on choosing a few to efficiently experiment with, using the following method.

MAKING A FIRST CUT

An initial winnowing can usually be done readily by considering the particular demands of your business model. For example, if you are selling a product to other businesses (i.e., business-to-business), you will often need a sales team and sales support operation to gain traction, a presence at trade shows, where sales staff can meet with prospective clients, and a content marketing strategy, which helps establish a company's expertise; therefore, content marketing, trade shows, and sales are likely to be among the most effective channels for reaching your target customer. An e-commerce store's business model revolves around driving the highest volume of potential shoppers to its site, and so search ads and SEO are obviously vital channels, while marketplace businesses like Uber and eBay must divide efforts between channels for bringing in suppliers and those aimed at shoppers (or riders).

This doesn't at all mean that businesses of each type should limit themselves strictly to these most obvious channels, especially as they continue to scale. A growing e-commerce company, for example, might discover that building a community, which is a viral channel, is also a good lever for driving growth; just think about Amazon's purchase of the book lovers' community Goodreads. Or a booming social network that has pioneered in new terrain, and that has attracted hefty venture capital, as Instagram and Snapchat both did, might decide to invest in TV, radio, and print ads to solidify its ownership of the territory, rather than relying only on viral mechanisms. But you've got to first focus on optimizing the channels that are most cost effective for you.

A next step in narrowing options is to consider the characteristics and behaviors of your users, and this means identifying the behaviors that they're *already* engaged in, such as the types of Google searches they are doing, the places they are shopping, and the social networks they are using. For example, does your product fill a need or solve a problem that people are currently searching for solutions to? Then channels where people are actively looking for answers (like search engines) are good bets. If you can't verify that there's a good volume of people looking (or searching) for what you offer, building awareness in other ways will be needed. That was the case with Dropbox. Services to help people easily share and store files online were brand-new when the company launched, so people weren't searching Google for the solution Dropbox was offering, which was a key reason that the effectiveness of paid search ads was so limited. The referral program solved this problem. If you know that your target customers are big purchasers of a certain product that is complementary to yours, a brand partnership or cross-promotion may be another solution.

Aatif Awan, the Vice President of Growth & International Products at LinkedIn, who helped take the company from 100 million users to more than 400 million, created this handy chart of types of user behavior that you can use as a guide in making these decisions.[13]

USER BEHAVIOR	CHANNELS TO EXPLORE
ARE PEOPLE USING SEARCH TO FIND A SOLUTION?	*SEARCH ENGINE OPTIMIZATION (SEO) OR MARKETING (SEM)*
DO EXISTING USERS SHARE YOUR PRODUCT VIA WORD OF MOUTH?	*VIRALITY OR REFERRAL PROGRAMS*
DOES HAVING MORE USERS IMPROVE THE EXPERIENCE?	*VIRALITY*
ARE YOUR TARGET USERS ALREADY USING ANOTHER PLATFORM?	*INTEGRATIONS AND PARTNERSHIPS*
DO USERS HAVE A HIGH LIFETIME VALUE?	*PAID ACQUISITION*

Once your growth team has selected a few channels to experiment with using the steps we outlined above, it's time to propose a set of specific tactics for each channel to experiment with, and prioritize them for testing.

EXPERIMENTING TO GET CHANNEL/PRODUCT FIT

We advise a prioritization method based on one devised by Brian Balfour, HubSpot's former head of growth, who created a simple scheme for ranking channels according to a set of six factors:

- Cost—how much you expect to have to spend to run the experiment in question.
- Targeting—how easy it is to reach your intended audience and how specific you can be in whom your experiment reaches.
- Control—how much control you have over the experiment. Can you make changes to the experiment once it's live? Can you stop it easily or adjust it if it's not going well?
- Input time—how much time it will take the team to launch the experiment. Filming a television ad, for example, has a much longer input time than setting up a Facebook ad.
- Output time—how long it will take to get results out of the experiment once it's live. For example, search engine optimization experiments or social media may have longer output times than a radio ad does.
- Scale—how large an audience can you reach with the experiment? Television has a much larger scale than advertising on topical blogs.[14]

Balfour suggests giving each channel a high, medium, or low score for each of the factors, as in the figure that follows. He notes that different channels will rank higher or lower on these factors depending on your product or business. For example, if the search words that you want to use for an SEM campaign are highly competitive, you'll have to pay more for them, which means that SEM will rank relatively high in cost for you in contrast to someone whose product is new enough that competition has yet to build up. If your product appeals to a very specific demographic of people who are highly networked, say, college age men, then targeting ability will be high for you for viral efforts, whereas if you're selling a product meant to appeal broadly to the masses, targeting could be a challenge, and therefore rated on the low end.

PRIORITIZING DISTRIBUTION CHANNELS

	COST	TARGETING	CONTROL	INPUT TIME	OUTPUT TIME	SCALE
SEM	*HIGH*	*HIGH*	*HIGH*	*LOW*	*LOW*	*LOW*
SEO						
VIRAL						
SALES						

We built on Brian's method to create a prioritization process for channel experimentation. We score each channel the growth team proposes for testing on a scale of 1 to 10, with 10 being the best possible score and 1 being the least favorable score (note that lower cost, input, and output time will receive higher, not lower, numbers, since low cost and input and output times are obviously more favorable). We then simply average the scores, rank them, and prioritize our experiments accordingly. Here's an example of the grid we use for the ranking, a template of which is available for download at growthhackers.com/resources:

	COST	TARGETING	CONTROL	INPUT TIME	OUTPUT TIME	SCALE	AVERAGE
SEO	*7*	*2*	*2*	*4*	*2*	*9*	*5.33*
EMAIL	*5*	*8*	*8*	*6*	*8*	*8*	*7.17*
SOCIAL							
TV							

To illustrate how this method can work, let's pick back up with the team working on the grocery store mobile app you read about in previous chapters, and see how they used it to both prioritize and optimize their first round of channel experiments.

You might remember that to drive initial adoption, the grocery chain, which has deep pockets, ran an aggressive radio and print ad campaign that generated an impressive 100,000 initial app downloads. But because not all that many of those people were *buying* much with the app, the growth team pivoted to focus on generating more revenue per user rather than on attracting more potential shoppers. Let's say that they've now succeeded in improving the average revenue brought in per active app user, so they're now turning their attention back to acquiring more users, and the mission (as it always should be) is to find more profitable channels.

First, they do another analysis of their user data. They've been monitoring the data continuously, of course, keeping a close eye on the metrics that matter most, but whenever a team shifts focus to a new growth lever, it's important to dive into the data with fresh eyes looking for insights specific to their new mission. Recall that they had discovered earlier that a large number of their best customers were coming from the grocer's main website, and that's still true. So they decide that they will focus on organic ways of leveraging the website more powerfully as one key channel, and will also experiment with new channels to help them cast their net wider and bring in more users who aren't regular visitors to the website, as was done at the initial launch. Facebook and Google advertising are obvious possibilities, so they conduct research to see how much of their existing user base is on those platforms, and how many similar types of users can be reached through advertising. They find that most of their users are quite active on both, so they dig deeper, scouring industry reports for benchmark data about where exactly their potential shoppers are spending time online and what other competitors have spent on Google and Facebook ad campaigns of what kinds, and what their relative success has been.

Armed with knowledge about their users' online behavior, they hypothesize that Google AdWords might not be such a great opportunity after all because people aren't searching on the wider Web for grocery items; they're searching on grocery retailers' websites. Facebook, on the other hand, allows them to target especially well by demographic groups and their interests, and they've got lots of demographic data about their customers, so they decide to put Facebook ads on their prioritization grid.

The team decides to also do some additional market research, running some feedback surveys on the company's main website and on the app, and also interviewing some existing customers. From those shoppers who visit the website, they want to learn whether they downloaded the app and if not, what held them back; for the existing app users they ask what would make them likely to refer the app to their friends. From these surveys, they learn that a significant number of the website visitors didn't know about the app, and those who did were happy ordering from their laptop and didn't see the need to use it. They also learn that a good portion of the app's users say that they would recommend it to others and would be even more likely to if they were given a discount off their next order or a coupon.

The team comes up with the following hacks to consider:

ORGANIC
- Improve app merchandising on main website
- Email regular shoppers who have loyalty cards but haven't down loaded the app with messaging about the benefits of shopping via the app
- Add a full page promoting the mobile app that pops up for website visitors when they access the site on their phones, also known as an app-install-roadblock page

PAID
- Run Facebook app install ads
- Run a set of radio ads based on the success from their initial launch campaign
- Retarget website visitors with ads to download the app, meaning: run a Web ad campaign shown only to previous website visitors

VIRAL
- Create a friend referral program for existing app shoppers that leverages their desire for additional discounts in exchange for inviting friends

So, which to try first? These all have strong rationales given the team's user research, and each has led to great successes for lots of companies. What's more, team members are quite partial to their own ideas, making objective prioritization a challenge. Here's where the scoring system is invaluable. The team members who made suggestions each provide an initial score on his or her own idea, and then, in the growth meeting, the team uses the scores as a guide to determine which ideas to try first. Disagreements about the scoring of one idea over another should be moderated by the growth lead. Again, the team should not use scores as the be-all and end-all but rather as a guide and one data point to base their decisions upon.

Let's say the scores come out as follows:

	COST	TARGET-ING	CONTROL	INPUT TIME	OUTPUT TIME	SCALE	AVERAGE
FACEBOOK ADS	6	9	9	9	9	6	8.0
WEBSITE PROMO	10	10	10	9	9	3	8.5
RADIO ADS	4	7	2	6	2	9	5.0
LOYALTY CARD EMAIL	10	10	10	7	7	3	7.83
RETARGET VISITORS	6	9	9	9	9	4	7.7
APP ROAD-BLOCK	9	10	5	3	7	3	6.2
FRIEND REFERRAL PROGRAM	5	4	2	3	2	6	3.7

It's easy to see they've got a set of clear front-runners. Their best shots for immediate acquisition growth come from two organic channel ideas: better website merchandising of the app and emailing their loyalty card members about downloading the app; and two paid channels: Facebook ads and retargeting ads to website visitors, urging them another time to download the app.

But what about the others? In discussing the scores in the weekly growth meeting, the team debates the value of experimenting with a referral program because the survey responses suggest it might be quite successful. But its total score is quite low, in part because it will take a relatively long time both to get up and running and to then get results. So the team decides to slot it into the development roadmap, aiming to launch it in eight weeks.

The radio campaign, too, gets relegated to the pipeline; its score is low because despite the advantage of the relatively good demographic targeting that radio advertising allows, and the fact that radio advertising the chain has done was initially quite effective, the team wouldn't be able to do detailed analysis of the results the way they'll be able to with the Facebook ads and retargeting ads. Radio is also relatively expensive and takes a good deal of time and up-front work to launch a new campaign. The team is also worried about the negative effect the full-page ad-overlay idea may have for their search engine rankings and the irritation it may provoke. It has a fairly high score, though, so it, too, will go high in their idea pipeline.

OPTIMIZING YOUR EXPERIMENTS

Fast-forward as the team conducts the first set of experiments and learns that the Facebook ads were especially effective with two demographic groups out of the six they targeted: one being new mothers, and the other shoppers in their twenties living in two specific cities. Of those urban dwellers, the data indicates that twentysomethings making $75,000 a year or more who got to the app through the ads went ahead to download and install it at a particularly high rate. The retargeting ads, on the other hand, showed disappointing results, so the growth team concludes that they will need to revisit their retargeting strategy and move on to optimizing the Facebook advertising effort, experimenting with additional ads, one set aimed specifically at new mothers nationally and the other at twentysomethings who make more than $75,000 per year in the 20 most populous cities.

As for the organic efforts, the promotion to loyalty card members turns out to be a major hit, with nearly 4 percent of all email recipients installing the app, while the new promotion on the website produced an interesting pattern: it generated lots of click-throughs, but a disappointing number of subsequent app downloads. So they decide they will also prioritize optimizing and expanding the loyalty card member promotion, and they will begin experimenting with new optimizations to better motivate downloads after people click through on the website promotions.

The process has helped them quickly identify two very promising promotion efforts to drill down on and has set a course for continuing to experiment. They are well on the way to identifying successful approaches to acquiring new customers.

KEEP TRYING NEW THINGS

As the number of possible channels for reaching users is multiplying, so are the potential strategies for *leveraging* those channels to attract people to your product. The ideation stage of the growth hacking process should provide a fountain of new ideas for making the most of the most promising channels. The recent trend of offering free online tools is a great example of how the tactics for optimizing existing channels—in this case, content marketing—are continually evolving. Take, for example, HubSpot's Website Grader, a free online tool by which customers can enter a URL and automatically get insight about which aspects of a particular website were performing well and which should be improved. New tools like these—and there are countless other examples—enable companies to grab attention despite the cacophony of free content, from blogs and whitepapers to infographics and video tutorials, that saturates the Web these days. In addition to standing out, one of the beauties of tools is that they can be "evergreen," requiring little continual upkeep to remain an effective new customer magnet, sometimes for many years. Other new tactics one could try could include building a community, as we have done with GrowthHackers.com, or getting the first user advantage on one of the hot new platforms—like the next Snapchat—that are popping up all the time.

The point is that even if you have found an established channel or set of tactics that work, new options are always emerging, and you should always be looking for which innovative ones to experiment with. In fact, it is precisely because there are so many new options, both for channels and for specific acquisition tactics, to choose from, that the growth hacking method is so efficient and effective; the data-driven, prioritized, and experimental approach helps you wade through that vast sea of options and smartly focus your efforts, and your marketing dollars.

Adding additional channels will be even more important as your growth takes off. One reason is that you will almost inevitably reach a natural ceiling with any given channel, after which you just won't be able to squeeze enough new customers from it to make it worthwhile. After all, you can only show so many ads to the same audience on Facebook before they tune you out, sending your click-through rates through the floor and your costs soaring, and there are only so many times you can hit up your loyalty card members with promotions before they start relegating your emails to their spam folders. When you reach these maximum capacities, you need to layer on additional channels to achieve additional growth.

As we've said, growth teams should periodically shift their focus to the next stage of the customer funnel, moving on from acquisition to activation and then on to retention, and we'll move on shortly ourselves, to activation, in the next chapter. But first, it's important to take a good look at the subject of viral user acquisition, which has become closely associated with the growth hacking process. Sometimes growth hacking has even been described, mistakenly, as being all about creating "viral loops" for bringing in users, meaning mechanisms such as referral programs. Such viral mechanisms can be remarkably powerful, as we saw with Dropbox, but there are a number of misunderstandings about both how to create them and the kind of growth to expect from them.

So before we move to the next step and talk about how to activate this new customer base you are building, we want to share the truth versus the hype and show you what the various kinds of viral loops look like, and how to experiment with making them best work for you.

DESIGNING CUSTOMER LOOPS

The rapid success of growth hacks that involve viral loops—like the Hotmail email signature line that encouraged recipients of emails to sign up and the Dropbox incentive program that offered free storage space in exchange for referrals—might suggest that creating such powerful incentives for users to share your product within their personal networks is a good deal easier to do than it usually is. One of the myths about a viral loop is that you can "set it and forget it," and let the word of mouth do all of your acquisition work for you. But the reality is much less idyllic. It's important to realize that not all viral loops are created equal. Creating effective loops is simply much easier for some products than others. At the easy end is a product like Venmo, a mobile payments app owned by PayPal. A product that is delivering money to people clearly has the edge; who's not going to sign up in order to receive the cash waiting for them? For most other products, though, incentivizing users to send out and accept invites is a good deal trickier, and most often, triggering anything even approaching truly viral growth requires a great deal of initial experimentation and then lots of continuous optimization.[15] Unfortunately there is no magic formula, but there are methods for finding strategies that work for you.

Here it's important to remember what we learned in Chapter Two about building a must-have product—if your product isn't delivering value, if it doesn't deliver the aha moment—then no viral loop strategy is going to help you. Remember, earlier, we described the news site Upworthy's skill for generating virality through brilliantly catchy headlines? A big part of their success comes from their recognition that the articles' content is equally important to creating viral attention. "We don't mind tricking people into seeing content they'll love," says founder Eli Pariser. "If they don't love it, they're not going to share it. Virality is a balance of how good the packaging is and how good the content is."[16] The takeaway is that while finding the right words to appeal to people is vital, offering true value is a necessary ingredient for achieving viral growth.

Another subject of much misunderstanding when it comes to viral growth is the very meaning of the term itself. For one thing, it's important to distinguish between the different types of virality, one being the traditional *word-of-mouth* variety and the other being a feature built into a product that provides a mechanism for users to hook in more users, which is often referred to as *instrumented virality*. A product can absolutely grow through both types, and, as remarked earlier, even some products that *seem* to have grown primarily through instrumented virality—Facebook being a leading case in point—in fact grew largely through word of mouth. As Chamath Palihapitiya at Facebook reminds us, he'd told the growth team not to even think about instrumenting virality at first and to focus instead on building a great product. Which brings up a key point: when you do focus on instrumenting virality, it's important that you follow the same basic principle as for building your product—you've got to make the *experience* of sharing the product with others must-have—or at least as user friendly and delightful as possible. Hotmail's email signature link, for example, was the epitome of a good user experience; one click and a very brief sign-up process and you've got free email. Similarly, Sean worked intensively with the Dropbox team on their referral program to make the steps fun and easy, from the welcoming design of the program to the ease of sending and accepting invites. All in all, the design of the program made it not only easy to invite friends, but even a joy. As a result, in both cases the viral loops were so effective that people not only took part, they felt good about the experience and raved about it to whoever would listen.

Another common misunderstanding about viral growth stems from the definition of a viral product as it's generally understood in the growth hacking community, which is that to be truly viral, the product must have a *viral coefficient* (or *K-factor*) of greater than 1. This means that each new user who signs up brings in one or more new people to the product. Yet achieving this degree of virality is extremely rare, and when achieved it's often for only very brief periods of time. To appreciate how unrealistic it is as a goal, let's just briefly look at how the viral coefficient is calculated. Don't worry, it's determined by a very simple equation:[17]

VIRAL COEFFICIENT (K) = INVITES SENT OUT BY CUSTOMERS × THE PERCENTAGE OF THOSE INVITED WHO ACCEPT THE INVITE

Let's say you have 25,000 users and you launch a referral program, and 25 percent of your users go ahead and take you up on the offer. The average number of people they send invites to is 5, and, on average, 10 percent of people invited go ahead and accept the invite. That would mean that you bring in 3,125 new users, which is 50 percent growth with just one pass through the viral loop. Such a response to any marketing effort would constitute a huge success, and yet the viral coefficient of this referral program would be 5 × 10% = .5, a far cry from the 1.0 definition of true virality.

But enough with the inside baseball about viral growth definitions. The takeaway isn't that growth teams *shouldn't* try to kick-start viral growth; rather, they need to be more practical in their assessment of viral potential. We encourage teams to experiment with creating viral engagement loops, and in fact to work on creating a number of them for any given product. But in doing so, teams should set and communicate realistic expectations, both within the team and with management.

Rather than worry about your viral coefficient (which we've shown is fleeting, and also fails to account for key factors that determine viral growth), you can come up with a helpful assessment of the degree of virality you're much more likely to be able to achieve by using a very simple formula devised by Sean Parker, cofounder of Napster and former president of Facebook. He taught early employees at the social network that the virality of any product is controlled by three factors: *payload*, *conversion rate*, and *frequency*, which can be expressed by the simple rule:

VIRALITY = PAYLOAD × CONVERSION RATE × FREQUENCY

Payload is the number of people to whom each user will likely send the promotion (or link, widget, etc.) at a time. So, for example, in Hotmail's case, most users sent emails to just one recipient, with a much smaller number sending emails to small groups, and only very few personal emails going to a long list. So the payload for Hotmail's email signature sign-up link was low. The second factor is the conversion rate of the invite, which for Hotmail was very high because at that time free email was unheard of and very appealing. The final factor is the frequency with which people will be exposed to the invites (i.e., how often emails will be sent). In Hotmail's case, this was again high because most people email some group of friends, family, and people they're doing work with quite often. So even with low payload, the high conversion rate and frequency made Hotmail's link extremely viral. Your goal in creating a viral loop is to optimize the three variables to create growth.

As you begin considering what sort of viral loop to experiment with, you've got to make a couple of key decisions. First, you need to choose how invites will be delivered. In the best viral loops, the delivery is a natural result of using the product, as was the case for Hotmail, where users didn't have to do anything in addition to sending their emails; the invitation to join was embedded in the email itself so the referrals were completely passive. Asking so little of users is not always possible, though; you'll often need to offer users an *incentive*. The best way to do this is to create a *double-sided incentive*, that is, one that offers something to both the sender and the recipient. If you have a high payload, you may not need as compelling an incentive in order to get good results because even a fairly small percentage of responses will add up nicely. But if your payload is low, you're likely going to need a more compelling incentive, for both parties, to drive up your conversion rate and frequency.[18]

A common trap companies fall into when trying to optimize a loop is to engineer ways to ratchet up the number of people being sent referrals to the point that users, and those they've made referrals to, are annoyed. Anyone who has accidentally sent an invite to download an app to their phone's entire contact list can appreciate how enraging this can be. User experience experts call tricks to get users to take an action they normally would not take *dark patterns*, and while some of these dark patterns may work in the short term, the backlash from users is a long-term drag on growth. The negative press and bad feelings these kinds of tricks stir up can even be enough to torpedo the best products—we've seen it happen.

Here are a number of best practices for experimenting with creating loops that will help you avoid such pitfalls.

CONSIDER THE POTENTIAL TO TAP NETWORK EFFECTS

The best loops are ones in which users are motivated to help sign up more users because doing so will improve their own experience of the product, such as with Facebook or LinkedIn. Network effect products have a great natural advantage with viral growth for this reason; they get better the more people are using them, so people are inclined to urge others to come on board. Social networks and messaging apps are obvious examples, as are big marketplaces that connect buyers directly with sellers, like eBay and Etsy, because more people using the site quite simply means: more potential customers for me as a seller and selection for me as a buyer.

Some products simply don't have this characteristic, such as the grocery chain's mobile app. For example, if you refer your next-door neighbor to the app, that will have no impact on your own user experience. But many companies have some degree of network effect potential that they can and should tap, even if it's not obvious on the surface. For example, with Dropbox, the more files I have stored, the more likely I will invite people to join Dropbox to collaborate on them, while the more people I know who use Dropbox, the easier file sharing is going to be.

That's why doing the legwork to learn about how your customers use your product and where potential loops can be created and optimized is essential for tapping into viral growth driven through network effects.

Eventbrite is a company that has created a powerful viral loop by tapping its network effect potential. The company is a hub for event promotion that makes money from taking a cut of ticket sales made through the site, and quite cleverly built in a social-driven loop by encouraging ticket buyers to share with their friends that they're going to an event. This clearly is a way to bring in more users and to drive more ticket sales, but it also offers an upside for ticket buyers, because having more friends attend an event you're going to usually (depending on the friends) enhances the experience. This loop has also helped Eventbrite attract more event organizers because it has been able to leverage these sharing loops to help organizers sell more tickets. In fact, Eventbrite found that each new share of an event generated $3.23 in incremental revenue for event organizers.[19]

CREATE AN INCENTIVE THAT'S IN SYNERGY WITH YOUR PRODUCT'S CORE VALUE

If there is no inherent incentive to share built into the user experience, you may have to create that incentive, generally by offering a reward of some kind. But it's critical that whatever reward users receive for making the referral be relevant to the core value of the product. If the grocery store app offered a free flower vase for making at least three referrals, for example, while some shoppers might find the incentive appealing, for many it would seem odd, an outlier to what they're expecting from a grocery store. But if the grocery chain were launching florist services, clearly that offer would be right in alignment with the product being promoted. We talked earlier about language/market fit and product/channel fit; think of this as product/incentive fit.

This was the genius of the Dropbox referral program. The product was about both storing files and easily sharing them with others. So not only was getting more people using the Dropbox service entirely in keeping with users' interests, getting more storage space for free was an incentive also totally in line with the core value of the product. A good rule of thumb is: whether you are selling a service, or a physical product, or some kind of information or content, the value of your incentive should be as closely aligned to that as possible.

Cash offers can work also, but for the best effect, it's important that they're also related to the core value of the product. Airbnb offers a $25 incentive for both inviters and invitees to use toward a future stay booked through Airbnb. Here, using messaging tied to the product or brand matters; in Airbnb's case they use language suggesting that customers share the great experience of living like a local that Airbnb delivers, rather than just blatantly offering the cash.

Similarly, for our grocery app team, offering a referral program where each shopper using the app gets a $10 discount on their next grocery order makes good sense, as it acts as a onetime discount on their purchase. The downside of offering cash, even in the form of discounts, is that it's very easy to calculate its value in relation to what you are asked to do to receive it, and this can make it hard to motivate people to act without larger sums to stir action. Contrast offering $10 to someone versus 250 free megabytes of space on Dropbox. How much is that space worth? It's hard to set a value on it as a user—it *feels* highly valuable—but for Dropbox the incremental cost is exceptionally low.

MAKE THE INVITE TO SHARE AN INTEGRATED
PART OF THE USER'S EXPERIENCE, NOT AN ADD-ON

There's a fine line to walk when it comes to inviting users to share with others: you don't want the prompt to be obtrusive, which can be irritating and perceived as too pushy, but you *do* want your users to see it. The best way to toe this line is to integrate the prompt as seamlessly as possible with the user experience. Too many companies add referral programs into their products as afterthoughts (another reason why the product managers, designers, and engineers should be involved in growth team efforts, so they can take these considerations into account when building the initial product) and include them on webpages or screens that are rarely visited; unfortunately, this low visibility all but guarantees that there is never enough critical mass to kick-start the viral loop. Far better to integrate the prompt into the more highly trafficked areas, like the new user experience, or on the home screen. At ScoreBig, a live event ticketing platform Morgan worked for, the team saw a massive spike in friend invites sent out when they integrated the referral program into the new user experience, whereas before it had only been accessible from a small link tucked into the corner at the top of the website home page.

If you start to pay attention to this on the websites and apps you visit, you'll quickly notice which do and don't do this effectively. LinkedIn prompts you as soon as you join to see who you are connected with and to import your email contacts to build your network. Uber prominently promotes an incentive to invite your friends right on the screen that details the status of the ride you're currently taking. Under close scrutiny, you'll find that most companies that have generated some word-of-mouth growth have gone through great pains to make their instrumented viral loops visible within plain sight, while at the same time appealing and intuitive to their customers.

MAKE SURE THE INVITEES ARE GIVEN A GOOD EXPERIENCE

Another common mistake is neglecting to optimize the experience that invitees receive when they *respond* to an invite—for example, abruptly hitting them with a request to create an account on the service before they even know what the site is about and why they should bother joining.

Contrast this to the masterfully appealing experience Airbnb has created for new invitees. First, the invite includes the name and a picture of the person who invited you, along with a personalized message about the incentive, which at the time of this writing was: "Your friend Morgan gave you $25 off your first trip on Airbnb, the best way to travel. Be sure to say thanks!" The call to action is also prominent and simple—a large box labeled "Claim Your Credit." The benefits are twofold here. Not only will invitees be more inclined to respond, they'll also be more receptive to sending referrals themselves because they now know they aren't spamming their friends with a shoddy or overly pushy invite.

EXPERIMENT, EXPERIMENT, EXPERIMENT

Remember, most "instant successes" have required extensive experimentation, and successful viral loops are no different. The brilliant strategies you've read about in this chapter didn't emerge out of thin air, but rather through a great deal of testing and optimization, which has involved plenty of surprises for growth teams along the way. At Dropbox, Sean and the team were surprised to find, for example, that if invites to share a file also promoted the value proposition of online storage space, it actually hurt the conversion rate! When the page that greeted invitees instead emphasized how the service facilitated collaboration and file sharing, however, the conversion rate spiked up. Why? Those invitees hadn't yet experienced the desire to get online storage space, but the beauty of being able to share files so easily with the people who had referred them, and anyone else of course, was immediately appealing. In hindsight it makes sense, but chances are the growth team would have never uncovered this insight, had they not experimented.

LinkedIn was equally surprised to discover that its invite program was more effective if inviters were prompted to send *more* invites than the original prompt had suggested—but not too many. At first, the prompt suggested that users invite two other people. But rather than just leave it at that, the team experimented with asking users to send a few more invitations, and they did. But when they got up to six invites, the response started to drop off. The growth team ultimately discovered that the optimal number of invites to recommend users to make was four.[20]

The point is: many of the best hacks are unanticipated discoveries. The methods you read about in this chapter are designed to help you find them—strategically, efficiently, and at low cost.

Okay, having explored how to bring in loads of new users, let's now take a close look at how to make sure they become active once you've hooked them.

CHAPTER SIX

HACKING ACTIVATION

N ow that you've worked so hard to attract all these potential customers, how do you engage them in actually using your product, or, in growth hacking parlance, to get them activated? Unfortunately, this is something many companies get wrong; in fact, 98 percent of traffic to websites does not lead to activation, and most mobile apps lose up to 80 percent of their users within three days.[1]

Improving activation is at its core about increasing the rate at which you get new users to your aha moment. The more visitors who experience what makes your product a must-have, the more of them will stick with you. The growth hacking process provides a rigorous set of steps for probing into the impediments to the aha experience, and then experimenting with hacks for improving activation. There is no one formula for improving activation; your efforts must be tailored specifically to your product, and your ideas for experimentation should be inspired by analysis of your specific data. Luckily, the growth hacking process offers the playbook to help get you there.

In this chapter, we will first introduce the three essential steps every growth team must take in order to identify the highest-impact activation experiments to run. Then we will introduce a set of best practices for increasing activation that have been implemented to great effect by fast-growth companies. A closing section takes a special look at one of the most effective, but also most often abused, tactics: the use of triggers, which are prompts to users that urge them to reengage with a product. We'll introduce the ins and outs of the sticky business of getting triggers right.

MAPPING THE ROUTE TO THE AHA MOMENT

The first step in hacking activation is to identify each point in your customers' journey toward the aha moment. We are assuming that you have already determined, in the process of making the product must-have, what constitutes this magical moment. To see how to create your map of points along the way, let's use the case of the grocery app. As you might recall from Chapter Three, the team has determined that the aha experience comes when shoppers realize they can use the app to easily and quickly order their groceries on the fly, in those in-between moments when they've got a bit of spare time, or as they randomly think of or remember an item they need as they are running around and going about their daily lives.

The next thing the team needs to do is list all of the steps that new users must take in order to have this experience: they need to download the app; find items they want; add them to their carts; create an account by adding in their name, credit card, and delivery information; then make the purchase itself. And, to truly make the experience must-have, they've got to receive their complete order as expected at home.

Just reading through these steps you can think of many ways in which users might lose interest or become frustrated and exit the app rather than making a purchase. The app might be annoyingly slow; users might find searching for items cumbersome; creating an account might be overly complicated. But in growth hacking, it's crucial that you never assume why users are behaving as they are; rather, you've always got to study hard data about their behavior and then query them on the basis of observations you've made in order to focus your experimentation efforts most efficiently on changes that will have the greatest potential impact. Even if you *think* you understand what the barriers to activation are, the true story can be quite surprising.

Once you've identified the steps that lead up to the aha moment, the next step toward homing in on stumbling blocks for customers and figuring out what's causing them to flee is to calculate the conversion rates for each of the steps on the way to the aha moment, or, in other words, the percentage of all visitors who are taking each of those steps along the path to success.

CREATING A FUNNEL REPORT OF CONVERSIONS AND DROP-OFFS

One of the best ways to measure conversion rates is through a *funnel report*, a tool that displays the rates at which people who come to your product are moving on to each of the key steps in the customer journey (and by the same token, where they are dropping off). Here's a very basic hypothetical one created by Kissmetrics, which shows a quite common drop-off between first visit and sign-up.

A SIMPLE FUNNEL REPORT

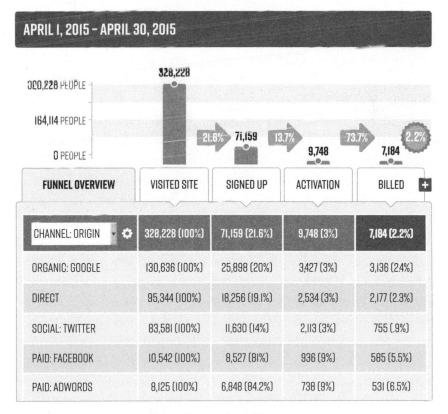

APRIL 1, 2015 – APRIL 30, 2015				
FUNNEL OVERVIEW	VISITED SITE	SIGNED UP	ACTIVATION	BILLED
CHANNEL: ORIGIN	328,228 (100%)	71,159 (21.6%)	9,748 (3%)	7,184 (2.2%)
ORGANIC: GOOGLE	130,636 (100%)	25,898 (20%)	3,427 (3%)	3,136 (2.4%)
DIRECT	95,344 (100%)	18,256 (19.1%)	2,534 (3%)	2,177 (2.3%)
SOCIAL: TWITTER	83,581 (100%)	11,630 (14%)	2,113 (3%)	755 (.9%)
PAID: FACEBOOK	10,542 (100%)	8,527 (81%)	936 (9%)	585 (5.5%)
PAID: ADWORDS	8,125 (100%)	6,848 (84.2%)	738 (9%)	531 (6.5%)

Funnel Report from Kissmetrics

Of course the steps for which you calculate percentages will be specific to your product. For this hypothetical product, they were: initial visit, sign-up, activation, and billing. For another company—let's say Uber—the funnel report might display the rate at which people are downloading the app, then the opening of the app, then the number who proceed to create a new account, the rate at which people book a ride, and the rate at which they rate their driver, and so on. For other businesses, steps might include, for example, inviting friends, downloading a whitepaper, watching a video, or visiting a retail store. The point is that whatever your product is, you should be tracking all essential steps of the customer journey to that moment of activation.

In addition to tracking the conversion rate of key action steps, the report should track the visitors according to the route or channels by which they've come to the product, whether from Google search or AdWords, from Facebook or Twitter, from online banner ads, from customer referrals, etc. Surprising differences in activation rate by channel can lead to high-impact discoveries that may cause you to go back and reexperiment with some of the acquisition channels you isolated following the steps in the last chapter. Once this data is available, you will look for differences between active customers, those who activated but then went cold, and those who never activated, or have "bounced." In essence, this report gives you a detailed overview of what the sticking points are for customers coming through each of your channels, which can be used to improve the rate at which you turn new customers into active ones.

Let's see how the grocery app team proceeds at this stage in the process. The data analyst on the growth team will create a funnel report that calculates the rates for downloading and opening the app, the rates at which people are searching for items to buy, the rate at which people are adding items to the shopping cart, and, finally, creating an account and purchasing. In addition, they'll also track key additional steps such as the rates at which people activate on any special offers or promotions, like the $10 off a first purchase offer we described them experimenting with earlier. Let's say that the team had gone ahead with creating the shopping list feature, which, as we noted earlier, was an experiment they put into their schedule for development, and that it's been available for a couple of months now. They are going to also want to calculate the rate at which people are adding items to their lists and also the rate at which they are then going ahead and purchasing the list of items.

Often, these activation funnel reports can be very straightforward, providing that your team has taken the steps outlined in Chapter Three to properly define metrics and establish ways to track them. Many analytics packages such as Kissmetrics, Mixpanel, Google Analytics, and Adobe Omniture SiteCatalyst offer the ability to create these funnels based on specific events and provide a variety of creative and useful funnel visualization and tracking tools. Other times, things can get a bit more complicated, especially if your activation funnel may need to be created by combining multiple sources of data. But a data expert will be able to identify the proper data sources to query and build the funnel report even if data lives in additional places (yet another reason why every growth team needs a data analyst!).

In sitting down to look at the data, the team now makes a set of intriguing observations. They learn that a large number of app users are adding items to their shopping carts and then leaving before they add their credit card information. They also see that quite a number of users aren't searching for many items, and also that the shoppers who are the most active in the first week after downloading the app browsed quite a few items on their first visit. Finally, they observe that a large percentage of visitors who use the shopping list feature to add items to it proceed to purchase them, and that many of those purchasers go on to become repeat purchasers.

Armed with this data it is clear that one major stumbling block is the checkout experience. So the team will want to consider experiments with making it easier to check out, perhaps by trying a new payment form design that's easier or quicker to complete. Since search volume is low among new users, they should also consider experiments aimed at encouraging first visitors to browse more items, perhaps by making it easier to search for items from the app home screen, or by making searching more enticing by highlighting special offers for various products, or by prominently recommending sections of the app (say, a screen for "most popular products") to explore.

So they've got lots of options to choose from. But before they start experimenting, there is one more step in data discovery. They must "get out into the wild" and conduct some surveys and interviews to probe into the reasons for the user behavior the data has revealed. This will greatly help them to narrow their focus and come up with the highest-potential hacks to try.

The growth team at Qualaroo, the online survey company Sean founded, followed this same process for coming up with ideas for possible hacks to boost activation. By deeply analyzing our user data, looking for differences in the experiences of people who used Qualaroo for free and then purchased versus those who tried the product but ultimately didn't buy, we learned that most people who ultimately purchased had run trial surveys that elicited at least 50 responses. Knowing that the aha moment for the product was getting actionable user feedback from surveys, we determined that 50 survey responses was the tipping point after which the value of surveys became clear.

So to get more users to experience the aha moment, we tried many experiments aimed at increasing the likelihood that new trial users would get at least 50 responses on a survey. These included a number of efforts to improve customer education about which surveys to run, through new email copy we wrote and also through tutorial videos about the types of surveys to run in order to get information about specific sorts of issues and suggestions about where to run them. We also changed the set of recommended surveys shown to new users to ones that would be run in broader uses and attract greater response rates, such as Net Promoter Score surveys. Finally, I (Sean) tasked the customer success team with doing proactive outreach to visitors in order to give them tips about deploying surveys. All of these experiments combined led to a dramatic increase in customer activation rate, even as we tripled the cost of the product!

SURVEY DOS AND DON'TS

You've probably had the experience of customer survey pop-ups on an app or website you were using just as you were in the middle of browsing, or on your way to buying something. These can be very effective discovery tools for growth hackers, but they can also be quite annoying to users. To get the most useful responses, while at the same time assuring a survey is not a turn-off to customers, it should be very brief, and should be delivered to users under two main conditions: (1) when their activity indicates confusion, such as lingering on one page for too long, or leaving the screen or page on the app or site; or (2) right after they've gone ahead and taken the step that many others *aren't* taking, such as creating an account or making a purchase. Both can also yield valuable insights about why that customer decided to take the next step—or not.

We advise asking one or two questions at maximum, which either can be open-ended or can offer a set of answers to select from. We have a preference for open-ended questions because they don't shoehorn people into your preconceived notions of what the problems users are encountering are. Letting them respond with whatever they feel like sharing allows them to surprise you. For example, maybe the grocery app team thought the obvious reason why shoppers weren't checking out might be that the payment form was too complex. But survey feedback may reveal that a bigger factor was that shoppers weren't sure if they were going to be charged for delivery or not, or perhaps that they forgot the code to enter to get their first-time-shopper discount. This is the type of qualitative information that can't be gleaned from hard data alone, which is why surveying customers is such an important piece of the process.

To get this information, if you have these customers' contact information, you can simply email or call them, to ask them these questions "voice to voice."

For those who've browsed and bounced without giving you any contact info, a survey can be programmed to pop up right as browsing patterns indicate that they're about to leave a page or screen (companies like Bounce Exchange, Qualaroo, Qualtrics, and others offer tools that can do this). You'd be surprised by how many people will stop and answer your questions before they leave (and keeping it as short as possible will only improve the rate of response). In this case you want to ask what has stopped them from moving forward, with questions such as:

- Is there anything preventing you from signing up at this point?
- What concerns are keeping you from completing your order?
- If you did not make a purchase today, can you tell us why not?
- What information would you need to feel comfortable signing up today?

Perhaps somewhat counterintuitively, some of the best information you will get about reasons people are abandoning your product at any given step will come from people who *didn't* give up. For example, to probe into why so many people visiting the grocery app aren't completing their purchases, the team should survey people who *just* completed a purchase. After all, these shoppers will also have encountered whatever obstacles are stopping other shoppers up—and may have insight on why they chose to continue along anyway while others did not. So the team might display a brief survey on the order confirmation screen that asks shoppers "What's the one thing that nearly stopped you from completing your order?" We've found this "one thing" question elicits a high number of responses, and ones that are very eye-opening. Of course the questions you ask will depend upon the drop-off point you're asking about. Others might be:

- What were you hoping to find on this page?
- Does this page contain the information you were looking for?
- What did you come to our site/app to do today?
- What convinced you to complete your purchase today?
- On this screen, it seems like I should be able to . . .
- Was there anything about the checkout process we should improve?

Once the grocery team has done all this, they now have both the data and the color commentary from customers they need to evaluate a first set of ideas for experiments. Let's say they decide to prioritize two experiments to start. Since surveys revealed that customers often left before making a purchase because they couldn't remember their discount code, the team could try automatically adding the visitor's first-time discount code on the checkout page. Not only would this change be likely to improve results, it would also be significantly faster and less expensive than a complete redesign of the app's shopping cart.

Additionally, the data showing that so many of those who added items to the new shopping list proceeded to purchase them may lead them to experiment with promoting the shopping list feature more prominently on the app home screen after installation.

And with that they're off and running. But they'll likely have to try many experiments for each of these ideas, and others as well, in order to optimize activation. Always remember that there are no silver bullets in growth hacking, and that even what seem like slam-dunk ideas can fail.

BE PERSISTENT AND YOU'LL GET THE PAYOFF

To illustrate how surprising the discoveries you can make through this process will often be, let's take a close look at the set of experiments that the growth team at HubSpot ran to try to stoke adoption for its new Sidekick product, a tool that allows salespeople to track the effectiveness of their email outreach. At the time, Sidekick was facing a problem common to newly launched products: they saw strong organic adoption via word of mouth, but activation was sluggish. To get to the bottom of the flagging activation rates, the Sidekick team first dug into the data to find the differences between users who tried the product and stuck with it, and those who installed Sidekick and disappeared.

They began by segmenting their users into buckets of people with similar attributes, starting with the general set of common differences, including the different traffic sources they were coming from, such as Google and Facebook. Then they went deeper, analyzing new users by job role, the type of email that they sent, whether they used Sidekick for sales prospecting or public relations outreach or other uses, and the email service they used, such as Gmail or Outlook. One discovery they made was that users who signed up using their work email address as opposed to their personal email account had a higher activation rate. So their first step was to experiment with getting people to use their work emails instead of their personal email addresses. (At Qualaroo, we found similar results with nonwork email addresses, so we used language on the sign-up form instructing users to use their work email addresses and would not let people sign up when they entered in an email ending in @gmail.com, @hotmail.com, and so on.)

Another discovery they made was that most people who didn't go on to become active users never sent more than a single email after installing the application. To probe into why, the team started to collect feedback from users who stopped using the product. And when they did, they were rather shocked to discover that people were saying that they jumped ship because they didn't understand how to use it. The team had been certain that the app was a breeze to understand and use; in fact, once installed, Sidekick simply worked in the background—but the data told another story. So they concluded that they should run experiments with ways of educating visitors on how to use the email tracking add-on.

The team tried adding various types of explanation on the landing page visitors arrived at once they had installed the app, and experimented with videos that demonstrated how to use the product and also tried showing a sample of the kind of report users receive about the activity seen on their sent emails. But to their surprise, every one of those tests failed to improve adoption. The team ultimately ran *11* separate experiments, and still, nothing took. At this point the bewildered growth team decided they needed to step back and take another dive into the data. Maybe more education wasn't the issue, but perhaps instead the key was to get people to the aha moment faster. What if, rather than sending people to the app's landing page after installation, they simply showed them a message that told them that the application had installed successfully and that they were ready to start sending email? Finally, this experiment worked. That message seemed to be a much-needed trigger to get people to go ahead and actually use the app. Then the beauty of its utility would quickly hit them. So the growth team added the messaging, and the activation rate dramatically improved.

But the team didn't stop there. They went on to run another *68 experiments;* some worked, some didn't, and many yielded more surprises, but they all produced insights that led to significant increases in activation, a perfect model of doing growth hacking right.[2]

The key takeaway here is that you cannot know ahead of time which experiments are going to be most effective. The best you can do is stay nimble and data-driven: continuously tailoring experiments according to the discoveries you make and then being ready to quickly adjust and try other approaches if experiments aren't working as hypothesized.

While there is most definitely a core set of best practices for improving activation, which we will now introduce, you must consider these as less of a playbook to follow and more as a set of examples and sources of ideas as you consider experiments to try. Remember that every product is different, and you won't get far by simply focusing on problems that are common but that aren't at the crux of what is getting in the way of activation for your particular customers.

The bottom line is: there are no shortcuts. But if you follow the three steps we have outlined above, you will rapidly discover ideas and insights that will produce dramatic gains in activation for your product. To recap, those steps are: map all of the steps that get users to the aha moment; create a funnel report that profiles the conversion rates for each of the steps and segments users by the channel through which they arrive; and conduct surveys and interviews both of users who progressed through each step where you're seeing high drop-offs, and those who left at that point to understand the causes of drop-off. You can then use this information to create new, highly targeted, and high-impact ideas to experiment with to improve your results.

Now let's look at the most common obstacles to activation, and how to design experiments for hacks to avoid them.

ERADICATING FRICTION

In user experience design, *friction* is the term used to refer to any annoying hindrances that prevent someone from accomplishing the action they're trying to complete, such as ads that pop up in the middle of an article you're reading or overly distorted letters in a CAPTCHA that force you to make repeated attempts at entering them successfully before submitting a form. For a physical product, such as a coffeemaker, it might be an annoyingly complicated procedure for setting an automatic brew time. The incredible irritation of friction is well understood; who hasn't experienced it? But what's tricky is that while we certainly notice the friction in the products we use, we often don't recognize sources of friction in the ones we've been involved in creating or marketing. Perhaps this is because we know how they work so intimately that our brains just can't see the impediments. Designers who watch people stumble in trying to use products they've worked on are often shocked to see how much difficulty people are having. A great deal of attention has been focused on the need to remove friction from the user experience of online products, and yet it is everywhere, from the e-commerce checkout forms that require you to create an account before making your purchase, to pop-ups that ask you to rate or review an app before you've even had the chance to experience using it, to zip code fields that don't recognize alphanumeric Canadian postal codes.

With every irritating hoop a new user has to jump through she's thinking to herself, "Is it worth it?" and if the value of your product isn't clear and compelling enough, even the slightest irritation can send people away, often for good.

Sean devised a simple formula to help keep the importance of continuously looking to reduce friction top of mind:

DESIRE – FRICTION = CONVERSION RATE

As the formula implies, the more visitors desire your product, the more friction they will generally be willing to work their way through. This is why early adopters are such a godsend for new or nascent products; they're often willing to use, and even pay for, your product even when it has some serious glitches. Morgan has an enviable Gmail email address because during Gmail's early beta period, he was willing to go to eBay and bid on a coveted invite to the service just so he could get the Gmail address he wanted. Customers with that level of desire (it might also be considered a form of insanity) are going to be willing to tolerate the inconvenience of bugs and annoyances, but the rest won't.

In order to improve activation, you can either increase your customers' desire or reduce the friction they experience—and making a product more desirable is generally a good deal harder than discovering and eliminating sources of friction. Eliminating friction, in other words, is the lower-hanging fruit, which is why many of the most successful growth teams have dedicated a great deal of effort to it.

Think of your funnel conversion report as your roadmap to the sources of friction in your customer journey. Sometimes just scrutinizing big drop-off points alone will reveal the impediments to begin experimenting with removing or redesigning. Slow download times and glitchy shopping carts are common examples, but perhaps the most problematic friction point is often right at the beginning of the customer journey, in the new user experience (NUX).

OPTIMIZING THE NEW USER EXPERIENCE

The first rule of designing and optimizing your NUX is to treat it as a unique, onetime encounter with your product; as such, you should think of it as a product of its own. This means that you will need to craft a special experience for it, one that entices users to engage with the product and appreciate what it has to offer. A great benefit of creating these separate experiences—which means a separate series of pages or screens either within the product if it is a Web product, or on the company or brand site if it is not—is that it makes experimentation with the NUX easier for a growth team because they don't have to worry about their tests interfering with the experience of the current users.

The second rule is that the first landing page of the NUX must accomplish three fundamental things: *communicate relevance, show the value of the product*, and *provide a clear call to action*. Bryan Eisenberg, who is widely considered the godfather of conversion optimization, refers to these three factors as the *conversion trinity*. Relevance stands for how well the page matches the intent and desire of the visitor—is this what they came for? Showing value is immediately answering the visitor's question "What's in it for me?" clearly and concisely. Lastly, the call to action provides a compelling next step for visitors to take. Doing all of these things may seem intuitive, but unfortunately most landing pages are lacking in one or another, if not all, of these must-haves.

Optimizing these pages generally requires running many experiments with the language: again, not just the taglines and call to action, but the text that accompanies images and that appears on subsections or farther reaches of the page. As much as the messaging here matters, so do the aesthetics. So you'll want to also experiment with size, positioning, and ratios of both the text and imagery. Experimenting with simplifying the page, stripping out text and/or images, is also important, as is sometimes adding in more explanatory text and/or imagery.

In short, all of the elements of the NUX should be scrutinized for problems, but there are two key tactics that have recently proven powerful in removing friction across a wide range of businesses and products.

SINGLE SIGN-ON

Simplifying the sign-up process is one of the key areas to experiment with, as often, reducing the amount of information people must provide up front can result in a big improvement in how many choose to sign up. This has been made dead simple now that Facebook, Twitter, LinkedIn, Google, and others have made simple login applications available to Web and mobile developers that enable their users to sign on with their existing accounts—a feature called *single sign-on*, or also *social sign-on*. This technology can be a game changer when it comes to reducing friction in the sign-on process: offering a single click to create a new account can dramatically improve conversion rates, particularly on mobile devices, where data entry can be especially challenging.

While single sign-on is more commonly used by companies offering consumer products, it can also work for B2B companies as well, as the growth team at Kissmetrics, a data analytics company, found when they tested using "Sign Up with Your Google Account" as the one and only call to action on their home page. There was no option to enter an email address and password; it was connect with your Google account or nothing. And seemingly overnight, cofounder Neil Patel reported, their sign-ups increased a stunning 59.4 percent.[3] But as we cautioned earlier, what works for one product may not work at all for others, which is why, as tempting as it may be to make this change, you've got to test it first. At Inman, when Morgan's team experimented with *removing* their single sign-on, they saw conversions increase 24.8 percent. It turns out that one size does not fit all when it comes to growth hacks.

FLIPPING THE FUNNEL

A particularly bold way to reduce the friction keeping your customers from experiencing the aha moment quickly is to *flip the funnel*, meaning to allow visitors to start experiencing the joys of your product *before* asking them to sign up. Hello Bar, a tool that makes it easy for Web marketing teams to display important, short-term messages to their website visitors, used this tactic to achieve a big win in increasing activation. They let users simply create their Hello Bar message first, and then once it was ready to go—that is, after the user had invested time in creating and customizing their first one—the company asked for the sign-up. Activation increased by 52.11 percent.[4]

Similarly, Stripe, an online payments company, allows its customers to grab a small snippet of code and start using it right away, only asking for account details when it's time to transact with real money. This gets more of their potential customers experimenting with their product—and experiencing the aha moment—before they commit to creating an account. And this technique works just as well for non-Web products; Warby Parker, the trendy eyeglass brand, will send anyone a set of five frames before making a purchase to help users decide which ones they like before they have to commit to a particular pair. Each of these companies flips some critical part of the typical funnel and eliminates friction in the process.

OPTIMIZING IS A PUSH AND PULL WITH FRICTION

Often, in trying to improve activation of new users, you may have to add some friction in order to direct them to take the next steps. A great example of how to strike this delicate balance between leading customers through a process that will ultimately lead to activation and not creating so much extra work as to turn them away is a set of experiments that Airbnb ran upon noticing in its data that most visitors who signed up did so only at the very last moment when they were ready to go ahead and book a room. The team wanted to get people to become active earlier than that, when they were merely browsing rooms, so they could learn about them and the kinds of locations and rooms they would be most interested in. That way, the team could work on ways of better tailoring the properties shown to people when they ultimately searched with the intention of booking, which the team expected would increase the booking rate and overall satisfaction of using Airbnb.

The team started with a very lightweight and somewhat rough experiment (remember, when prioritizing which experiments to run, it pays to start small!), by adding a prominent strip across the bottom of the website with a small bit of text explaining the benefits of signing up. If a visitor ignored that call to action, she would be shown another sign-up prompt on the next page she went to, and on each subsequent page.

The results of the first experiment were intriguing. They saw a good uptick in sign-ups, but also a drop-off in bookings. The prompts seemed to be causing friction that stopped some people from proceeding to search and book. But as they analyzed the data further, they saw that the increased sign-ups led to many valuable payoffs, such as more invites sent out to potential new users, and new users adding more properties to a wish list feature, thus providing more information about users' desired bookings. So the team decided to next experiment with reducing the friction of the prompts in an attempt to find the best of both worlds: more sign-ups *and* more bookings.

They focused on optimizing how they displayed the prompts, including their design and the frequency with which they appeared. In one experiment, instead of showing the sign-up prompt on every page, they dropped the frequency to every five pages a visitor viewed. By changing the rate at which they prompted users to sign up they lost just 4 percent on the improved sign-up rate and entirely eliminated the negative impact on bookings. The team also tested adding more text around the call to action to encourage sign-ups, inserting a testimonial from a happy Airbnb customer as well as some text about the value of signing up. Here they got a real surprise. They found that adding this additional text actually *hurt* sign-ups, and they reasoned that was because it actually distracted users.[5] This is an example of a more subtle type of friction, which isn't actually experienced as annoying, yet still deters visitors or users from taking the action you want them to. You can really only discover whether this kind of friction exists—and how it is impacting your activation rates—through experimentation.

The Airbnb team ran many more experiments in order to optimize this experience, testing all of the design of the elements in the sign-up prompts, from the color of the sign-up bar on the home page to the styling of the buttons on the sign-up form, and eventually found the sweet spot for improving the company's overall sign-up rate and other important metrics.

THE POWER OF POSITIVE FRICTION

One of the great ironies of improving activation is that not all friction is bad. Dumping people with no context or clue right into your product as fast as possible is not always optimal; sometimes you *want* to put some *positive friction* in their way. Creating positive friction is a delicate art of putting manageable, ideally engaging steps in the path of visitors that help them understand what the value is and get to the aha moment with greater predictability. Videogame developers have honed the practice to a level of perfection. They face a particular challenge in getting users hooked on new games because the rules of games must be introduced (after all, users will never get to the aha moment—the joy of playing—if they don't know how to be successful in the game), and in many cases, the rules and the strategies for play are quite complicated. To solve the problem, developers drew on insights from psychological research to craft marvelously enticing introductions to game play.

One of the key findings they drew on was introduced by psychologist Robert Cialdini in his business classic *Influence: The Psychology of Persuasion*. In a number of studies he references, it was discovered that once people take an action, no matter how small, as long as the experience wasn't onerous, they are more inclined to take any action in the future. The explanation for this, he says, is that they have made a form of psychological commitment by taking the action, and people have a bias for honoring commitments with subsequent, follow-on actions, often regardless of the change in size of request. Game designers shrewdly realized that rather than providing instructions about how to play a game, they had to get people committed; they had to get them to start playing through small, easy steps to get them oriented and rolling.

Game developers draw on many other powerful insights from psychology as well. One is the well-established principle of conditioning people to engage in behaviors by offering them rewards. The other is taking advantage of the enormous satisfaction people feel when they are in the brain state known as *flow*, a theory pioneered by psychologist Mihaly Csikszentmihalyi, who showed that people get into this optimal state when they feel challenged just the right amount by a task they are engaged in; not so challenged as to feel frustrated, yet challenged enough so as not to feel bored. People who are "in flow" are so engaged that they lose track of time; three hours of working on a painting or on writing an essay or coding an app can feel like much less, and people will look up from their work shocked by the time that's passed. Anyone who's ever been told by someone playing a videogame "Just give me ten more minutes!"—then another ten minutes then another ten minutes—knows how easily game players tend to get into flow.

Game designers combined this wisdom to craft new user experiences that lead people gently into playing their games, starting with simple challenges that can be mastered quickly, and providing them with rewards for each hurdle cleared, while orienting them to the rules of the game and the environment in the process. They then ratchet up the level of challenge, as well as the degree of reward, in exquisitely refined increments (both of which they experiment a great deal with), so that users are hooked and get into flow. And this doesn't just work for videogames; designers of many other types of online products have incorporated similar tactics to create new user experiences that greatly increase activation rates, tailoring a set of actions for users to engage in that show them how the product works, and then providing some kind of reward for doing so. For example, when Facebook prompts new users to fill out their profile, add a photo of themselves and some biographical information, they are not just gathering personal data that is valuable for analysis and for selling advertising (though those things are true also), they are establishing commitment (*Since I already spent all this time picking out a picture and drafting my bio*, we think, *I might as well keep going*) and providing a psychological reward (the satisfaction of a completed profile). And as anyone who has spent hours crafting their Facebook profile knows, there is something about this process that provides an utterly satisfying state of flow. In the process Facebook brings people closer to discovering the aha moment, because the core value of the site is based on people finding their friends—which they can only do once everyone has filled out their profile.

The more information people put into the product, the more their commitment increases, through a concept called *stored value*. Much like putting money in a safe deposit box, putting information into a service instantly creates a sense of ownership for users and an inclination to commitment to add to and maintain that value. So while prompts for information can be a source of friction, if done properly—i.e., in a way that is rewarding and through actions that slowly increase the level of commitment—they can also be a catalyst for activation and growth.

CRAFTING A LEARN FLOW

While the new user experience is ripe for friction, it is ripe for opportunity as well. That's because the first experience people have with your product is also the time that they are most consciously trying to figure it out. As former head of growth for Twitter Josh Elman, who we met earlier, says about the new user experience, "This is your moment. You have more attention than you ever will have again, from that user, to try to teach them what your product is really about. To really help them learn the product in a meaningful way." Elman's team designed something he dubbed the *learn flow* to enable Twitter to take advantage of this attention. *Learn flow* is Elman's definition of a new user experience that's designed to more than just sign people up, but rather purposefully educates new users about the product, its benefits and value, and how to use it in the process. This NUX design takes advantage of the abundance of attention and patience new users credit you in that first visit to make sure they're primed for activation by the time they finish. For Twitter, this involved not only creating a new account, but also showing new users what Twitter was all about in the first place. They designed a learn flow that showed users how the Twitter timeline worked, suggested categories to follow (such as Fashion, Sports, and News), prompted people to follow notable accounts, and then to complete their profile. By the end of this learn flow, not only are you all signed up for the service, you've customized your profile and you have a Twitter feed full of news you care about. In one visit, Twitter got you to commit to the service, experience the aha moment, and build stored value. Not bad for one visit![6]

Of course because Twitter was offering such a novel service, one that required people to adopt a new habit, teaching them about the value of following people and how to use Twitter was not optional. For some products, no such explanation is needed. For e-commerce sites, for example, people generally just really want to start browsing for goods as fast as possible and most often have a good idea of what they're shopping for, so just about any effort to get people to move through some kind of orchestrated process will be resented. For yet other products, the judgment call about whether or not to require some of a user's time to go through a set of steps is harder to make, because while they may be able to make a rough assumption about how to use the product, getting some information from them and showing them some aspects of the way the product works as it relates *specifically to them* can enhance their appreciation of its value. Making this call, of course, requires experimentation; Pinterest is a great case of this.

Just as Twitter had to educate people about what a "tweet" was, exactly, and what this foreign process of "tweeting" entailed, Pinterest, too, had to introduce users to the novel concept of *Pins* and show users how to create them. The growth team worked hard on educating new users: through three mobile learn flow screens that showed how to discover pinned content, how to add their own Pins, and how to create *Boards* (collections of items that users create to store and share Pins). After going through those three screens, new users were delivered a stream of the most popular content on Pinterest and from that point were on their own.

By all accounts, a solid first user experience. Yet in exemplary growth hacking fashion, the team decided to experiment with improving it even more. They realized that the most popular content wasn't always relevant to any given user, so they decided to test a more personalized new user experience on the mobile app. Now users were first shown just one screen, which asked them to select five topics that they were interested in following, such as camping, weddings, motor sports, and home decor. After they made their selections, the app delivered them to a feed made up solely of that type of content, where they could practice pinning and saving items. The change resulted in a 20 percent increase in activation rate, a massive win.[7]

If you do decide to introduce some positive friction, there are two additional tactics in particular that have proven quite successful: questionnaires and gamifying the new user experience.

THE ART OF THE QUESTIONNAIRE

Neil Patel, a leading expert in growth hacking, has highlighted the effectiveness of asking users a set of questions as you greet them. These should be questions that are clearly asked in the interest of serving the user better; almost like a mini questionnaire. A great example Patel notes is a questionnaire that online golfing retailer Revolution Golf asked users to fill in as part of the sign-up process, and one that the company credits with gains in activation that helped it reach $20 million in annual revenue. It asks questions such as a visitors' gender, age, average driving distance, average score for 18 holes, and biggest problems with their swing. When Patel tested similar questionnaires with Hello Bar, which he owns, he was able to increase the number of leads generated by 281 percent.[8]

Asking customers about their interests or about the problems they are seeking solutions for immediately creates a form of commitment, as they must invest a little time in responding, while at the same time they have forged a deeper personal connection with you and your product. It also conveys to them that you are interested in them individually and in providing the best service for them you can. And as with Pinterest's method of onboarding users by showing them Pins of particular personal interest, it also allows you to start customizing their experience of your product as part of their first exposure.

The tactic works best if it's clear to the customer that customizing the product to their needs and desires will be to their advantage. In an era when people are becoming increasingly fearful of Big Data (or as some think of it, Big Brother), customization is not always a plus. For example, when people learned that Google was customizing search results according to a complex algorithm that factored in lots of information about the searcher from prior search history, many people were put off and the company received lots of criticism in the press.

A key caution here is that you also don't want to ask too many questions. Patel recommends no more than five, and making them multiple-choice rather than open-ended, with no more than four possible answers each. Including images and visuals will also likely improve engagement. And as with all hacks, these mini questionnaires should be put through the process of rigorous experimentation.

GAMIFICATION PROS AND CONS

Gamification is, in essence, offering rewards, such as perks and benefits not available to all people, to customers for taking certain actions. Adobe, for example, used gamification in their activation hacking to increase the number of people who took a free trial of Adobe Photoshop and then purchased the product. The company launched LevelUp for Photoshop, which was a new user experience that turned boring tutorials into "missions" for trial users to complete. The missions helped the trial customers learn the most powerful benefits of the software and showed them how to make the most of it. They added incentives for completing missions and new levels that could only be unlocked by completing other tasks. Adobe saw a 4x increase in trial to purchase from the effort.[9]

By adding a pleasing element of challenge and fun, and also offering meaningful rewards, gamification can be a powerful activation tool, but it can also backfire. If rewards offer no value, or value that has little relevance to the core value experienced by users (i.e., don't achieve product/incentive fit), then the tactic can come across as blatantly manipulative, or just downright strange. That was true for a gamification effort that online shoe retailer Zappos launched for their VIP program. The company was trying to create a new level of higher-frequency shoppers; they tried to gamify the shopping experience by offering badges for doing things like favoriting a shoe model and buying multiple pairs, but the badges offered no value—no higher discounts or other benefits—and left customers confused, leading Zappos to ultimately shutter the effort.[10]

Brian Wong, founder of Kiip, a company that helps mobile apps provide rewards to their users, says that gamification should be thought of as a toolkit of options to choose from, rather than a predefined set of tactics that work for all businesses. What you choose to deploy can range from subtle to more overt; as with anything, you've got to experiment with what will be best for your product and customers. He suggests focusing on three main aspects of any gamification effort: meaningful rewards, creating surprise and delight by varying how rewards are earned and presented, and providing some element of instant gratification. Beyond assuring the relevance of rewards is clear and that they are actually of value to users, there are few hard and fast rules about what perks to offer. LinkedIn gamifies in a gentle fashion, including a progress meter on people's profile pages that shows them how complete their profiles are, nudging them to fill in more information. This offers the reward of the instant satisfaction of a completed profile, and receiving the implicit approval by those who view it. Khan Academy, an online education website, takes the more overt approach of offering points and awards as users take more courses, creating surprise and delight with rewards as users hit new milestones. The company is careful, though, not to make these the centerpiece of its user experience, as they are aware that such explicit rewards can undermine the actual intrinsic reward of skills acquisition that is offered by learning.

On the very overt side of the spectrum are loyalty programs employed by businesses ranging from Starbucks to credit cards to restaurants. Gabe Zichermann, a leading gamification expert, has identified that the most effective rewards in a gamified setting come in the form of status, access, power, and stuff (stuff being financial incentives or physical gifts).[11] Credit cards, such as American Express Membership Rewards, deploy all of these elements, from new levels of status to achieve through spending, power, and access to special events and travel opportunities, and of course free stuff, which can be redeemed with the points earned. Similarly, the Starbucks Rewards program boasts more than 12 million members who use a Starbucks gift card or the company's mobile app to earn "stars" each time they buy a cup of coffee. Those stars turn into more free coffee and other Starbucks merchandise. The more stars they earn, the bigger rewards they can redeem and they also move up in rank, accumulating more status as a member of the Starbucks faithful. The program has been so successful that the company now has more than $1 billion in customer cash from the preloaded gift cards and app.[12]

INS AND OUTS OF TRIGGERS

While gamification doesn't work for every situation, *triggers* are everywhere. And even more so than gamification, the use of triggers to stoke activation requires careful consideration to get it right. Triggers are any sort of prompt that provokes a response from people, common ones being email notifications, mobile push notifications, and, less obtrusively, calls to action on a landing page. There is no denying that triggers are one of the most powerful tactics for increasing the use of your product. But for every benefit there are plenty of potential pitfalls. We're targets of so many triggers these days, from Facebook notifications that a friend has liked a photo, to LinkedIn emails about a new connection request, and Amazon updates about the delivery status of a package, that it's easy to cross the line from helpful to annoying. Who hasn't been utterly infuriated by the desperation of a steady drip of email messages hollering "Come back!!" "Are you sure you don't want to come back?" "We'd really love to see you come back!!!" Often they come from a company whose product we long ago dismissed, making them even more irritating—while at the same time making the company look desperate. So you want to tread lightly with triggers, experimenting with great care.

The power of triggers comes from two key factors: how much they motivate users to take the action you want them to and how easy it is for users to do so at the time they receive the trigger. BJ Fogg, a psychology researcher at Stanford, developed the following useful model for thinking about how to make triggers effective. The curved line represents the threshold of whether a user will or will not take a particular action, which depends primarily upon the combination of her level of motivation and what Fogg dubs her ability to take that action, meaning essentially how convenient it is to do so.[13]

Nir Eyal, the author of *Hooked: How to Build Habit-Forming Products*, helpfully uses the scenario of receiving a phone call to illustrate this interplay of factors. Whether you answer a call is dependent on whether the phone is handy and you're free to take it—your ability—as well as on motivating factors such as whether you know the name of the caller, wish to talk to him or her, or perhaps need some information that he or she possesses. The trigger in this case is clearly the phone ringing. If you hear it ring when you're motivated and available, you'll answer.

Because triggers can be so invasive, you want to be judicious in how you use them and experiment in measured steps. Making matters more complicated, you've also got to follow some rules dictated by the platform on which you wish to deliver them. For example, mobile push notification rules differ for Apple phones than for those that run on Android; whereas Apple users need to opt in to receive notifications, Android users are opted in to get notifications by default. Rules have also been established in consumer protection law for sending emails, such as the CAN-SPAM law in the United States.

FOGG BEHAVIOR MODEL

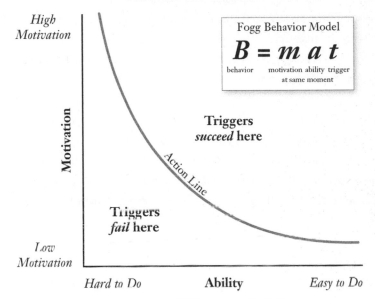

© 2007 B.J. Fogg. For permissions, contact B.J. Fogg at www.BehaviorModel.org

And finally, for opt-in notifications, a trigger's impact will vary greatly depending on how many users agree to receive them. The range of opt-in agreement can vary a great deal across products and product categories. For example, for mobile notifications, opt-in rates range from

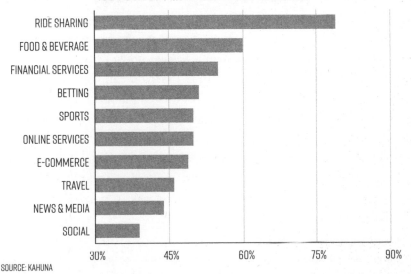

IOS PUSH OPT-IN RATES BY APP INDUSTRY

SOURCE: KAHUNA

80 percent at the high end, for services like ride sharing, to 39 percent at the low end for news and media offerings, according to Kahuna, a mobile messaging company.[14]

One of the biggest mistakes companies make is asking visitors to opt in to receiving triggers such as notifications and emails too soon, often as a necessary first step to setting up or accessing the product. This can scare people off because they have no idea, or only a vague inkling yet, about why they would want these messages. Many companies also abuse triggers in an attempt to gin up their product use statistics—a move that may make their short-term activation stats look pretty, but does nothing to create long-term use (often in fact having a negative effect as people tune out, turn off notifications, or delete the app).

A great rule of thumb about deploying triggers is that your rationale for getting in touch with the users should be to alert them of an opportunity of clear value to them. For example, the grocery app team could send notifications when an item that a person has saved in their shopping list goes on sale, or when there's a special offer on free delivery, or when the chain is running a Thanksgiving holiday promotion. These types of triggers would make sense to users because they relate to the core value of the shopping app. However, sending notifications weekly about new sales or product features that aren't particularly relevant to customers might quickly irritate them and prompt many of them to disable notifications or delete the app from their phones altogether.

In experimenting with different trigger notifications, it's important to keep some users in what's called a *holdout group*, which is subject to none of the experiments. This assures that you can compare not only the effect of new triggers, but the effect of using none of them as well.[15]

Some common types of notification triggers to experiment with are:

- Account creation—encourage users who have downloaded an app or visited a retail website to complete their account
- Purchase messages—encourage users to make a purchase with a short-term discount
- Reactivation campaign—encourage users who haven't been to your site or app in a while to come back and reengage

- New feature announcement—share the news about updates to the product
- Top user incentives—for heavy users of the product, let them know they're special and encourage greater affinity and use
- Activity or status change—such as a friend taking an action or an item in a shopping cart changing price[16]

You can, of course, invent your own types of triggers as well. In coming up with ideas, it's helpful to know about a categorization of the types of triggers that BJ Fogg introduced. He divides them into three basic types, based on the motivation and ability level of the user: a *facilitator trigger*, which helps those with high motivation but low ability take action; a *signal trigger*, which helps keep people with high motivation and high ability headed in the right direction and encourages repeat action; and a *spark*, which spurs people with high ability yet low motivation to take action. Many email and mobile notifications fall into the "spark" category, but they shouldn't be the only ones considered.[17]

The grocery app team, for example, might devise a facilitator trigger that pops up after a certain amount of time that a user has been on the checkout page without completing the purchase, asking if they'd like to have the credit card that was used before be used for this purchase. They might also experiment with a signal trigger, which could be a message on screen that notifies a user about how much he's saving by having made a set of purchases. A spark trigger they might try out would be offering an especially high discount on a favorite item of a shopper who has logged in but hasn't moved any items into her cart after a certain period, to try to spark that first critical purchase.

In crafting triggers to try out, the set of six principles of persuasion that Robert Cialdini presents in his book *Influence* are also invaluable. We mentioned one earlier, in discussing his insight that once people take an action of whatever kind, they are more inclined to take that action again. Here is the full set:

- Reciprocity—whereby people are more likely to do something in return of a favor, regardless of the favor done and the ask now presented to them

- Commitment and consistency—people who have taken one action are likely to take another, regardless of the size or difference in action
- Social proof—in a state of uncertainty, people look to the actions of others to help them make their own decisions
- Authority—people look to those in the position of authority to decide which actions to take
- Liking—people will do business more readily with people and companies they like over those they don't or are indifferent to
- Scarcity—people will take action when they are worried that they will miss out on the opportunity in the future

A trigger can draw on the principle of reciprocity by offering users a free resource, such as a downloadable whitepaper, or free shipping. HubSpot's Website Grader is a great example. A case of using the principle of consistency and commitment is the way in which the Obama presidential campaign team broke down the donation request form on its website into a series of smaller steps rather than having all of them appearing on one page. Having taken the first small step, users were more inclined to take the rest, which led to a 5 percent increase in the rate at which people responded with donations, and millions of additional dollars in the campaign fund.[18]

Triggers can incorporate the principle of authority by showcasing that influential people, or companies, have taken the action they're urging users to take, which is, of course, the rationale of celebrity endorsements. Including the logos of well-respected companies that have used a service, or testimonials from respected individuals, can also act as triggers, by reassuring the visitor that people and companies they know and respect have made a similar decision.

Lots of triggers make use of the principle of liking, such as the messages sent by Airbnb with the name of a friend who referred you to the service, or Nasty Gal, where founder Sophia Amoruso tracked which models customers responded to best (i.e., who seemed to sell the most merchandise) and paired them with items that needed a boost in sales.

All of us have surely received some notifications that draw on the principle of scarcity, warning us, for example, that a sale is about to end, or that there are only a few tickets left for the show or concert we were thinking of attending, or only a few seats left on a flight we were thinking of booking. Booking.com makes great use of this tactic, showing all browsers the number of people actively looking at hotel rooms in the same search area and the number left on the site. Amazon, too, shows browsers how many items are left when inventory is low, trying to spur them to go ahead and purchase.

The final (and most powerful) type of trigger is the internal type, which occurs involuntarily within your customers; these are at the core of habits and spur long-term use. Few of us need any external trigger to visit Facebook or Instagram; we do it on our own volition now. The same could be said for our favorite clothing retailer whose website we routinely check for new sales or inventory, the news source we visit every morning, or the convenience store we always stop at to grab coffee on the way to work. No matter what your product is, these habits are at the foundation of strong relationships with your customers. So we'll revisit them and some more nuances about them in the following chapters.

The bottom line is: do experiment with triggers, because they can be extraordinarily effective, but do so with a very thoughtful understanding of how they can actually be of service to your users. Otherwise, rather than activating users and starting to build a good relationship with them, you are almost sure to push them away.

Now, speaking of building relationships with your customers, let's move farther through the user experience to examine how growth teams have used the growth hacking process to achieve great successes in retention.

CHAPTER SEVEN

HACKING RETENTION

egendary business expert Peter Drucker famously wrote many years ago that the purpose of business is to create and keep a customer.[1] But even though no one would argue with the famous business maxim, the fact is that for most businesses, the rate of customer *churn*—the rate of loss of new users—is appalling.

This is unfortunate because high retention is generally the deciding factor in achieving strong profitability, for any kind of company. As we mentioned briefly in Chapter Four, widely cited research by Frederick Reichheld of Bain & Company has shown that a 5 percent increase in customer retention rates increases profits by anywhere from 25 to 95 percent.[2] The flip side is that *losing* customers comes at great cost. One reason is that, as we learned in Chapter Five, it takes so much money to acquire a new customer, especially at a time when advertising costs are skyrocketing due to a surge in competition for prime online real estate. And the more you have to spend up front to attract new customers, the more costly the loss of each customer becomes—making retaining customers that much more essential, both for recouping your spending on expensive ad campaigns and for preventing customers from defecting to the competition.

Homejoy, a home cleaning start-up, once had a bright future, raising more than $64 million from some of Silicon Valley's best investors. But the company is a prime example of the danger of poor retention. Despite having attracted an impressive number of initial customers through an aggressive promotional discounting strategy, Homejoy failed to live up to its promise, delivering service that customers described as "hit or miss." In addition, many customers couldn't swallow a steep jump in price from a promotional first cleaning, at a special discounted price, to the regular price for the service; the result being that only 15 to 20 percent of customers ended up ordering a second cleaning. Meanwhile, Homejoy's competitors were achieving retention rates double those numbers. Making matters still worse, the company had spent heavily on customer acquisition. This combination of high acquisition costs and low retention led to its rapid demise.[3]

Amazon, in contrast, is perhaps the gold standard example of retention prowess. The company's subscription program, Amazon Prime, has been a particular triumph in retaining customers, largely due to the two-day free shipping included on thousands of items, but also many ancillary benefits that have been added to the program, such as its video and music streaming services. Seventy-three percent of free trial subscribers convert to paying subscribers, and ninety-one percent of first-year subscribers renew for a second year. What's even more impressive is that retention continues to increase the longer customers have been subscribers, with the renewal rate for customers heading into their third year in the program at an almost unheard-of high of 96 percent.[4]

THE COMPOUNDING VALUE OF RETENTION

It should go without saying that the longer you retain customers, the more opportunity you have to earn more revenue from them, whether that's from selling them more items or services, from ongoing subscription renewals, or from bringing in more advertising revenue due to advertisers wanting to target your large and loyal customer base. If you consider the fact that subscribers in Amazon's Prime program purchase more than twice as much as non–Prime members, it becomes easy to imagine the compounding gains in revenue one can see from high retention rates. In fact, some analysts believe that without Amazon Prime, the company would not be profitable.

Increasing the average revenue you earn per customer in turn allows you to invest more in growth, creating a virtuous cycle. This is both because strong retention generates higher current earnings and because it allows you to predict better that your future earnings will be strong. Amazon's reliable earnings per subscriber have allowed the company to invest significantly in continuing to build up the Prime program, such as by adding original programming to its video streaming service. The longer you retain customers, the more you can learn about them and their needs and desires, and thus the better you can tailor services and promotions to them, which of course allows you to earn more from them. When Amazon launched Prime, some analysts argued that the company would be spending too much on free two-day shipping and discounts for Prime-eligible items and therefore the program would be unsustainable. But Amazon saw that with so many subscribers renewing and spending far above average, the program was on a highly profitable trajectory.

Yet another benefit of higher retention is that it allows you to see stronger results from both word of mouth and your viral marketing efforts, because the longer users stay with your product, the more opportunities they'll have to talk about it and even to show it to friends and others.

HOMING IN ON BEST BETS FAST

Given the increasingly high costs of customer acquisition and the ever more heated competition most businesses are up against these days, it's vital that companies are attuned to problems with their customer retention and work to stop defections, or what marketers call churn, as early as possible. Growth hacking is the ideal means of achieving this. To give just a quick example, let's return to the grocery app team. What if, by keeping close track of customer data, the team identifies a slide in usage by a large number of customers after the first month or so of use, a fate far too familiar for mobile apps. Where should they begin trying to get more customers to stay actively engaged in using the app? Should the team increase the number of mobile notifications it sends its users to entice them to come back? Should they offer special pricing and savings available only within the app on popular items? Perhaps they should build some new features, like the successful shopping list, to increase the utility of the app. All of these ideas might work, but they all involve significant costs, and in addition, the team must be sensitive about not annoying users with too many promotional messages or triggers. As discussed in the last chapter, more mobile notifications could spur short-term use but might quickly lose their luster as people tired of the interruptions. In-app promotions might lead to increased purchasing by loyal app shoppers but not reach most of the customers the team wants to reengage, because those people aren't on the app much, if at all. Building new features is expensive and there's no guarantee that users will become more regularly active and for the longer term due to them.

Growth hacking allows teams to quickly choose which out of such a set of ideas to start testing first, and rapidly produce results that clarify how to move forward. The grocery app team could easily test all three of the ideas above in short order. The email notifications and app promotions are a snap to create, and an idea for a new feature can be rapidly tested by surveying customers about how appealing it would be to them or building a quick prototype to test with a set of users. Perhaps they would decide to experiment first with sending more email notifications, and within only a few weeks, they might be able to learn that sending one additional mobile notification per week led to only 10 percent of lapsed users to returning to the app, but that if two more notifications were sent in a week, 35 percent of them returned. They might then go ahead and schedule sending the two additional notifications to all lapsed users the next week. Meanwhile, the responses to the new feature prototype might be so positive that the team could convince the product development group to fast-track work on it, and that might begin to improve retention shortly after it's introduced.

These results would, of course, only be the beginning of nonstop crafting and testing of hacks to boost retention, the topic of this chapter.

WHAT DRIVES RETENTION?

Before we get into more specifics about how to apply the growth hacking process to improve retention, it's important to return to a brief consideration of the basics of what builds customer loyalty and keeps customers coming back.

As discussed in Chapter Two, retaining customers most fundamentally depends upon providing them with a product or service of high quality that continually addresses a need of theirs, or perhaps simply delights them, and which they come to regard as a must-have. We also discussed there that a great measure of having achieved product/market fit is a stable retention curve. Recall that this looks like the black line in the graph below, versus the gray line, which indicates that an increasing number of customers have been abandoning the product over time.

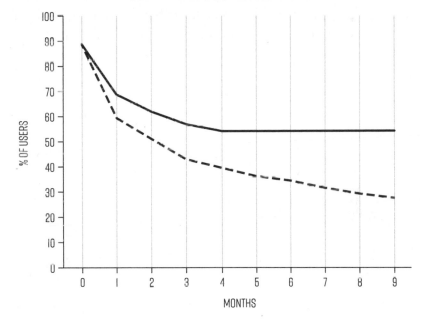

Now, in focusing on hacking retention, we will look closely at what growth teams should be doing to assure that retention at the very least remains stable, or ideally, how they can work to increase retention from that baseline over time. First, it's important to highlight that even after having initially achieved a stable retention curve, a company may begin to see its retention erode, for various reasons. Perhaps a competitive product has come out and is stealing users away, or perhaps an existing competitor has launched a new feature or promotion that has the same effect. Another key reason customers defect over time is that a company is not communicating with them optimally; the company hasn't found the right sorts of messages to be sending to them, with the right frequency, to keep the app "top of mind," leaving them ripe for the picking by competitors. Companies may also be failing to take advantage of opportunities to build loyalty by working to create a regular habit or strong feeling in customers that they are appreciated and understood. Or perhaps the need the company fills is no longer an urgent one for its customers, or is being fulfilled in a way that is more satisfying or convenient, as might happen when the technology in the product has become outdated or obsolete.

Growth teams are perfectly equipped to look for early warning signs of erosion in retention. But they shouldn't stop there. Teams ought to apply the rapid experimentation process to pushing retention higher and higher, as Amazon has achieved with its Prime subscribers. A stable curve is by no means the be-all and end-all of retention. Take a look at the figure below, which Evernote calls its Smile Graph, showing that the longer people use Evernote, the more likely they are to continue using it.[5]

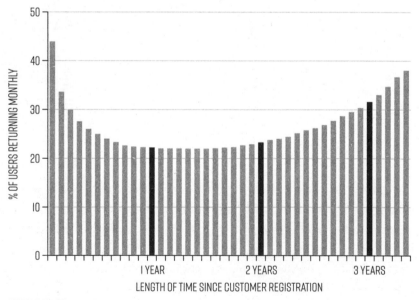

EVERNOTE'S SMILE GRAPH

SOURCE: EVERNOTE

Evernote's retention graph looks that way essentially because the service's usefulness improves over time. The core value is enhanced the longer you use Evernote because as a note-keeping product, the more information that is saved within it, the more likely people are to return to access those ideas and notes and add more to them. Many successful digital products achieve a growing retention rate over time: whether it's for Instagram, which becomes more valuable the more photos you post and people you follow, or a business product such as QuickBooks, which gets more valuable to the company the more financial data stored within it, which, remember, is referred to as *stored value*.

Companies with the opportunity to capitalize on the power of stored value have an advantage in increasing retention over time, but no company, even those with this built-in opportunity, can simply assume that customers will continue to be actively engaged. They must steadily work to improve their offerings for customers. Just think about how many new features and services Facebook has offered since its launch and how many different kinds of notifications and prompts they've devised to keep you using the service. From adding live video and slideshows, to prompting you to share news about your favorite sports teams or letting you know when you have a Facebook anniversary with a friend, the company continually works to improve how engaged and retained its customer base is. Any kind of company can, and should, work to keep increasing the value it's delivering to customers and their level of engagement over time.

THE THREE PHASES OF RETENTION

The methods for retaining users evolve according to the phase of retention the user is in. Brian Balfour, whom we've met earlier, highlights that retention breaks down into three phases: initial, medium, and long-term.[6] The *initial retention period* is the critical time during which a new user either becomes convinced to keep using or buying a product or service, or goes dormant after one or a few visits. Think of the initial retention rate as a measure of the immediate stickiness of the product. There is no fixed definition of the initial retention period; it might be as short as a day for a mobile app, or a week or two for a social network. For a software as a service (SaaS) product, the initial retention period might be more like a month or quarter, whereas for e-commerce companies it is often the first 90 days.[7] You should determine this period for your product based on both the data you can get about the standards for products of your type across the sector you're in and by your own analysis of the behavior of your own customers over time.

The good news about this period is that research shows that users who get more value from a product during the initial period of use are more likely to stick around longer term. Also, generally, there's lots of opportunity to improve the user's experience in this phase. This was the main impetus behind the start of the growth team at HubSpot, as explained by cofounder and CTO Dharmesh Shah. "The *reason* we decided to kick off a growth team in the first place was that we felt there was a lot of low-hanging fruit in our trials/onboarding process."[8] We covered the work of the HubSpot team in improving its onboarding process in the activation chapter, and this initial retention phase is essentially an extension of activation; think of it as assuring that customers or users are *truly* active; that they haven't just given your product a cursory once-over and then lost interest.

It might seem to make better sense to just consider this as part of the activation process, but the distinction is meaningful. For many products, solidifying the appreciation of the value of a product or service requires new customers returning for an additional experience with it a certain number of times within a certain time period. For example, Pinterest might determine from analysis of user data that if a new user doesn't return to the site at least three times within the first two weeks after signing up, they are highly likely to abandon use. This means that the growth team would want to work intensely on getting them back that minimum number of times within that time frame, and anyone who has signed up for Pinterest will find that the company is indeed vigorous in encouraging return visits beginning right after initial sign-up.

Once new users have crossed the threshold of initial retention, they move into the **medium retention phase**, a period when the interest in a product's novelty often fades. The core mission for growth teams in retaining users who are in this midterm phase is to make using a product a habit; working to create such a sense of satisfaction from the product or service that over time, users don't need to be prodded to use it again because they have incorporated the use of the product into their routine. Think of the Snapchat user who constantly checks her friends' stories while having breakfast and again after dinner. Or the Amazon shopper who always thinks of searching there first for any given product he's looking for, no prodding required. In the coming sections, we'll introduce a little about the psychology of habit formation and then introduce tactics growth teams can employ for increasing the number of initially retained users who become habitual ones.

Then, we'll move on to the tactics for **long-term retention**. This is the phase in which growth teams can help to assure that a product keeps offering customers more value. Teams must experiment with ways to keep improving the product, helping product development teams to determine the timing for introducing enhancements of existing features or entirely new features. The key here is to keep refreshing the customer's perception of the product as must-have.[9]

WHAT DOES GOOD RETENTION LOOK LIKE?

Before we get into the specifics of how to improve retention in each of these phases, it's important to discuss the data that growth teams must be tracking and how they should be parsing it in order to find opportunities for hacks to try. First, different companies will want to measure their retention rate in different ways. This is due to the fact that the frequency with which customers return to purchase items or use a service will in large part be determined by the nature of the product or service. Some things we need or want often, and others much less so. While Facebook wants users to be returning daily, Apple knows that purchasers of an iPhone will likely not buy a new phone for several years (except for the raving fans who always immediately purchase the newest version), so it won't know if a given iPhone buyer has been retained until perhaps three years, maybe more. This is a key reason that Apple's evolution into a provider of the services people use with their products in addition to the devices themselves, was such a brilliant growth tactic; it allowed the company to capitalize a great deal more on its retained customers in between product releases. The frequency with which buyers search for listings on sites like Zillow also varies from how often diners search Yelp for restaurant recommendations, just as the search and purchase frequency for customers looking for mattresses will differ from those looking for a new pair of shoes.

For e-commerce, the basic metric of retention is the *repurchase rate* of customers, which might, for example, be the number of times customers make a purchase per month. Many e-commerce companies, for example, measure the repurchase rate per 90 days, but again, this time frame varies depending on the product sold. Since most people shop for groceries at least once a week, our grocery app team would want to be looking for more frequent purchases, say, every ten days or so, as a sign of healthy retention.

The key point is that in crafting your retention metrics, it's important to benchmark your results against the best information you can get from market research about the typical retention rates for your kind of product or service, and any information you can find about the performance of successful companies you are competing with. These benchmarks are the only way to tell whether what you're seeing with your customers is typical, better, or worse than expected. A company like Airbnb can never expect to get as much engagement and retention as a social network, so these benchmarks become important in pinpointing how your retention is faring. Sources such as industry publications, trade associations, and research companies Forrester and Gartner can offer industry-specific insights.

While we've so far discussed retention in terms of the customers you keep, it's also critical to track the flip side, the customers who defect, or churn, from your business each week or month. Your churn rate is essentially the inverse of your retention rate; so, for example, Costco's 91 percent membership retention rate is also a 9 percent annual churn rate.[10] Some churn is unavoidable, even for the best-loved products. But clearly, for all businesses, the lower rate of churn, the better.

IDENTIFY AND CHART YOUR COHORTS

Once you've determined the metrics you will use for measuring your retention rate, the next step is to break your retention data down more finely, determining the specific rate for various subgroups of users, through a technique called *cohort analysis*. This allows you to probe more deeply into your data to make discoveries about why those who are staying are doing so—and why others are not.

You can break users down into many different types of cohorts. The most basic way is by the time of acquisition, meaning the date they signed up or first purchased from you. This is most often done by month, but as said above, for some business types it might be important to identify them by week or day. This may sound like drudge work, but the power this process gives a team to identify issues with retention makes it well worth the effort. Tracking groups of customers by the date of their initial acquisition allows teams to discover the overall health of the customer base. As sales and marketing efforts ramp up, are the customers that are acquired today being retained at as high a rate as some of the earlier customers, or vice versa? If the company is successfully bringing in lots of new users, which means that sales or new sign-ups are improving nicely, churn can easily get hidden if you're not tracking retention by time acquired.

Problematic trends can also be uncovered with this type of cohort analysis. For example, a growth team might discover a particularly high churn of users who were acquired during a particular campaign effort, or during a particular time of year. Or they may find that engagement stays high during the first two months, but during the third month after acquisition, a large number in each cohort go dormant.

To see how this might be revealed, and how the growth team would then have valuable information for figuring out why, let's say that a video streaming service for which users pay a month-to-month fee, and can cancel their subscription any given month, has decided to break down the new users it acquires by the month they are signed up. Take a look at the following table and graph that display this data. We should note that the spreadsheets displaying retention data by cohort can be a little daunting to read, so it's sometimes helpful to also translate the data into the format of retention curves for each cohort, which can make it easier to see patterns worth investigating in the data.

COHORT TRACKING WORKSHEET

Conversion month	New customers	# of retained customers in month									A1
		Jan-15	Feb-15	Mar-15	Apr-15	May-15	Jun-15	Jul-15	Aug-15	Sep-15	Oct-15
Jan-15	150	140	130	125	118	105	102	97	95	95	95
Feb-15	180		172	160	150	140	130	121	118	118	118
Mar-15	200			190	178	169	155	142	135	132	128
Apr-15	270				188	175	170	153	144	137	131
May-15	350					247	228	216	202	189	178
Jun-15	450						307	288	269	258	244
Jul-15	225							210	195	180	166
Aug-15	235								218	207	197
Sep-15	240									224	211
Oct-15	250										233
		140	302	475	634	836	1,092	1,227	1,376	1,540	1,701

Conversion month	New customers	% of retained customers in lifetime month									B1
		0	1	2	3	4	5	6	7	8	9
Jan-15	150	93.33%	86.67%	83.33%	78.67%	70.00%	68.00%	64.67%	63.33%	63.33%	63.33%
Feb-15	180	95.56%	88.89%	83.33%	77.78%	72.22%	67.22%	65.56%	65.56%	65.56%	
Mar-15	200	95.00%	89.00%	84.50%	77.50%	71.00%	67.50%	66.00%	64.00%		
Apr-15	270	69.63%	64.81%	62.96%	56.67%	53.33%	50.74%	48.52%			
May-15	350	70.57%	65.14%	61.71%	57.71%	54.00%	50.86%				
Jun-15	450	68.22%	64.00%	59.78%	57.33%	54.22%					
Jul-15	225	93.33%	86.67%	80.00%	73.78%						
Aug-15	235	92.77%	88.09%	83.83%							
Sep-15	240	93.33%	87.92%								
Oct-15	250	93.20%									
		83.49%	77.04%	71.65%	65.32%	59.63%	58.52%	59.75%	64.34%	64.55%	63.33%

Chart via Christoph Janz[11]

To the left of the table, you can see the number of customers signed up each month. These are the groups of cohorts that we want to track over time. In the body of the table, the top part tracks the absolute number of users in each of those cohorts who are retained each month. You can see that of the 150 new customers who signed up in January, 140 were still retained in February, 130 in March, followed by fairly steady drop-offs each month, until the cohort stabilizes at around 95 subscribers who remain paying for the service in July through October. Following down the chart, you can see that the customers who sign up in February and March exhibit similar retention rates.

In April, May, and June, however, something dramatically different occurs. The first thing to notice is that the number of new customers acquired in each month jumps dramatically from the high 100s to a new high of 450 in June. If the team managing this company's growth were only looking at new customer acquisition, they would be ecstatic because they dramatically grew how many people were signing up for the service each month. But by looking more closely, it's clear that these April through June cohorts are not being retained as well as previous ones. Among customers who joined during those months, the data shows a sharp decline in retention after the initial month of sign-up, and their numbers show no sign of stabilizing as the ones in January through March did.

To make this data more visual for reporting dashboards, the team may convert these cohort charts into retention curve graphs. To simplify it we've shown just two cohorts on this graph, one for the January group and one for May, but growth teams often look at every curve from every month on the same graph. You can see how different the curves are below, and May's continues to point downward while January's has leveled off.

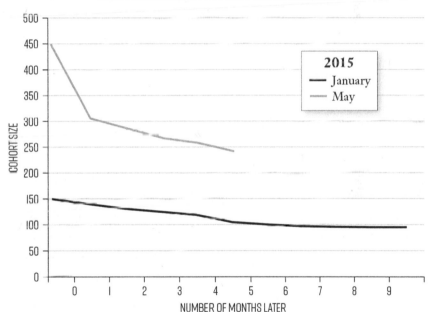

COMPARING COHORTS SHOWS BIG DIFFERENCE

Clearly the growth team that's been presented with this data has something important to learn about what happened in those three months. The April, May, and June cohorts show a precipitous drop in retention right after initial sign-up. To begin to investigate why the drop-off occurred, they should dig more deeply into the troubled cohorts.

This pattern might be seen when a company runs a new ad campaign that brings in lots of new customers for whom the product is not actually particularly well suited. Perhaps the campaign offered a steep promotional discount, and when prices increased lots of these new customers quickly abandoned ship. Or maybe they decided to advertise in a new channel to reach a particular demographic better, say, running a campaign on radio targeted at stay-at-home moms. Maybe the ads were very effective, hitting a sweet spot for those moms, but once those moms watched a couple of movies with their kids they realized that the selection of that kind of movie wasn't very rich and so rather than renew, they canceled. Knowing the correlation between the ad campaign and the drop in retention gives the growth team valuable information for experiments to try: clearly, these moms are good candidates as new customers, but before targeting them so aggressively again, the service should add more movies that will appeal to them to its inventory. Or perhaps the existing movie inventory needs to be better highlighted to these customers as soon as they join. Or, there could be an issue that's not as readily apparent to the team causing this churn. The team should follow up on this observation by surveying these churned customers to ask them why they canceled, with a set of questions to test their hypothesis that the selection of movies available was what indeed caused them to unsubscribe.

Breaking down users by month acquired is only the beginning of cohort analysis, however. You'll also want to create many other sets of cohorts, such as the specific channel that brought the new customers to your product—for example, by a customer referral program versus a paid ad campaign, and so on. Another distinguishing factor might be the numbers of visits to your website or purchases made. For the video streaming growth team, then, cohorts might include breakdowns by number of shows or series watched in the first month, by subscribers who have watched particular series, or by number of days in a month that someone uses the service. Parsing the data this way would allow them to look for correlations between frequency of use of the service and the rate of retention, as well as whether there are particular movies or shows that are leading to higher retention.

To consider how the breakdowns might be done for a different business model, say, e-commerce, our grocery app team might break customers down into cohorts by those who have only made one purchase within the first month from signing up, those who have made two purchases in that time, those who have made three purchases, and those who have made four or more. By tracking the retention of these cohorts for six months, the team might discover that making three purchases within a month after first sign-up is a tipping point that leads to much higher retention, which would point them toward experiments focused on getting shoppers to increase the number of purchases that first month.

It's important to note that tracking retention by cohorts and in the many ways suggested above requires more sophisticated analytics capabilities than basic Web analytics tools, like Google Analytics, offer. A data analyst can put together these reports relatively easily, assuming that your user database has been set up to allow for separating out users by the right set of variables. But if you don't have a dedicated data analyst, you can use one of a number of programs, such as Mixpanel, Kissmetrics, or Amplitude. While Google Analytics has recently added some cohort analysis capability, these more robust tools allow you to do much more refined analysis such as the one above, and they are easy for anyone to use.

HACKING INITIAL RETENTION

Once you've analyzed the cohort data to identify drop-off points in initial retention, and deployed surveys to probe into the causes of the defections, you can begin to experiment with solutions. The hacks for improving initial retention will be essentially the same as those introduced for improving activation, as this period is really a prolonging of the activation experience. Refining the new user experience and getting users to experience the product's core value as quickly as possible are two of the most important strategies at this stage. The use of triggers, such as the mobile notifications and emails, can also be effective in helping to cement the usefulness and value of the product in the user's mind. However, as we discussed in the last chapter, growth teams should not fall into the trap of relying only on triggers to keep people coming back in this initial stage; they've got to also keep their eye on the experience the product is offering and any refinements that could be made (for a refresher on these tactics, turn back to Chapter Six).

BUILDING HABITS

Recall that the core goal during the medium phase of retention is to solidify users' commitment to your product by making the use of it habitual for them. For some products, this means making use a daily or weekly habit, while for others, the use might be much less frequent than we tend to think of as being habitual, but simply means that regardless of frequency, whenever that customer wants to buy a product or use a service of the type you sell, they turn to you rather than a competitor. They are, in other words, loyal to you.

The key to habit formation is convincing customers of the *ongoing rewards* they will receive from returning to your product or service. In *Hooked*, customer behavior researcher Nir Eyal explains how the most engaging products do this, which is through a process he describes in his Hook Model (depicted below), or what's referred to in growth hacking as an *engagement loop*. Here is where the external triggers we talked about in the activation stage—like mobile notifications, emails, and in-app prompts—come in again. They will serve as the prompts to action that kick off those powerful engagement loops that lead to habit formation. Here, growth teams should work to identify the optimal number, method, and cadence of triggers needed to build habits, and keep those habits reinforced.

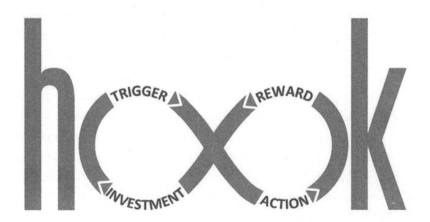

Hook Model by Nir Eyal[12]

To understand how habit formation works, think of the psychology of joining a gym. When people first decide they want to get in shape, they often need an external trigger to psych themselves up to go and work out, maybe setting alarms in their calendar or committing to a schedule with a trainer or friend. But once they receive enough of the rewards from going—feeling healthier, seeing how their muscles are firming up and their weight dropping—many people don't need these external prompts anymore. The same basic process is involved when people regularly check Facebook while having breakfast, when they post Instagram on their way home from work, or turn to Yelp when considering a place to meet up with a friend for a meal. The mere act of having breakfast, or driving home, or choosing a restaurant, becomes the internal, subconscious trigger: no other prompting needed.

Amazon's Prime program is the quintessential case of powerful habit creation. Recall that many analysts predicted the program would fail because the free shipping would be too expensive for Amazon to sustain. It's easy to understand why they were wrong when you consider the nature of the program with the Hook Model in mind. First, Prime offers two essential, and very compelling, rewards every single time subscribers purchase an item included in the program—meaningful savings in the form of free shipping and instant gratification with two-day delivery. The program also creates a reward for members when they shop by validating the decision they made to invest in the $99 Prime subscription in the first place. Every time they make a purchase and are shown how much they've saved due to the free shipping (and often additional savings from the item list price), they say to themselves, *See, the $99 is so worth it because I'm saving so much.* In fact, Vijay Ravindran, the director of Amazon's ordering systems, told Brad Stone, the author of *The Everything Store*, that the subscription fee "[w]as never about the seventy-nine dollars. It was really about changing people's mentality so they wouldn't shop anywhere else."[13] Indeed, the Prime program proved so habit forming that, according to a *Businessweek* story, while Amazon had forecast that it would take two years to break even on the program, it did so within just three months.[14]

The engagement loop with Amazon Prime is clear and continues to reinforce itself with repeated use, which is why it works so well. Of course this model won't work for everyone; growth teams should map out their own engagement loop based on the core value their product delivers, and then set out to measure, monitor, and optimize it. By using data and experimenting with triggers that lead to the most valuable rewards for customers, the team can ascertain how to build habit formation around their product. For example, the video streaming service team could measure the effectiveness of triggers that lead to discovery of new shows compared with triggers that lead to completion of series or shows already in progress.

One general rule that holds true across most product types is that improving the perceived value of the rewards leads to greater retention. To make a product or service more habit forming, growth teams should experiment with providing customers with a range of rewards, and encouraging them to take action to receive them; the more action taken, the greater rewards, and the greater perceived value. They should do cohort analysis about which customers are using the product most avidly and what features they're using most, and also which features provide the greatest reward and subsequent retention rate. The team should also identify which customers are less active who might be motivated to make more use of the product if only they were exposed to more compelling rewards.

The video streaming service, for example, could break subscribers into cohorts by the amount of viewing time. That analysis might reveal that a group of avid users are watching several episodes of shows all in one viewing; in other words, that they are binge watching, a new viewer habit that Netflix has capitalized on well. This discovery might lead the growth team to consider how the company might create a new type of reward by allowing customers to do more binge watching, as Netflix did when it started to offer its original series for viewing all at once rather than making episodes available one at a time. The team might also analyze what types of series are the most popular for bingeing and experiment with highlighting similar series that have proven to also be great for bingeing.

OFFER REWARDS BOTH TANGIBLE AND EXPERIENTIAL

Many popular strategies for offering rewards to customers are focused on allowing them to "earn" savings, or sending them coupons or cash vouchers or gifts. This is especially true in retail businesses, which have a long-established repertoire of such tactics. These are powerful rewards, and teams should definitely experiment with an array of them. But it's also important to experiment with offering rewards that are not about money or savings, but instead about the *experience* customers have with your product. And in fact, some of the most habit-forming rewards are the intangible ones. There are many kinds of rewards to experiment with in this category. There are social rewards, such as Facebook's "Like" feature, which has been a strong driver in making the posting of photos and comments habitual. Similarly, frequent-flier programs have long used social rewards such as improved status, access to exclusive lounges, and preferential boarding order, and found them to be far stronger motivators of loyalty than discounted airfare. Teams should be creative about thinking of ideas for such nontangible rewards to offer, and they should also experiment with blending both tangible rewards and experiential and social ones.

In keeping with the principle of incentive/market fit, rewards should be tied to the value your specific product provides to customers, but there are three noteworthy strategies for offering customers rewards beyond special offers and discounts that have proven powerful in boosting habit formation and retention (among other growth levers) in recent years. While by no means exhaustive, these examples are representative of the broad and scalable strategies available.

I. BRAND AMBASSADOR PROGRAMS

These programs generally combine the power of social rewards with that of tangible ones. By designating members as high-status users, these programs confer social recognition, and most also offer a series of perks.

The Yelp Elite Squad program has been one of the most successful at using this approach to increase retention. By offering special recognition to those who are first to review a business, as well as letting other users give kudos for reviews that are useful, funny, or just plain "cool," Yelp confers powerful social benefits that incentivize users to keep coming back to write more reviews.

Yelp conferred the "Elite Status" as a reward for its most engaged users, and the company explains that doing so is ". . . our way of recognizing and rewarding yelpers who are active evangelists and role models, both on and off the site. . . . Members of the Squad are recognized with a shiny Elite badge on their account profile, as well as offered perks like invites and early entrance to Yelp events."[15] The results are impressive; a study of Yelp by Northeastern University economics professor Zhongmin Wang found that while only between 5 and 10 percent of the users of leading competitors, Citysearch and Yahoo! Local, contributed six or more reviews to those sites, more than 65 percent of Yelp users had contributed that number or more, and that a full 44 percent of reviews on the site were contributed by Yelp Elites.[16]

Web companies aren't the only ones who have taken advantage of ambassador programs to spur loyalty and customer retention. Restaurants, hotels, credit card providers, and many retailers have a long history of success with programs that smartly pair social rewards, such as the feeling of belonging, community, and status, with more tangible ones. The American Express Centurion card, better known as the Amex Black card, is the quintessential example. Coveted by many as the ultimate status symbol, the card is limited in the number of people who have it (a requirement of spending and paying off at least $350,000 per year on your Amex account ensures it), shrouded in secrecy about exactly what the benefits are, and comes with loads of perks (such as exclusive offers, travel and concierge services) that make even the wealthiest American Express customers feel special.[17]

A particularly impressive recent example of such a program is the one that the fast-growing media company theSkimm, which provides daily news, hand-curated for professional women, has used to grow its way to 3.5 million daily readers.[18] To become a "Skimm'basador," readers must refer 10 friends to the service, and are rewarded not only with public recognition on the site, but also with perks such as branded T-shirts, handbags, and cellphone cases, networking opportunities, and birthday shout-outs in the daily newsletters.[19]

2. RECOGNITION OF ACHIEVEMENTS

All customers appreciate recognition from companies, whether that recognition is big or small. One great way to show them this recognition is by recognizing some achievement or action or what's called in marketing circles the *behavioral email*. One kind is when a customer has passed a milestone, such as when Fitbit sends you a congratulatory notification upon recording your 10,000th step in a day or when Runkeeper sends emails when you've hit your first 10-miler, or clocked your longest- or fastest-ever trip. Similarly, Medium, the publication platform founded by Twitter cofounder Evan Williams, sends an email when an article you publish on the site receives 50 or 100 recommendations. These achievement notifications are fixtures in most referral programs as well, sending an email when a friend joins and encouraging you to invite additional friends.[20]

These notifications can also alert you about the actions of other users that essentially constitute an achievement for you, such as when LinkedIn sends an email that you've been endorsed by someone and when Twitter sends word that someone has liked or retweeted a post of yours. Facebook and Instagram have made particularly smart use of this dynamic, using mobile notifications to both let users know when their Facebook friends join Instagram and also to encourage users to "like" photos posted on Instagram by other users, particularly those who haven't added a new picture in a while. Both types of notifications drive retention in two ways: by bringing users back to Instagram to see what their friends are up to, and by rewarding new users by increasing the number of new followers, likes, and comments they get on Instagram.

3. CUSTOMIZATION OF THE RELATIONSHIP

With the ever-ballooning databases of customer information being built by companies and powerful new tools for analyzing that data available, a company's ability to serve customer needs and desires more precisely—even individually—has been vastly improved. Shouvick Mukherjee, the vice president of product and engineering at @WalmartLabs, notes that one of the most important shifts in growth for the company has been the transformation from a traditional "one-to-many" marketing mindset, to one of delivering fully customized, one-to-one experiences. Companies can now, for example, customize email communications and product recommendations specifically to each customer, no matter how many millions of individuals shop with them. This mass personalization is "about understanding the customer, understanding the business you are in, and making sure that you are building a perfect match," Mukherjee says.[21]

This technique, much of which was pioneered by Amazon, has been made possible by the development of such large data sets about customers and programming that they enable systems to efficiently search through them to extract a customer's information about his or her preferences. Personalization can be based not only on information customers have provided, or on their activity on the company's website or in its app, but also on data about their wider behavior on the Web, which is readily obtainable from data providers such as Demandbase. Many companies offer personalization technology, such as Salesforce Marketing Cloud, Optimizely, and HubSpot.

Cara Harshman, a former content manager at Optimizely, has shared how the company improved a number of metrics, including activation and retention, by delivering a personalized home page experience to their most important audiences. The company went from having one home page to more than 26 variations based on key accounts, time of day visiting the site, business vertical, and more. A person visiting from the *New York Times* offices, for example, will see a message specific to how Optimizely can help publishers, while someone from, say, Microsoft will see information about how Optimizely can help technology and software companies, and so on.[22]

The next wave of personalization is being powered by machine learning algorithms. Machine learning is exactly what it sounds like. Rather than humans making the rules about which customizations to make, the software uses customer responses to refine and improve the customizations. This technology is sophisticated, but it is rapidly being made more accessible. For example, at Inman, Morgan's team customizes which news stories users receive in their weekly newsletter, delivering a unique, highly relevant newsletter to each subscriber. This customization is enhanced by data from a company called Boomtrain, which uses machine learning tied to personalization to continually optimize the newsletter's relevance, without Morgan's team taking any additional action. It's just one of a number of companies offering this type of service. Open source software such as the Machine Learning Library (or MLlib for short), offered by Apache Spark, can be used by teams to build their own software to achieve the same result.

As we touched on briefly in Chapter One, Pinterest's growth team has been experimenting heavily with machine learning customization and optimization, and have built a program, which they call Copytune, that allows the team to rapidly test dozens of variants of notifications sent to users, across more than 30 languages, with the program picking winning versions and teeing up subsequent tests on its own. The graphic below shows just how intricate this testing can be. The program tested messages with every one of the variations diagrammed. The results of the program have been extraordinary, driving the growth of users who return to the site each month (monthly active users, or MAUs) by a high single-digit percentage, which, given Pinterest's massive user base of more than 100 million, translates into millions more people using Pinterest actively each month, and an untold amount of additional revenue generated from the advertising that gets served to all of those additional visitors.[23]

EXAMPLE OF COMPONENT VARIATIONS

'Hey' vs. 'Hi' vs. None   'some' vs. 'new'

'!' vs. ','   keyword vs. topic

add 'Hey Emma!'   'found' vs. 'picked'   2 variables vs. 1
                                                      If 2, reverse order?

"We found some {pin_keyword} and {pin_topic} Pins and boards for you!"

'Pins and boards' vs. 'Pins' vs. 'Boards'   '!' vs. None

Pinterest Copytune Optimization

Teams that want to experiment with personalization can start by doing so with the triggers they're sending customers. Most email marketing software allows for a variety of personalization options. These can be as simple as inserting the recipients' names in a message, but can also include delivering different content and offers based on their past behavior. Our grocery app team could create different emails to send to customers who've made only one purchase, customers who haven't purchased at all, and customers who average more than $100. By starting this way, growth teams can get some early data on how effective custom experiences may be and then decide to invest further if results warrant doing so.

MORE VALUE *COMING SOON*

If you've ever purchased a gadget or device in its "1.0" version, or been involved in the selection of enterprise software such as Salesforce or Oracle, you've experienced the power of the promise of new features as a retention hook. Communicating to customers that some new features or product offerings are just around the corner, and telling them how they'll benefit, can be a powerful inducement for them to stick with you. This works particularly well for SaaS products, videogames, and content providers like Hulu and HBO. Netflix uses this tactic effectively in spacing out the release of new seasons of their original series like *House of Cards* and *Orange Is the New Black* to make sure you keep your subscription active as you await the next show to binge-watch. Salesforce similarly holds the release of their big product updates to new yearly events—one in the summer and one in the winter—to keep customers subscribed with the promise of must-have new features. Apple, too, has employed the tactic brilliantly, by keeping customers anxiously awaiting the day when they can upgrade to the shiniest new object the company puts out.

Bing Gordon, a venture capitalist at Kleiner Perkins Caufield & Byers, shared how powerful the "Coming Soon" hack can be when he recounted a conversation that he had with HBO chief executive Chris Albrecht. Albrecht had okayed the production of *Rome*, an original production that is famous for being one of the most expensive shows ever made for television, with a per episode cost of $9 million. When Gordon asked Albrecht if the exorbitant cost was tough to swallow for a show that ultimately didn't draw a ton of viewership, the HBO CEO shared with Gordon the power of "Coming Soon" by revealing that HBO experienced almost no customer churn between the time the show was announced and the first episode aired; subscribers, it turned out, were intent on sticking around to see what the fuss around the new show was all about—even if many didn't end up ultimately watching it. Indeed, for those two intervening months the company experienced near-zero customer churn, with those captured revenues more than paying for the cost of production.[24]

Of course there's the potential to irritate customers if you seem to be baiting them by promising a fabulous new thing but making them wait too long for it. This is another reason why experimenting is so important: it can help teams calibrate the timing of these notifications. For example, the team working to boost retention for the video streaming company might learn that the company has just made a deal for the rights to an extremely popular series that hasn't been previously available. The show won't be available for three months, but they might decide to see whether notifications that it's coming spur more subscription renewals in the next few months leading up to its release. Then, a simple A/B test could be run with email notifications to viewers who watched shows like it. The control group would have a typical experience, while the experiment group would receive one or a series of email messages about the new show "coming soon." The retention of these two groups could be compared to get the quantitative impact of the test. If the "Coming Soon" message resonates and retains more of the subscribers who view that show and others like it, the growth team can move forward with making the "Coming Soon" strategy a permanent part of the customer communications.

LONG-TERM RETENTION

Once you've achieved strong retention for a good base of users, the next step is to focus on continuing to keep them happy and highly active over the long haul. Here we recommend a two-pronged approach that involves (1) optimizing the current set of product features, notifications, and subsequent rewards from repeated use; and (2) introducing a steady stream of new features over a long period of time. Getting this balance right is extremely important. Too many companies make the mistake of introducing too many new features too rapidly, called *feature bloat* by product teams. This often results in making products overcomplicated and actually obscuring their core value. In a 2005 study, researchers for the Marketing Science Institute, Debora Viana Thompson, Rebecca Hamilton, and Roland Rust, found that companies routinely hurt long-term retention by packing too many features into a product, explaining "that choosing the number of features that maximizes initial choice results in the inclusion of too many features, potentially decreasing customer lifetime value." They concluded that "firms should consider having a larger number of more specialized products, each with a limited number of features, rather than loading all possible features into one product."[25]

David Pogue, a technology columnist, brought this painful reality to light in a 2006 TED talk in which he showed the cringe-inducing screenshot below indicating what the Microsoft Word screen would look like with every toolbar option turned on.

MICROSOFT WORD TOOLBAR OVERLOAD[26]

Timing the rollout of new features can be particularly challenging with online products, in part because they're so much easier to launch than physical products. People become attached to how products look and work, and rolling out changes too quickly or abruptly can result in backlash. Look no farther than the outcry over Instagram's new algorithmic timeline or Twitter altering the visual elements involved in bookmarking tweets by changing the icon from a star to a heart, and renaming the action from "Fav" to "Like," as just two recent examples.

Growth teams can play a pivotal role in evaluating the appeal of planned new features by experimenting with offering customers prototypes or beta versions. New features should be road tested with a very small percentage of users, as these experiments create rafts of data that help companies refine new features before making them widely available. While the product teams in most organizations are responsible for designing new features, the growth team will undoubtedly come up with new feature ideas for the product team to try from the constant surveying and data analysis they conduct. Similarly, data that the team synthesizes can uncover new product optimization opportunities that may not have been discovered in market research or strategic planning. In other words, all members of the growth team should constantly be looking for opportunities both to refine features for maximum retention and to introduce new ones.

To see how this works, let's return to the grocery app team and see how they could collaborate with the grocery chain's product team to introduce an important new feature. The product group has been working on a prototype of a major new feature for the app: a meal planner. The feature uses past purchase history from users and the popularity of items offered in the app to recommend whole meals to buy, making the purchase of the necessary ingredients a breeze. All the shopper has to do is input the number of people to be served and with one click, the items are added, in the appropriate quantities, to the shopper's cart. The growth team works with the product team and marketing group to agree on a testing strategy for offering the planner to a select number of customers as well as for experiments to improve its use among those that have access to the new feature. For example, the growth team could use the data about how effective free delivery is in driving retention to suggest that the meal planner should be programmed to recommend recipes with items that, when ordered, will result in a purchase over the free-delivery threshold. They might also experiment with triggers to notify users when new meal recommendations become available in the app. The team should also experiment with when and how to roll out the planner to customers, as well as how to communicate about any changes to the feature to those customers using the beta version.

ONGOING ONBOARDING

As new features are added, and also as more discoveries are made about how the most avid and satisfied of your customers are using your product, it's important to continue to educate your customers about the value they can be deriving from your product. The ideal scenario is one in which you are leading them on a continuous journey of discovery. So another important element of long-term retention is figuring out how to move your users along a learning curve. This developmental process—called *ongoing onboarding*—is similar to how you would learn any subject, such as an instrument or language or technical skill: by starting with small, simple objectives and then building on your mastery incrementally over time. The same choreographed progression should be built into any new features customers need to master to get the most value out of their product. User experience designer Harry Brignull calls this process *ramp up*.

As users become more experienced at using your product, features they haven't used yet—and new ones being introduced—should be brought to their attention, gradually and in a way that allows them to tackle learning a new feature only after having achieved mastery of the previous one. Brignull highlights the way in which Google Analytics uses a series of progressive notifications to drive the user deeper into the product experience as one of the better examples of this ramp up. "[T]hey monitor user behavior, they have a decision-making engine that works out what notification to show, and they track which actions are completed, to make way for new ones," says Brignull.

All ongoing onboarding messaging can be tested by growth teams, such as by sending email to test groups with different versions of explanations and imagery explaining the features being promoted. If email messages prove effective in driving more use of the features, the team might then experiment with including highlights about the features in the product itself, such as by adding a promotional video about a feature to the landing pages of several other features.

RESURRECTING "ZOMBIE" CUSTOMERS

Winning back users who've abandoned a product is called *resurrection* in growth circles. The growth hacking process can again help you discover experiments to run to win back "zombie customers" who have disappeared off your radar. The first thing to do, of course, is investigate why people disappear in the first place. Getting to the bottom of this can be done quite simply by interviewing people who canceled or no longer use your product about why they left. For example, when Evernote was struggling with their retention, their growth team found that one of the big reasons people stopped using the service was that when they purchased a new computer or phone, they didn't immediately install the app again on their new device.

Dan Wolchonok, product manager at HubSpot, says the first step in considering experiments to try based on zombie customer feedback is to understand whether the reasons people leave are ones that you can actually control or address.[27] For example, if our grocery app team learns, as Evernote did, that one of the biggest reasons people stop using the app is because they don't install the app after they get a new phone, the team can design new email and retargeting ads encouraging people to reinstall the app if the team notices a period of prolonged inactivity. However, if people are leaving because the grocery chain doesn't carry an important brand that they want to buy, the growth team may not be able to prevent their churn. In that event, the best the team can do is alert the purchasing department of the high demand for that brand (which they certainly should, as the absence of the brand may be stymieing not only the retention rates for the app, but the growth of the chain overall).

Most of the work of resurrecting past known customers is done through emails and advertisements. When teams notice that a customer's purchasing or a user's activity has dropped to zero, after some designated time—which the team should experiment to determine—these people should be added to a *resurrection flow*, which means that they should be sent a series of email communications or targeted ads designed to win them back, often by reminding them of the aha moment, or core value that once drew them to the product. By creating specific custom email and push notification campaigns just for customers who have become detached or inactive, companies can sometimes bring them back in considerable numbers; and because these customers already are familiar with and have experienced the aha moment of the product, this can often be done with less cost and effort than it would take to recruit brand-new customers.

At Inman, for example, Morgan identified users who had read articles on the site in the past, but hadn't visited in three weeks. Because many subscribers pay monthly, he hypothesized that those who don't visit the site at least once monthly would be more likely to cancel their accounts. So the team ran a test wherein they emailed those users with the most important news of the previous weeks accompanied by a call to action to come back to the site. Of those who received the email notification, 29.4 percent more returned to the site than those in the control group who didn't receive a follow-up email.

Of course, as with any targeted email notification or advertising strategy, such efforts can be overdone. First and foremost you'll want to make sure to experiment with frequency, duration, and wording of your messaging to ensure that you aren't annoying or further alienating your lost customers with pleading "come back" messages; doing so will only tarnish their view of you and dash all hopes of their returning to you in the future. At some point, companies should accept that a user simply isn't coming back and stop sending notifications. Sometimes, they will end up coming back on their own for reasons entirely out of your control, maybe because a friend talked about how much she liked the product (which was what Twitter discovered was behind a large number of "comatose" users returning to their service), or because she took a new job for which the product would be useful, or because the competitor she fled to went out of business, or failed to deliver continuous improvements, or a celebrity, or maybe their boss, started using the product, and so forth.

Attempts to resurrect such "cold" customers may seem low priority.

There's no question that if your retention is suffering, your first area of focus should be on early retention of new users. But remember that every customer who is ultimately retained represents ongoing opportunities to earn more revenue for your company, so efforts at resurrection are valuable. Now, to look closely at methods for taking the best advantage of the opportunities to earn more revenue from increasing retention, let's move on to explore how growth hacking can help companies earn more from each customer.

CHAPTER EIGHT

HACKING MONETIZATION

T he ultimate goal of acquiring, activating, and retaining customers is, of course, to earn revenue from them. Ideally, you want to earn more revenue from each customer over time, which is referred to as increasing the *lifetime value (LTV)* of customers. So in this chapter, we'll focus specifically on this mission of earning more money from the base of customers you have. Growth hacking offers many ways to devise experiments for optimizing earnings from your customer base. We've noted that many growth teams fail to capitalize on these tactics, focusing mostly on acquisition and customer activation. But in doing so, they're leaving considerable growth potential on the table. We hope this chapter changes that.

The basic means of increasing revenue per customer vary according to a company's business model. If you're a retail company, greater monetization of your customer base is fundamentally achieved by persuading customers to purchase more of whatever it is you sell. If you're a software as a service (SaaS) company, it is achieved by getting more subscribers to renew their subscriptions, and to do so for more years, as well as by persuading more of them to upgrade to higher-fee levels of service (or in the special case of freemium services, by getting more users to upgrade to paid plans). If your revenue comes from selling advertising space, then driving revenue higher comes essentially from creating more available space to sell and convincing more advertisers to purchase and to pay more for the space they purchase. Each of these models require different tactics, but in all cases growth teams should start with the same fundamental diagnostic process to generate ideas for experiments to try for boosting earnings.

MAP YOUR MONETIZATION FUNNEL

As with all growth hacking efforts, the first step is to perform data analysis that will help you home in on the highest-potential experiments. When it comes to monetization, analysis starts by returning to the basic mapping of the entire customer journey, which, recall from Chapter Six the team should create when it first starts the growth hacking process. The goal at this stage is to highlight all of the opportunities in the journey—from acquisition to retention—for earning revenue from customers. You should also identify all junctures along the way that are presenting barriers to generating revenue, such as friction in the payment process.

For retail companies this mapping is often referred to as the purchase funnel, and the particularly important junctures for increasing revenue are screens displaying items for sale, the shopping cart, and the payment page. For SaaS companies, particularly important junctures are the page or pages explaining the features and prices of different services or plan levels and pages promoting add-ons and upgrades. And for companies that generate their revenue from advertising sales, the most important junctures are all pages where the company has an opportunity to display ads, whether or not the company is as of yet doing so.

The next step after doing this basic mapping is to analyze where in the customer journey the company is making the most money, and where there seem to be *pinch points*, meaning steps where potential earnings are lost, which vary by model. By identifying high-value pages and features within a product, website, or app, growth teams can experiment with ways to generate even more revenue from them, while identifying those pinch points with poor conversion rates and high friction will generate ideas for patching up revenue leaks.

Each of these different business models has typical pinch points within the customer journey. For e-commerce companies, the steps between selecting an item to completing the purchase are a danger zone, with many purchases often abandoned along the way; as a study conducted in early 2016 by Monetate (a service that provides customization capabilities for e-commerce companies) found, while approximately 9.6 percent of website visitors add an item to a shopping cart, only slightly less than 3 percent of them go ahead and make a purchase.[1] For SaaS businesses, the pages displaying the options for plans and their prices are often underoptimized, hurting rates of purchase. For advertising-revenue-driven companies, ads that are too intrusive and turn users off, or that are not visible or compelling in their message or design, are common monetization sinkholes.

These common pinch points are good starting points for assessment, but doing a more detailed analysis of your particular monetization funnel is vital and will almost surely surface additional weak spots specific to your product for the growth team to experiment with. For example, an online retailer might find that some of its product pages are inspiring fewer purchases than industry research about sales for those categories indicates they should be generating. The growth team would likely then decide to focus on experimenting with hacks to boost sales in those categories. Or for a content provider or media company driven by ad revenue, the analysis might reveal that video ads in a particular ad space are not performing nearly as well as the text ads in that space. The growth team might then choose to focus on improving the performance of video ads, by experimenting with their size and placement or the nature of the video itself, such as its length, its call to action, or whether it includes captions or not, among other potential changes.

For a SaaS company the analysis might show a pinch point in the step from free trial sign-up to paid subscription. Digging into causes of the drop-off, analysis may uncover that users who don't make use of a particular feature during their free trial period are half as likely to purchase the lucrative enterprise plan than those who do. The team might decide to focus on experiments to increase the rate at which trial customers use that feature to lead to more purchases when the trial period ends.

As far as the tools for doing this mapping, many of the common analytics packages that we've mentioned so far offer the ability to display simple purchase funnels for e-commerce companies. And advertising services such as DoubleClick provide software for ad response analysis to Web-based companies selling ad space. But the complete mapping of all of the steps in your company's monetization funnel will often require additional work by a data analyst.

HOW MUCH ARE YOU MAKING FROM COHORTS?

In analyzing your customer data to assess opportunities you also want to divide customers into a number of cohorts, as you did for hacking retention. This time, however, the emphasis is on how much *revenue* groups account for. Thus the first set of cohorts to break out are the higher-profit versus lower-profit customers. For a subscription service, these will generally break down by the level of subscription plan. For an e-commerce company, you can break customers into groups according to how much they spend per year (or month, or week, depending on your model) on purchases. For an ad-revenue-based company, the breakdown will be a little more complex. Because the level of users' engagement is one of the primary factors in determining the number of ads the company can show and the rate they can charge advertisers for space, ad-based companies should track not only the *average revenue per user (ARPU)*, which is the most basic monetization metric for this business model, but also look to segment specific groups of users according to their degree of engagement, and specifically their engagement with ads, such as the amount of time spent on the site or in the app, the number of pages or screens viewed per session, and other engagement metrics that will be specific to the company (such as number of videos a user watches).[2]

In addition to these revenue-related breakdowns, growth teams should again break customers down into many other groups, as was also recommended for hacking retention. These should include, but not be limited to, groups by location, age and gender, types of items purchased or features used, the source through which the customer was acquired (such as from a Google ad or from a referral program), the type of device they used to access the site or app (desktop vs. mobile, Microsoft Windows vs. Apple), the Web browser used, the number of visits to the site or app in a given time period, and the date of their first purchase or action taken. But again, instead of looking for patterns in retention rates, at this stage you want to look for correlations to revenue being made from each of these groups, which will provide ideas for experiments.

To give an example, HotelTonight, a mobile app that allows customers to book last-minute hotel rooms at a significant discount, made an important and unexpected discovery when they analyzed the purchase behavior of their customers based on how they connected to the app (that is, either over Wi-Fi or via 3G or 4G cellular connections). Their hypothesis for the rather confusing finding that customers who connected via 3G or 4G booked at twice the rate of those using the app over Wi-Fi (after all, shouldn't it be easier to book on Wi-Fi?) was that comparison shopping on *other* travel sites was easier over Wi-Fi than over a spotty data connection; that with spotty data the sluggish competitive websites were too slow and unreliable, leading those customers to more readily book with HotelTonight rather than doing the comparison shopping that could have easily been done over fast Wi-Fi. Using this insight, HotelTonight focused its advertising to target only users who weren't using Wi-Fi to connect to the Web, and drove higher purchase rates from new customers who saw their ads as a result.[3]

For e-commerce companies, particularly important cohort groupings to look at beyond how much they spend on purchases include number of items purchased, the average amount of a customer's order, the types of items they purchase, the date of their first purchase, the number of times they make a purchase within a selected time frame (say, per month or per year), and also the time of month or year they typically purchase. So, for example, consider a team that discovers that 55 percent of customers who make one purchase within 90 days go on to spend $500 or more over the next 12 months, whereas 95 percent of customers who make two purchases within 90 days reach or exceed $500 spent over the same period. They might design a series of experiments to encourage all users who make one purchase to buy again within 90 days, such as by offering a steep discount or special perk (such as free shipping), just to those users, via an email sent after 30 days, and then again via a follow-up email sent after 60 days.

For advertising-revenue-model businesses, a more refined break-down of the user base allows companies to experiment with ways of fur-ther monetizing the ad space that already generates high engagement, as well as increasing ad performance—and thus revenue—in spaces where engagement is soft. For example, the growth team for a media company could find that readers who spend at least two minutes on a site are three times as likely to click on an ad as those who spend less time. Armed with that knowledge, they could devise a series of experiments to increase the amount of time the lower-use readers spend on the site, such as by improving the selection of articles they are shown after finishing the one they're reading. Alternatively, if they were to find that many readers are spending large amounts of time on pages that don't have particularly ef-fective advertisements on them, such as on the video gallery page or on long-form articles, they could devise experiments with new types of ads on these pages and with alternative placements, such as between videos or embedded in articles to appear as readers progress through them.

For SaaS companies, whose customers tend to be businesses, particu-larly important cohorts to investigate are the different types of business, as some businesses will have deeper pockets than others, making them more willing to purchase the higher-ticket plans and add-on features. For example, when the growth team at SurveyMonkey, which provides a survey service that can be used by many different kinds of companies for many different purposes—everything from marketing teams doing mar-ket research, to customer service teams measuring customer satisfaction, to students running surveys for research papers, among many others—did this analysis, Elena Verna, who leads the company's growth efforts, and her team discovered (perhaps not surprisingly) that users from edu-cational institutions and nonprofits, as well as college students, were not purchasing the premium services at nearly the rate of other groups of users. So they experimented with offering specially discounted plans to these groups in order to earn more revenue from them by converting them from free to paid customers at a higher rate.

The features of software customers will be the most inclined to pay for will also likely differ by cohorts. For example, a large corporation may have its own internal customer relationship management software system, and therefore be willing to pay a premium for software that explicitly integrates into that existing system, whereas a start-up without established systems may value getting more capabilities out of the box, but not care much about system integrations.

If a product or service is offered internationally, companies should also be sure to look at monetization by country, since different countries have different norms about the types of payment options, and also the fees charged, for services. For example, users in Germany may be more likely to purchase using a specific set of payment options, which are different from the preferred payment method in Russia, resulting in markedly different monetization rates for each country. By the same token, certain business models may be better understood in one country compared to another. Subscription businesses are well understood in the United States, for example, but may be less well received in other countries. Growth teams can experiment with offering different sets of options to different countries to increase monetization within each.[4]

LEARNING WHO YOUR CUSTOMERS ARE

As we've seen already, there are numerous ways to segment your customer base to find new insights. And one of the first steps for growth teams trying to better monetize that base is to identify the general groupings of customers who share similar characteristics. These may be that they share the same location, same experience, spend roughly the same amount of money, have the same needs from your product, or a combination of factors (many of which we've identified in our potential cohort breakouts). The goal of creating these groupings is to better generate ideas for ways to satisfy customers' specific wants and needs. Many marketers will be familiar with the exercise of creating *personas*, which are fictional dossiers of a representative customer from each group, for this very purpose. For example, at Inman, we have identified four primary types of customers: new real estate agents with less than three years' experience; agents with five to ten years of experience; real estate brokers;

and franchise and technology executives. These general groupings represent the large common clusters in our customer base, and our growth team has focused on designing experiments such as customized email communications, landing pages, and promotional offerings to drive increased revenue from each group.

ASK CUSTOMERS WHAT BENEFITS THEY WANT

Growth teams should also again make use of surveys and find out directly from customers what improvements in the product, such as possible new features, new plan levels, or perhaps improved selection of items for sale, each of your key customer segments would most like to see. It should go without saying that at the very core of the mission of increasing revenue is providing customers with the services and products they find most appealing and that best serve their needs. And, of course, those desires may differ by different groups of customers.

It should also go without saying that one of the best ways of driving up the volume of your customers' purchases is to offer them additional items to purchase or features to pay for. (Or, for ad-based models, additional experiences and content to consume more time and engage them further.) Earlier we covered the danger of feature creep, and now it's important to emphasize the flip side, which is that it's generally important for companies to steadily, and very judiciously, introduce new items to buy or features to use in order to keep growing revenue. Just think of how relentlessly Amazon has increased the number of categories of items it sells and the choices within those categories, and how vigorously Facebook has continued to introduce new features. The key to making good additions is to focus intensely on offering customers the *benefits* they find most valuable and are willing to pay for, not just bolting on more choices that the company conjectures customers will want.

Growth teams should systematically present ideas for new product or feature offerings to customers through surveys, and then experiment with those products or features before going wide with them. A great example is the survey question that follows that the BitTorrent team sent out to users in order to decide which of a number of possible new features to build. Note that rather than asking users open-ended questions,

BitTorrent presents users with a range of benefits and asks which would be most valuable. You can incentivize responses while at the same time validate that users actually want the features they say they do by offering to give a few survey respondents a free copy of the product with the new features included, as you can see BitTorrent did.

SURVEYING USERS ABOUT NEW FEATURES

* FIVE SURVEY TAKERS WILL RECEIVE THE PRO VERSION OF μTORRENT FOR ANDROID, WHICH WILL INCLUDE ALL FUTURE PRO FEATURES.

FOCUSING ON FEATURES, WHICH ONES WOULD YOU MOST WANT THE PRO APP TO INCLUDE?

	(LEAST WANTED) 1	2	3	4	5	6	(MOST WANTED) 7
WATCH/PREVIEW MEDIA WITHOUT DOWNLOADING THE ENTIRE FILE	○	○	○	○	○	○	○
SCHEDULE TORRENTS TO RUN WHEN I WANT THEM TO	○	○	○	○	○	○	○
PAUSE μTORRENT WHEN MY BATTERY GETS LOW	○	○	○	○	○	○	○
ANTIVIRUS SCANNING	○	○	○	○	○	○	○
PREMIUM CUSTOMER SUPPORT	○	○	○	○	○	○	○
TURN μTORRENT OFF WHEN MY TORRENT HAS FINISHED DOWNLOADING	○	○	○	○	○	○	○

By asking respondents to rank each option, you may well end up with a couple or a few good choices for next offerings, which the growth team can suggest be added to the product development roadmap schedule. The BitTorrent team went ahead with developing the battery saver feature largely on the basis that it got the strongest responses in this survey, and as a result drove a 47 percent increase in daily revenue. The auto-shutdown feature, which also got a strong response, was subsequently tested as well and, after finding favorable response, was introduced to all app users and increased daily revenue 20 percent.[5]

USING DATA AND ALGORITHMS TO CUSTOMIZE
OFFERINGS TO CUSTOMERS' WANTS AND NEEDS

In Chapter Seven, we discussed personalization as a tactic for building a stronger relationship with customers and thereby helping you retain them. Personalization is also a good monetization tactic, and particularly effective are customized recommendations, usually delivered on the site or in the app while a customer is visiting, and also through email and mobile push messages. Amazon is, once again, a leading practitioner, having developed one of the most powerful "recommendation engines," the term for the algorithmic programs that customize which items are recommended to you while browsing the site. The selections are based on a combination of a customer's search history and buying habits, and data about the habits of other shoppers like that customer. All Amazon shoppers in effect see their own version of Amazon with a unique experience tailored to their preferences.

Some recommendation engines, such as Amazon's, as well as those deployed by Google and Netflix, are incredibly complex, but many are based on relatively simple math. As Colin Zima, the chief analytics officer at Looker, a business intelligence software, explains, it can be relatively easy to generate recommendations based on a simple formula called a *Jaccard index*, or *Jaccard similarity coefficient*, which determines how similar two products are to each other. This helps to recommend additional items that a customer might want to buy because the software has calculated that the items, when purchased, are often purchased together.

JACCARD INDEX

$$\mathcal{J}(A, B) = \frac{|A \cap B|}{|A \cup B|} = \frac{|A \cap B|}{|A| + |B| - |A \cap B|}$$

While the formula looks a bit intimidating, in reality it is straightforward. What the equation says is that the similarity between two items, A and B, is equal to the size of the *intersection* of A and B divided by the *union* of A and B. Let's use our grocery app to walk through a quick example of how it works. Let's say they want to test the hypothesis that recommending products that are typically purchased together in the app will increase the average order size of each shopping trip. In order to make these recommendations effective, they need to calculate the likelihood that people who purchase one product, such as peanut butter, will also purchase the recommended one, such as jelly, is greater than that likelihood for other product combinations. The team will want to recommend items that are most often purchased together to increase the likelihood that shoppers accept a recommendation and add that additional product to their shopping cart.

The intersection size in the Jaccard index is how many people buy both peanut butter and jelly together, while the union is how many people bought either peanut butter and jelly independently. For example, if you find that 30 people have purchased both peanut butter and jelly together, while 100 people have purchased either peanut butter or jelly independently, you'll get a Jaccard similarity score of 0.3, which is actually quite high as these scores go. In contrast, the score for peanut butter and, for example, laundry detergent will almost surely be much lower.

This calculation can be done for a host of combinations of every item in the store, creating powerful recommendations that lead to more purchases. And with the best recommendation engines, these product suggestions will only get better and more personalized over time because the more customers shop, the more data is available not just about what an individual customer has purchased, but also about common patterns among a large pool of shoppers. The grocery app recommendation engine might, for example, recommend seltzer water and limes when a shopper puts Red Bull in her shopping cart—even if that shopper has no history of buying any of those products—based on data that shows most people buying Red Bull are purchasing mixers for vodka.[6]

DON'T BE INTRUSIVE

An important word of caution about customizing is that it can backfire if you're not sensitive about how you're doing it. If you seem to be prying too deeply into people's lives, customization becomes, for lack of a better word, creepy. A notorious case is that of the big-box retailer Target inadvertently outing a teenage woman for a pregnancy that she was trying to hide from her parents. The company targeted her with coupons for baby clothing and cribs, and as reporter Charles Duhigg recounted in the *New York Times Magazine*, the girl's father stormed into the store and confronted a manager, fuming: "She's still in high school, and you're sending her coupons for baby clothes and cribs? Are you trying to encourage her to get pregnant?" When the manager called to apologize a few days later, the father reacted very differently. "I had a talk with my daughter," the man said. "It turns out there's been some activities in my house I haven't been completely aware of. She's due in August. I owe you an apology." Regardless of the father's forgiveness, the much-reported story ignited a firestorm among Target customers and consumer rights advocates, who saw the data mining and personalization as an unforgivable intrusion into private life.[7]

You can just as quickly turn people off if you miss the mark about what they would like to see from you. When customers receive suggestions that aren't appealing, whether from a clothing retailer recommending clothing in a style that's not their taste, or from Netflix recommending a genre of movie they hate, they are apt to not only be unimpressed, they may even be offended. Think of when you receive a birthday gift from a close friend—or worse, from a spouse—that is not at all your taste. Getting personalization wrong can dramatically hurt revenue rather than improve it.

This is another reason that the experimentation growth teams are set up to do is so vital. A good way to test how effective any planned customization will be is to start by sending personalized email and text notifications to just a small segment of customers to gauge their response and effectiveness. By starting this way, growth teams can get some early data on how effective custom experiences may be and then decide to invest further if results warrant doing so. Most email marketing software allows for a variety of personalization options, ranging from simply inserting the recipients' names in a message to the ability to deliver different messages and offers based on their past behavior.

Our grocery app team, for example, could send a free delivery coupon to customers who've made only one purchase, seeking to spur an additional purchase, and then if that test was successful, the team could experiment with building in notifications in the app itself, promoting free delivery to all users who have made at least one purchase.

OPTIMIZING YOUR PRICING

One of the trickiest issues in growing revenue has always been determining how to price products and services—price them too low and you're leaving revenue on the table, but price them too high and you're losing revenue by turning away customers. Companies can get it wrong in a multitude of ways, from not doing enough analysis before setting initial pricing, to running experiments on pricing too infrequently, to pricing above what the market will pay or being too quick to lower prices when they shouldn't. Growth teams can be of great assistance with getting pricing right by working with product and finance teams to conduct surveys and customer research to find the optimal pricing range to start experimenting within.

Companies selling physical goods have a relatively straightforward path when it comes to setting prices. They need to account for the production or purchase of the items they're selling, plus the associated costs of marketing and delivering those products to the customer, all while making a profit. But even within this equation, growth teams can experiment based on the information they've gained about the purchase behavior and lifetime value of customers. They can also take inspiration from the many principles that have been found to trigger purchases in retail over decades of study. For example, in his book *Priceless: The Myth of Fair Value (and How to Take Advantage of It)* William Poundstone cites the power of using "charm prices," those that purposefully end with a 9 or 99 or 98 or 95 instead of the full round dollar amount. Hard as it may be to believe, those pricing strategies actually work; Poundstone writes,

"In 8 studies published from 1987 to 2004, charm prices were reported to boost sales by an average of 24 percent relative to nearby prices."[8]

Additional psychologically rooted tactics such as anchoring the value of an item compared with others for sale, and including the dollar sign on prices shown, can all impact behavior. As with anything, these strategies won't work for every product and every purchaser, but with so many options, a growth team has plenty of opportunities for the continual testing and optimization of pricing to improve revenue growth.

While pricing a physical item is relatively straightforward, what about a piece of software that is delivered over the Web and doesn't have raw materials costs? Patrick Campbell, CEO of Price Intelligently, offers a wealth of advice about best practices for finding the pricing sweet spot for SaaS products, and suggests starting with, as we've recommended with many other growth initiatives, sending out a survey that asks the recipients not only what features are most important to them—but also how much they are willing to pay, by asking the following four questions in the following order:

- At what price point does [your product] become too expensive that you'd never consider purchasing it?
- At what price point does [your product] start to become expensive, but you'd still consider purchasing it?
- At what price point does [your product] start to become a really good deal?
- At what price point does [your product] start to become too cheap that you'd question the quality of it?[9]

The responses will give you a range of prices that people think are too high, too low, and just right, which the growth team should map onto a graph like this:

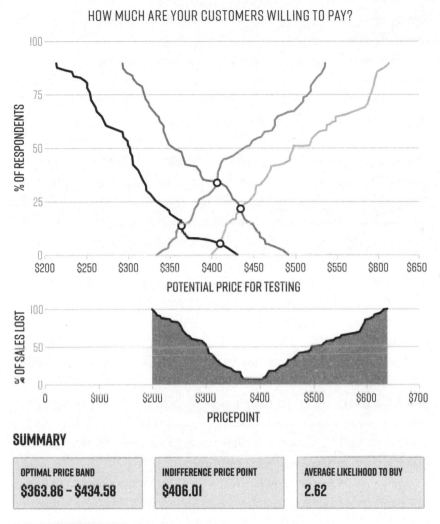

HOW MUCH ARE YOUR CUSTOMERS WILLING TO PAY?

SUMMARY

OPTIMAL PRICE BAND	INDIFFERENCE PRICE POINT	AVERAGE LIKELIHOOD TO BUY
$363.86 – $434.58	$406.01	2.62

SOURCE: © PRICE INTELLIGENCY

The roughly diamond-shaped terrain in the middle of the graph is the ideal testing range for your pricing experiments. Of course the customer responses shouldn't be the only data taken into consideration; a complex set of factors must be considered in pricing, such as the costs of production and distribution, marketing, and general overhead, as well as market research about competing products. And the range of prices that growth teams should run experiments with must be determined in collaboration with, and be approved by, the finance team, and by executive leadership.

Some would also argue that asking customers directly for a price only gives you "lowball" insights, because the customers will always be looking out for their own interest. Yet, even for those who feel pricing can't be directly gleaned from customers, most agree that using customer feedback in the form of surveys and interviews should at the very least be used to guide you in deciding what you're charging for the product—as well as who your target customer is who will be willing to pay that price. And, in fact, that's why the experimental approach to pricing is so critical. Too many companies set a price and then treat it as if it's set in stone, when in reality the team should be continually experimenting with it just as they do with other elements of the business. Whether you choose to use the exact wording of the pricing questions listed above, modify them to fit your specific needs, or come up with entirely new ones of your own, the key is to leverage customer feedback to inform your ongoing experimentation.

You'll then want to combine this pricing research with the feature research we covered earlier to create a matrix of the features that people find most valuable and the price points for which they're willing to pay. This gives you what Campbell calls *persona/pricing fit*, which helps you confidently build product plans and pricing that meet the needs and expectations of the buyers in your audience.

Let's return to the hypothetical video streaming company we met in Chapter Seven to see how this works in practice. Through surveying and cohort analysis, they may have identified two very different types of customers using the service: a group that only wants the basic ability to watch shows and movies when they want, without ads, and another group, which wants a much more robust entertainment experience. As discussed earlier, the growth team comes up with prototypical customers that represent each group: Basic Bonnie represents the customer type that is no-frills and wants simple video streaming, while All-Access Andrew represents a customer who wants (and is willing to pay for) all the bells and whistles the service offers.

BASIC BONNIE	ALL-ACCESS ANDREW
VALUED FEATURES:	*VALUED FEATURES:*
· FAVORITE TV DRAMAS	· WATCH FROM ANY DEVICE
· NO ADVERTISEMENTS	· KIDS LIBRARY
	· MULTIUSER LOGIN
LEAST VALUED FEATURES:	
· WATCH FROM ANY DEVICE	*LEAST VALUED FEATURES:*
· MULTIUSER LOGINS	·NO ADVERTISEMENTS
WILLING TO PAY: $9.99 PER MONTH	*WILLING TO PAY: $19.99 PER MONTH*
COST TO ACQUIRE (CAC): $27	*COST TO ACQUIRE (CAC): $52*
LIFETIME VALUE (LTV): $109.89	*LIFETIME VALUE (LTV): $479.76*

Understanding these differences in preferences will give the growth team areas of experimentation to explore. For example, since some customers are willing to pay a good deal more than the basic $9.99 monthly subscription, the team might experiment with offering some of these customers an even higher-priced plan, which might give them access to watch on more devices, or allow more family members access to the service at once.

No matter what product you are trying to monetize, as you create options for customers, you want to be sure that your pricing is in proportion to the value they are getting from the use of your product. And in the case of certain products, most notably software, often you should charge according to usage. For example, HubSpot's marketing software charges for the number of contacts stored in its databases, because that is a good metric of the use that customers are making of the service and the value they are deriving from it. If instead Hubspot charged per user account a company signs up for, a likely outcome would be that companies would sign up for just a couple of accounts and have many employees share them, which would mean that the revenue HubSpot made was out of proportion with the use of the product. Unbounce charges for the number of visitors that come to the landing pages created through the software, and SurveyMonkey charges for the number of responses collected through their survey software; both are metrics directly tied to the value users are getting from the services. These metrics on which charges to customers are based are called *value metrics*.

To determine your value metric, Campbell recommends asking yourself three questions:

1. Does the value metric align with where your customer perceives value?
2. Does the metric scale as the customer uses the product more?
3. Is it easy to understand?[10]

SurveyMonkey's value metric clearly meets these criteria; it's easy to understand why they charge based on the number of answers that surveys produce, because the more answers that result from a survey, the higher the value of that survey is, and, obviously, this value scales up the more surveys a user creates and sends.

But it's not enough to just set the right prices; equally important is how you present and communicate those prices to customers on your pricing page and elsewhere. If your model involves multiple pricing options, it's important that the features of the various plans can be easily compared with one another so that customers can evaluate readily whether or not the extra charge for any given plan above the basic level is worthwhile to them. They should be able to see all of the basic features in the list of features for each plan, and then the added benefits of each plan should be clearly listed. You can see this in action on this hypothetical pricing page that follows.

Growth teams working on ad-revenue-based products should experiment with the pricing of the advertising units. Experiments should be run with different ad unit types—such as with standard banner ads, those that include animation or interactive elements (i.e., rich ads) versus video ads—and also with their placement to compare user engagement. With that data about engagement in hand, teams can experiment with the payment models for various ad space offerings, such as plans based on a price per user who clicks on an ad, pay per view, or perhaps the affiliate

TYPICAL SaaS PRICING PAGE

BASIC FREE	SILVER $5/MONTH BILLED MONTH-TO-MONTH SAVE WITH AN ANNUAL PLAN	✓ BEST VALUE GOLD $10/MONTH BILLED $120 ANNUALLY
SIGN UP ▶	SIGN UP ▶	SIGN UP ▶
–	–	FREE PICK OF THE MONTH
–	NEWSLETTER SUBSCRIPTION	NEWSLETTER SUBSCRIPTION
GLOBAL SEARCHING	GLOBAL SEARCHING	GLOBAL SEARCHING
5 GB OF STORAGE	20 GB OF STORAGE	UNLIMITED STORAGE

model, according to which the ad space provider is paid a referral fee for users who click through an advertisement and then take an action or make a purchase on the advertiser's site.

But remember, once pricing is set, it should not be checked off the list and never revisited. Like all other growth levers we've covered so far, pricing should be continually experimented with. We recommend that growth teams for SaaS products run tests of pricing changes at least once a fiscal quarter, whereas e-commerce companies are advised to experiment much more fluidly and continuously with pricing, as Amazon does. Called *dynamic pricing*, this strategy draws on data about many different factors, such as inventory, seasonality, time of day, a shopper's past purchase history, the type of computer they're using, and more, to continuously change and test different prices in order to arrive at the one that results in the most purchases at the highest profit. But beware: as with personalization, dynamic pricing can backfire if done wrong, as the travel website Orbitz learned when news broke that users who shopped for travel deals on the site using a Mac computer were routinely shown higher-priced hotels and travel packages than those who accessed the site on a PC. Indeed, Orbitz research had shown that Mac users were willing and able to spend up to 30 percent more on hotel rooms, and the company used the data to extract more revenue from them.[11] Needless to say that upon learning this, Mac customers were not pleased.

Ad-based growth teams should be optimizing pricing in a similarly fluid way. The largest advertising platforms, such as Google and Facebook, use an auction model to set the value of their ad inventory, which essentially means that when advertisers want to place an ad they set a bid price for what they're willing to pay, then the site gives the ad space to the highest bidder (this is a dramatic oversimplification; the auction processes are dauntingly complex). When that bidder's budget is exhausted, often by hitting a daily cap or other restriction, the next highest bidder is given the inventory, and so on, until all available inventory is used. These companies also use elements such as ad quality and customer response to factor into which advertisers get what space and which ads are shown more prominently, which is a strong incentive for advertisers to make higher-quality ads. That is, of course, in the interests of both the advertiser and the advertising platform. Smaller publishers who don't have this kind of bidding system should continuously experiment with pricing of their inventory based on supply and demand to drive the best revenue growth.

PRICING RELATIVITY

As teams collaborate with management to craft pricing experiments, a number of findings about pricing that have been established by long practice and research should be considered. One of these is *pricing relativity*, which is the principle that people's perceptions of prices are influenced by the prices of other options they are offered. In his seminal book *Predictably Irrational*, Dan Ariely describes an experiment that revealed just how much consumers' decisions about the price they would like to pay are affected by the set of options they have to choose from. The idea for the experiment was born when Ariely noticed that *The Economist* magazine was using a rather perplexing pricing plan for subscriptions: the online-only edition for $59 per year, the print edition of the magazine for $125 per year, or the print-and-Web combo also for $125.

Intrigued by the two differing subscription options offered at the same price, Ariely gave the subscription page pictured above to a group of 100 students at MIT and asked them to choose an option. Understandably, they all either chose the Web-only edition or the print-and-Web

SUBSCRIPTIONS

**Welcome to
The Economist Subscription Centre**

Pick the type of subscription you want to buy
or renew.

❑ **Economist.com subscription** – US $59.00
One-year subscription to Economist.com.
   Includes online access to all articles from
   The Economist since 1997

❑ **Print subscription** – US $125.00
One-year subscription to the print edition
of *The Economist*.

❑ **Print & web subscription** – US $125.00
One-year subscription to the print edition
of *The Economist* and online access to all
   articles from *The Economist* since 1997.

The Economist *subscription from* Predictably Irrational

edition, with 84 percent choosing the latter package. He then removed the middle, print-only option (which nobody chose) and then asked a fresh batch of 100 students to make a choice between just two options. Suddenly the results were astonishingly different. Now, 68 percent of the students (as compared with the 16 percent) chose the first, lower-priced Web-only option. Why? Because simply seeing that middle option gave potential customers a much easier way to compare the value of each offer, and many saw that they were essentially getting the Web subscription for free—what a deal!—leading them to choose the higher-priced option. The middle package is sometimes called a *decoy package* and can be a powerful way to drive customers to higher-priced products.[12]

Digital marketer Steve Young used this decoy product to profound effect at SmartShoot, a marketplace that connects professional videographers and photographers with people who need their services. Originally, when the company offered two options, a monthly option and an annual option, 40 percent of visitors bought the annual plan and the remainder purchased a monthly package. Young and team hypothesized that by offering a slightly inferior (and slightly cheaper) offer to their $299 plan they could leverage the pricing relativity phenomenon and drive more annual purchases. So they added a decoy product that cost just $10 less than the $299 plan and severely limited the features available. As a result, their conversion rate soared by 233 percent with 86 percent of buyers choosing the $299 annual product.[13]

The lesson is unmistakable: teams should experiment with a product option that is priced to help customers better understand the relative value of the items and plans you hope to sell.

LESS IS NOT ALWAYS MORE

When trying to increase purchase volume, the impulse to lower the price can be powerful. Lower prices do often lead to a higher volume of sales—but not necessarily. In some cases, lowering the price can actually hurt sales or at least fail to provide the boost in demand hoped for. That's why it's so important to experiment with lowering prices before going ahead and making them available to your whole customer base.

At Qualaroo, we boosted our revenue significantly by conducting experiments that showed us we should actually *raise* prices. We started out with the hypothesis that if we improved the features of the freemium version of the online survey widget that Qualaroo sells, more of those who started using it would be more willing to upgrade to the paid version so they could also get the extended features and additional surveying capability. But that hypothesis failed; the improved free version generated no uptick whatsoever in paid product sales. We then hypothesized that perhaps our target customers had little sensitivity to the price and feature combinations, so we reversed course and experimented with *higher* prices, and as it turned out, our second hypothesis was right: by charging more, we made the product more appealing to large customers who were looking for best-in-class product, not necessarily the lowest-cost option. Psychologist and bestselling author Robert Cialdini explains this phenomenon: he says this is the result of people using price as a signal for quality, and it's particularly common in markets such as technology and professional services. And indeed we found it to hold true as we proceeded to raise prices three times over the course of the next year and a half, driving big revenue growth and opening up access to a whole new market of much bigger companies who wanted the surveying capabilities.

Even if you aren't selling a Web service or a tech product, the point is that your customers might be less price sensitive than you think— and the growth hacking process provides a simple way of figuring out just how price sensitive they actually are. This doesn't just apply to the pricing of the products and services being sold, but also to the discounts being given to customers to take action. At Inman, the team tested giving a discount to visitors who were abandoning their purchase in the middle of checking out by offering a limited-time 25 percent off their purchase to complete the checkout process. Not surprisingly, this discount drove a significant lift over offering no discount at all, increasing the rate at which people completed the purchase by 39 percent. But when they ran another test, testing the 25 percent discount against a 10 percent discount, they found that the smaller discount still converted roughly the same amount of additional customers— and by offering a smaller discount they were able to improve the revenue captured from the sign-up process by 18.9 percent.

PROCEED WITH CAUTION

While testing pricing is critical, it can also be tricky because customers generally don't react well to noticeable changes in prices. So the growth team must ensure that the customer experience remains consistent; for example, once customers see an experimental variant of a pricing page they should always see that variant on subsequent visits. To understand how shifting pricing and features can turn off potential customers, just imagine how you feel when you see something you paid $100 for listed just the next day for $75!

Another challenge specific to products that are sold by a sales team is that it can be difficult to coordinate pricing tests with the reps who are actively working to close prospects (and who may receive a higher commission when a product is priced higher). Sales teams must also always know which version of the page the visitor is seeing (just think of how embarrassing and detrimental it could be to have a salesperson offering one price, while a prospect is seeing an experimental pricing page that looks completely different or has different pricing), which means connecting the growth team experiments with the sales team's internal customer management database. Building connections between the two can be done by the software team or by connecting third party tools such as Optimizely and Salesforce with a technology such as Zapier or Segment, which act as plumbing to send data between disparate technology systems.

A final challenge is that growth teams often don't have the individual authority to test changes to pricing on their own, as it requires the co-ordinated effort of the product, finance, and sales teams (if the company uses a sales-based model). Therefore, it's essential the pricing and discounting tests are done in a considered, well-coordinated fashion, ensuring that all stakeholders in all parts of the business are aware of the various pricing experiments being run and their impact on both the user experience and other critical business metrics, such as margin, recurring revenue, and average order size for each customer.

THE PENNY GAP

At the opposite end of the pricing consideration is the challenge that arises when customers have become so used to getting products like yours for free—as is often the case for online software or apps—they don't want to pay anything for it at all. Venture capitalist Josh Kopelman dubbed this pricing conundrum the *penny gap*, which refers to the large difference consumers perceive between a product being free and paying even a small amount for it.

In fact, in some cases, particularly with Web or digital products, the friction of asking people to pay even a small amount can be so great that sometimes offering your product for free is actually cheaper than the cost of paying to acquire a customer who is willing to pay for it. Moreover, monetizing free users through ads, or by charging for add-on features, can be extremely lucrative. Take the case of Stuart K. Hall's 7 Minute Workout app. After promoting the app as a pay-up-front product for a

few weeks, sending out press releases with promo codes with minimal effect on downloads, Hall decided to make the app free to see what would
happen. Within three days, the app's downloads had grown to an average
of 72,000 per day, or around 2,500 times what they had been for the paid
app. It became the number one fitness iPhone app in forty-nine countries. But it wasn't just downloads that surged; the app's revenue soared
as well. That was because when Hall made his app free, he added in-app
purchases by way of a pro upgrade that provided workout tracking and
customization. These few simple upgrade features led to a 300 percent
increase in overall revenue, even though 97 percent of users didn't pay
anything to use the app.[14]

The fact is, if your product is a mobile app, you may not really have
any option but to offer it for free. A quick look at revenue for the top-
grossing iOS games makes this case. At the time of this writing, of the
highest-grossing games in Apple's App Store, not one of the top 50
games is a pay-up-front product. They are all free for download and either make their money from ads or charge for in-app upgrades to unlock
additional features.[15]

If your primary source of monetization is add ons and upgrades, it's
even more critical to optimize your strategy for persuading more of the
free users to upgrade. Luckily, several tactics have already been developed that growth teams can experiment with. One is displaying features
that are only available to paid users while free users are making use of the
product. Spotify, the popular music streaming app, does this brilliantly,
by displaying some of its premium features within the free user experience. When free users try to access these features, they encounter a call
to action to unlock the premium features by upgrading from the free
version of the software to a paid subscription.

Beyond offering premium features for purchase, growth teams can
experiment with charging a subscription price for upgraded versions, or
introduce virtual goods or in-app currency, a strategy that many popular games—from Candy Crush to Pokémon Go—have successfully used
to drive monetization. Electronic Arts is one prominent game company
that offers a variety of games that use digital currencies that allow game
players to advance more quickly in the games or to add characters to
them and more. These in-game virtual goods are so popular that they

contributed more than $173 million in revenue for Electronic Arts in its fiscal Q4 of 2015.[16] And this strategy doesn't apply just to games. There are examples of everything—from dating apps to photo apps and beyond—that offer virtual currency as a monetization strategy. For example, the popular dating app Coffee Meets Bagel sells "beans"—a currency that can be used to do things like get a second chance with a missed match, or see the identity of friends a user shares with a potential match.

Growth teams should also experiment with *combinations* of the ways in which they can generate revenue for a freemium product. Many successful apps use a mix of advertising, referral fees, and sponsorships to generate revenue. Teams may also consider monetizing user data and activity by selling access to it. For example, an app may charge other companies for access to its user activity via a subscription model, or via revenue sharing, such as by partnering with an online retailer to sell goods within the app.

In all cases, the growth team should let data lead the way, measuring what's working and what customers are interested in paying for, and experimenting to meet those needs and maximize the revenue over time.

BONE UP ON CONSUMER PSYCHOLOGY

Surveys can be powerful to uncover what people are willing to pay for, but we all know that consumers are not always rational or predictable. They say they want one thing, yet pay for another. So while customer feedback is a powerful way to come up with hacks for experimentation, understanding the psychology of consumer behavior is enormously valuable in monetizing those customers, and in growing revenue.

A wealth of fascinating research has provided powerful insights into the psychology of why people make purchases that growth teams can use as inspirations for experiments to increase earnings. Daniel Kahneman, the Nobel Prize–winning psychologist who has studied and written extensively about behavioral economics, shared many such insights in his book *Thinking, Fast and Slow*. Similarly, economist Daniel Ariely covers eye-opening experiments he has conducted about how consumers make purchasing decisions, such as we saw earlier with *The Economist* subscription example in his book *Predictably Irrational*. Another fascinating look at how consumers make choices is *The Art of Choosing*, by one of the world's leading specialists on the psychology of choice, economist Sheena Iyengar. A deep dive on all that these researchers—and many others who have conducted important work in the field—have uncovered about consumer behavior is outside the scope of this chapter, but we recommend that you consult these books to learn more and generate new revenue ideas to experiment with.

However, here we will offer a revisit of Robert Cialdini's six principles for influencing consumer behavior, which we discussed in Chapter Five in regard to activating customers, and look at how they can be used to inspire hacks to try for monetization as well.

THE PRINCIPLE OF RECIPROCITY

In essence, this is the principle that we as humans are hardwired to return a favor. Companies and marketers can put the power of reciprocity with growth experiments that center around *giving* before asking for a commitment to purchase.

Costco is a master at applying this principle, making in-store samples and demonstrations a highlight of the shopping experience at the chain. Company spokesman Giovanni DeMeo has said that some of the product demonstrations have increased purchasing by as much as an astonishing 2,000 percent, in part because when customers feel that they have received something for free—whether it's a slice of pastrami or a tutorial on how to use a state-of-the-art veggie peeler—they feel compelled to reciprocate with a purchase.[17] The HubSpot marketing grader that we discussed earlier uses this principle as well. It gives you a robust analysis of your website for free, because growth experiments have shown that you are likely more inclined to talk to a HubSpot salesperson, subscribe to their emails, or recommend the brand as a result. Giving away webinars, videos, whitepapers, and other content can also trigger this reciprocity, as can free upgrades to shipping costs and timing and on-the-spot discounts for e-commerce. In fact, the freemium model in SaaS is also a take on reciprocity, in that they are giving a set of free features away with the expectation that some people will upgrade as a result of their successful use and need of the product.

THE PRINCIPLE OF COMMITMENT AND CONSISTENCY

Recall that Cialdini found that once we've taken an action we are likely to take another one that is consistent with that previous action. It's why car salesmen are instructed to get potential buyers to initial a term sheet with no binding obligation, because the act of initialing one piece of paper makes you more likely to sign the purchase documents for the car later in the process. This same idea is used by the eyeglass retailer Warby Parker. Its home-try-on program lets prospective customers select and receive up to five sets of eyeglasses to try on before buying. Once you have a pair of their glasses on your face, it's unlikely that you *won't* move forward with the purchase.

You can use this principle to drive revenue by asking users to make small commitments up front to lead to larger purchases later on. Amazon uses this principle with their Wish List feature. They know that when you add books or items to your Wish List, you are more likely to buy the item because you have already acknowledged your desire to do so. As another example, sending a customer who recently purchased something on your site a quick follow-up with an incentive to make another purchase can lead to additional purchases from people who want to be consistent with their earlier purchase decision. Even asking a recent shopper if they'll buy again from you in the future can be enough to trigger additional purchases down the line.

THE PRINCIPLE OF SOCIAL PROOF

The desire to follow social norms or conform to the behavior of others is among the most powerful motivators to purchase. Cialdini highlights the case of Her Majesty's Revenue & Customs (England's version of the IRS), who in 2009 faced an incredible amount of unpaid debts from citizens behind on their taxes. Their collection efforts in the form of mailings were proving ineffective, so the HMRC teamed up with Cialdini's

coauthor Steve Martin to try a new approach leveraging the power of social proof that proved incredibly simple and effective. The HMRC added
a single sentence to the collection letters to a pilot group of delinquent
taxpayers: a statement of the fact that most UK residents pay their taxes
fully and on time. As a result, collections jumped from 57 to 86 percent
in the pilot group, which added up to collections of 560 million pounds
(out of the outstanding 650 million pounds) of tax money. Simply reminding people of the social norms around paying their taxes produced
a staggering improvement.[18]

Too many companies get social proof wrong, featuring unbelievable
or nonspecific testimonials to try to persuade customers to buy higher-
priced items, such as a restaurant that might include a testimonial on
the back of their menu like "Best steak in town. Love it!" Yet this can
actually *dissuade* shoppers from ordering that higher-priced item by raising doubts about the authenticity of the claim. Conversion expert Angie
Schottmuller identifies seven core factors that make reviews and testimonials effective, for which she coined the acronym CRAVENS, which
stands for Credible, Relevant, Attractive, Visual, Enumerated, Nearby
purchase points, and Specific.[19]

Flower delivery shop daFlores drove revenue higher when they added
a testimonial that met these simple criteria to their e-commerce site.
The original version of the site displayed some text-based testimonials, but after discovering that new visitors didn't know much about their
brand, they replaced those testimonials with an image that celebrated
the company's 600,000 Facebook fans. Turned out that showcasing their
large social following in a credible, relevant, attractive, enumerated,
visual way resulted in a 44 percent increase in revenue from shoppers
who likely felt in better company shopping on a site with so many happy
customers.[20]

One monetization opportunity for growth teams is to increase the
visibility of social proof along the conversion path to purchase. Adding testimonials, the logos of prominent customers, the results garnered
from users of your product, and the number of people currently shopping or booking on your website are all ways to validate the decision-
making process of your customers with information based on what other
users have already done. For example, ModCloth, the women's online

retailer, uses their Be the Buyer program to let users decide which styles and sizes of clothes to sell, but they also indicate these items with a badge to indicate to shoppers that these are "buyer approved" items. Those with the Be the Buyer badge sell at twice the rate of other items on the site.[21]

THE PRINCIPLE OF AUTHORITY

Research shows that we are more likely to trust experts and people in positions of authority than an average person. Even the inclusion of subtle language that indicates authority can increase purchase behavior, as Kaya Skin Clinic proved when they generated a 22 percent increase in sales simply by adding the word *expert* to their call to action on their website, which then read "I want an expert opinion. Sign me up!"[22]

The principle of authority explains why one out of every four television commercials features celebrity endorsements, and why brands founded by celebrities—like actress Jessica Alba's Honest Company—have been so successful. Depending on your industry and budget, celebrity endorsements may be out of scope, but each niche has influencers and tastemakers who have credibility within the audiences you're targeting. Growth teams can experiment with featuring such influencers to drive improved revenue growth through the principle of authority.

THE PRINCIPLE OF LIKING

We also buy more when a product or service is recommended by people we like. Airbnb leveraged the principle of liking when they reengineered their friend referral program by including a photo of the person sending the referral with the invite. The addition of this personal touch was part of the reason why their new referral program saw a 300 percent increase per day in sign-ups and nights booked from friend referrals to Airbnb.[23]

If you're looking for experiments to try to leverage the principle of liking, consider using images of real people—like your salespeople, or your customers—on your website. In addition, friendly, welcoming copy on your landing pages can trigger a similar response. Recall how Nasty Gal's founder, Sophia Amoruso, took poorly selling items and styled them on the site's most popular models to stoke sales? This is liking in action. The good news is that many of these changes don't require massive technical overhauls, and can be quick experiments the growth team can run to generate higher volume or purchases or to drive people to higher-priced items.

THE PRINCIPLE OF SCARCITY

When we feel like we're going to miss out, we're more likely to take action. Booking.com uses the principle of scarcity to increase revenue exceptionally well. The travel deals site shows deals that you've already missed, letting visitors know that these deals won't be around forever. They also show how many other people have booked the deals today, how many rooms are left at the hotels, and even how many people are looking at the listing at that moment—another trigger that says to customers, "You better buy now, before it's too late."

Using scarcity as a purchasing tactic is about triggering the *fear of missing out* (or *FOMO*) in your shoppers. You can run experiments that limit the time of promotions, show remaining inventory when there are only a few of each item left, limit the number of appointment spots available to book through for consultants, or limit the number of people who can take advantage of a special offer. When something is about to sell out, is hard to get, a deal is expiring, or your customers may miss out one way or another, you're more likely to make the sale than otherwise.

Having now made the full circuit through the four key types of experimentation for driving growth—acquisition, activation, retention, and monetization—in the next, and final, chapter, we'll explore how vital it is for growth teams to continue to work on all of these fronts to avoid falling into the common trap of growth stalls: lulls in growth that can, and often do, spell disaster, even for leading brands. Remember, growth teams should never rest on their laurels. In a twist on the old adage "You snooze, you lose," today's hypercompetitive business environment assures that if you stall, you will fall.

CHAPTER NINE

A VIRTUOUS GROWTH CYCLE

A s we've seen throughout the book, driving growth is a job that is never truly done. The breakout companies that sustain their success are those who constantly push for more, leveraging their success, capitalizing on new opportunities, and creating a virtuous cycle of growth.

In 2017 the Facebook growth team will celebrate its 10-year anniversary. Going from a team of five tasked with reversing the social network's slowing adoption, to multiple teams, across numerous initiatives, responsible for sustaining the seemingly unstoppable growth of the largest social network of all time, the growth team has been instrumental to Facebook's extraordinary growth over that decade, breaking all preconceived notions about just how large an online community could become. The company now serves more than one billion people per day,[1] with plenty of room for further growth around the world, and untold opportunities yet to be discovered for increasing revenue from that massive user base. Moreover, the unrelenting growth both in the number of users and in their level of engagement, has been the fuel of the company's strong support among financial investors and the public market who have rewarded it with plentiful capital to fund innovation, including long-term moonshot bets like the company's foray into virtual reality with the purchase of device maker Oculus, and its Internet Everywhere initiative, which includes an audacious plan to deliver wireless Internet to remote corners of the globe with solar-powered drone aircraft. That's what we mean when we talk about a virtuous growth cycle.

Whether yours is a growth team of 5 people or 500, and whether you work for a company valued in the millions or one that is still getting off the ground, you, too, can follow their example of continuously and relentlessly experimenting on all fronts with new ways to push growth.

AVOIDING GROWTH STALLS

One of the greatest threats to long-term success is when companies aren't vigilant enough about responding to the changes in their market— whether it's by failing to spot product or channel fatigue, acknowledge new competition, make needed updates to products or marketing adjustments in a timely fashion, or embrace new technology coming online. One prime example of the dangers of such complacency is Skype, which was once massively successful by any measure, but which failed to continue to innovate after its acquisition by Microsoft. As a result, it is now rapidly losing ground to mobile apps offering chat service, such as Facebook Messenger and WhatsApp, and the fast-growing group chat company Slack that is sweeping the corporate world. Where did Skype go wrong? Put simply, the product and executive teams failed to grasp the appeal of mobile messaging and perceive how rapidly mobile phones and tablets were being integrated into workplace communication.

Such lapses in strategic vision and product innovation often lead to a company experiencing what is called a *growth stall*, a phrase coined by Matthew Olson, Derek van Bever, and Seth Verry of CEB, a leadership advisory network. These slowdowns in growth are often unforeseen, sneaking up on companies without warning, and they happen both to major established brands and to once-fast-growth start-ups. They are devilishly hard to predict, and many ironically follow a period of strong growth. Reporting in the *Harvard Business Review* on a major study of growth stalls they conducted, Olson and his colleagues cite the case of the iconic brand Levi Strauss, which hit a historic high mark of sales in 1995, reaching revenue of $7 billion, but then, starting in 1996, saw a decline in sales so precipitous that by 2000, revenue was down to $4.6 billion, a 35 percent drop. Other major brands the authors identify as having suffered stalls include 3M, Apple, Banc One, Caterpillar, Daimler-Benz, Toys "R" Us, and Volvo. Though one might think that such abrupt reversals must be due to some dramatic disruption in the market, the study showed that often stalls are not caused by the entrance of a bold new competitor or a disruptive innovation, like smartphones, but by chronic failures on the part of companies to closely monitor customer satisfaction and to zealously look for early warning signs of disaffection. Often, erosion of customer loyalty has been going on for years but the company has failed to perceive it—until it's too late.

Stalls are also often caused, the authors report, by companies becoming overconfident of having secured a premium position in the marketplace. That is to say, they detect competitive threats but don't take them seriously enough. This false sense of security tends to lead to a failure to innovate aggressively, making only incremental improvements in existing products rather than pursuing new market opportunities for growth. Even the most vigilant of product teams can be ambushed by breakout companies that introduce a new technology, or apply a new one in an innovative way.

Conversely, stalls can occur because companies lose focus on their core products or services, becoming distracted by the launch of shiny new products, bells-and-whistles extensions, and making an entry into new markets. The drain of talent from a company can also lead to stalls, as stars who have been instrumental in driving growth defect, leaving the organizational machinery inadequate, without their superior vision and drive, to sustain vigorous growth.[2]

These pitfalls are not limited to product development. Complacency and failure to innovate in marketing efforts can also lead to massive slowdown in growth. One common growth stall occurs when companies become overreliant on particular channels, which may be losing their effectiveness. As marketing channels that once brought in endless streams of new customers mature, those streams can quickly become mere trickles, as a result of anything from new competition, to changes in consumer behavior (often brought about by technology, like the shift to mobile), to new rules that govern the channel. Online publishers like Upworthy and Buzzfeed are a prime demonstration of the latter example. These brands suffer from an uneasy reliance on Facebook's News Feed algorithm, which they use to drive a great deal of traffic to their sites. Each time Facebook chooses to tweak the rules for the stories they show to users, the publishers hold their collective breath, as even a tiny modification to the News Feed algorithm could easily cause a huge drop in their readership—and thus advertising dollars. Some companies have made the mistake of relying so heavily on the Facebook News Feed that such a change has been life-threatening. For example, Viddy, a video app that rose to a $370 million valuation, relied so much on Facebook for promotion and distribution to users that when Facebook tweaked the rules of its News Feed algorithm in a way that resulted in much lower visibility of the app on the site, Viddy saw a rapid drop from 50 million users per month to less than 500,000, and its developers ultimately shut down the app as a result.[3]

Facebook isn't the only culprit in such channel volatility; many channels institute regular changes in rules that can have serious growth consequences for companies relying too heavily on them to reach their target market. Google, as another case in point, constantly tweaks its search ranking algorithm—often sealing the fate of companies for whom search is the primary channel of acquiring costumers.

While customer churn and loss of market share through one or several of these lapses is often quite avoidable, it's also true that dramatic disruptions, whether due to competitor innovation or changes in market conditions, can blindside companies in ways that they have little or no control over. Disruptive technology can also suddenly affect the effectiveness of marketing channels, such as with the advent of ad blocking. With the pace of innovation increasing, and powerful new tools—such as cloud storage of big data sets and machine learning algorithms for mining that data—now affordable and accessible to even fledgling start-ups, even the most powerful incumbents, such as Walmart and Microsoft, must learn to be more agile in both product development and marketing. Today, no company can afford to leave any potential customers up for grabs by competitors. This is why newly hatched start-ups and market-leading powerhouses alike are instituting growth hacking.

Growth teams help to keep companies on their toes, constantly on the lookout for changes in customer behavior and experimenting with new ideas for growth. Growth teams are both active and proactive; they are detectors of early warning signs, and they are entirely dedicated to acquiring, activating, retaining, and monetizing the maximum number of customers and even driving the innovation of new opportunities for growth.

But, of course, growth teams are only human. They too can become complacent and distracted from the growth mission, or blindsided by market forces and disruptive technologies. But the high-tempo growth hacking process enables them to make effective course corrections at optimal speed. This chapter will introduce some of the common pitfalls that can stop growth teams in their tracks—and show how they can be mitigated or avoided.

SWIMMING WITH SHARKS

Certain species of sharks must always keep moving to survive; if they stop swimming, they literally die. Growth teams are like those sharks. Teams that aren't constantly innovating, that aren't continuously diving into customer data and surveying, and that aren't rapidly experimenting and producing results are not long for the world. Competing priorities, limited resources, and corporate inertia can quickly swallow up even the once-highest-performing teams. This is a particular danger for start-ups once they reach a rapid rate of growth. Understaffed and scrambling furiously to serve the growing number of customers, employees have so much to do just to keep the business running smoothly that growth team members may get pulled away by those demands. Moreover, after a big push of rapid-fire experimentation to drive for, example, the launch of a new product, slowing the tempo of experimentation once widespread adoption has been achieved can be justified. After all, in this envious situation, growth is hardly the problem. But it's important to keep in mind the danger of sliding into such complacency. Remember, growth stalls very often sneak up on companies when they least expect them. We know about the danger of taking the focus off growth all too well from our experience building GrowthHackers.com.

It was the end of 2014, and the community was just over a year old. Though we'd been seeing a huge increase in visitors over the previous 10 months, we had suddenly hit a plateau. For three frustrating months, traffic to the site remained flat, and we couldn't figure out what was happening. We had stalled. Had the online community lost the interest of growth hackers? Had we failed to serve their needs, leading them to flee and congregate elsewhere? Or had the number of people adopting the method slowed? On a hunch Sean decided to look into how many experiments we had been running during the three months that the stall had kicked in, and he was shocked to discover that we'd run fewer than 10 tests in the entire quarter. Ironically, we had all succumbed to the false confidence that growth had been assured. Our early stage hustle had fallen prey to administrative routine, and valuable growth experimentation had taken a backseat to busywork. Sean quickly rallied the team.

We agreed that from that point forward we would practice what we preached: we would run a minimum of three experiments per week (three tests per week may not sound like a lot, and for some teams, it won't be, but for our small team, it was a vigorous pace), and would always prioritize growth efforts over administrative work. We vowed that we'd dedicate time and resources to the initiatives the growth team deemed important, at the expense of everything else. With the gauntlet thrown down, we rejuvenated our ideation process, quickly building up our backlog of ideas to test from 50 to 100 and then 200 and beyond. We immediately felt reenergized as a team, and by the second week, we started to see some traction for our efforts as experiments started to hit their mark. Each week as we flew through the cycle, our growth increased that much more. Our experiments pointed us to ways to better activate visitors who came to the site—converting more of them from onetime visitors to engaged members who were participating in the community. We improved retention through reengagement loops, notifications, and working to get more users to our own aha moment faster and more frequently. In short, we did more to drive growth in the subsequent three months than we had done in the previous year.

The results were astounding; we pulled out of the stall, and into a rapid trajectory upward:

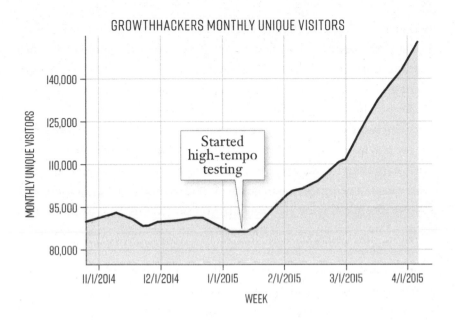

GROWTHHACKERS MONTHLY UNIQUE VISITORS

Started high-tempo testing

The high point was when we added 20,000 new visitors within 2 weeks, and then ultimately increased our site traffic by 76 percent in that quarter, nearly doubling where we had started from. During this time, we made no extra investment in paid traffic or ads. The results came 100 percent from running cycle after cycle of growth hacking process as fast as we could, learning what worked and then doubling down on those winning tests to drive even more growth.

After this renewed push, we have settled into a steady and vigorous—if somewhat less intense—testing schedule most of the time, with periods of more rapid tempo when launching new initiatives, such as new software or a new marketing test. Such ebb and flow is to be expected, but the key is to stay on top of growth metrics rigorously, and to constantly ask if the team is slowing down for a valid reason, or if complacency is creeping in. If it's the latter, the team needs to pick up the experimentation pace immediately.

DON'T UNDERESTIMATE THE POWER OF DOUBLING DOWN

Another reason that growth teams can slide into complacency is that they think they've reached the limit of the results they can generate from their growth levers. Yet before a team moves on to a new initiative, they should push themselves to find new ways to make the most out of the channels and tactics that have already proven successful. Teams can leave lots of growth on the table by not doubling down on successes.

Brian Balfour and Andrew Chen describe the way teams should push more and more on levers they've had success with as being like the strategy for playing the board game Battleship. When you have made a first "hit" in looking for the ships hidden on your opponent's board, you become a heat-seeking missile in going after that ship, calling out more and more spaces in the same vicinity until you sink it. Growth teams want to be just as intense in pursuing their "hits" and pressing on to get the most out of every avenue of success.

At GrowthHackers, for example, the launch of our email newsletter, which highlights the top posts of every week, was an important early success in driving readership. We could see it in our analytics clear as day—each week we saw a flood of users come back to the site to read the articles. Yet we didn't declare victory and hang up our hats; we focused intensively on ways to make it an even more powerful driver of growth. For example, we experimented with moving the sign-up form for the newsletter from the bottom of the landing page to the top, which, as we recounted before, drove a 700 percent increase in sign-ups, massively boosting the size of our email list, which would go on to pay dividends each and every week. Then we asked ourselves how could we get even more from this optimization to really max out our email marketing opportunity. So we redesigned the process of creating a GrowthHackers.com user account, adding a step to get people to choose to opt in to the email newsletter. That experiment added another 22 percent to our email sign-ups. But we weren't done; we knew the results were too good to abandon this line of experimentation just yet. We suspected that the email sign-up form wasn't as alluring as it could be and hypothesized that even more users might sign up if they were told how popular the newsletter was (a perfect example of the principle of social proof you read about in the last chapter). So we designed a new sign-up bar with a more prominent call to action, encouraging users to sign up with the line: "Join more than 60,000 growth professionals from Twitter, Facebook, Google, Uber, and more who get our best content each week." That experiment resulted in an additional 44 percent increase in sign-ups.

In short, when growth teams hit on something that works, they should invest in getting the most out of it, rather than moving on to the next battleground. Doubling down is a powerful way to stack one growth win on top of another.

MINING DEEPER FOR DATA GOLD

Growth teams may also come to (incorrectly) think they've reached the limit of results they can generate from a certain lever when they have tapped out the potential of the pool of data they have access to. In such cases, teams must consider investing the time and money into creating a more comprehensive data bank by ramping up on their analytics capabilities, as advised earlier. Recall that after nearly a year of operation, the Facebook growth team ceased all experimentation and for a full month, January of 2009, invested in improving their analytics tracking, which allowed them to perform more refined and powerful data analyses. That was done in specific response to the dwindling number of ideas the team was coming up with for driving growth. By investing in deeper analytics insights, the team was able to better track and measure how Facebook users moved from page to page on the site. The new data unearthed a rich new vein of potential experiments for the team to try, fueling growth that propelled the company ever higher.

To determine where to dig deeper for data, growth teams should review each of the major tasks and pathways customers and users take to reach the aha moment of the product. Within each of these key tasks and experiences, the growth team should identify gaps in their data or areas where it is thinner or less granular than in other places and work to fortify it. A growth team for a fashion brand, for example, might ask if they can identify how many images of a piece of clothing a visitor looks at before adding it to a shopping cart. Or whether they can calculate how much time it takes a customer to fill out each field when inputting their shipping information. By enhancing their data system to allow for these queries, the team may find that customers who view 4 images of an item of clothing add it to the cart 50 percent of the time, compared with only 20 percent of the time when they view 2 images or less. This more nuanced insight should lead them to a host of new growth experiments, such as adding more photos for each item, or improving how easy it is to view and navigate through multiple product shots.

Beyond patching data gaps about product use and customer behavior, the team should also ask if it has the requisite analysis skills to make the most of the data at hand. If the growth team has been working without a dedicated data analyst or data scientist, the company should consider hiring or moving one over to work with the team full-time.

DIVE INTO NEW CHANNELS

In Chapter Five, we discussed how focusing on one or two channels for acquiring new customers is optimal at the beginning of the process of driving growth, but that over time, teams should experiment with adding new channels. This can be a powerful way not only to reach even higher levels of growth, but also to escape the danger of growth stalls that can occur when a channel suddenly changes the rules of the game, as we've said can happen with Facebook or Google. If teams have reached an impasse where additional ideas are hard to come by within existing channels, this is a sign that experimenting with new channels is a good move to try. For example, for a company that has been reliant solely on paid acquisition the growth team should experiment with developing organic channels such as search engine optimization, content marketing, or social media marketing to complement the paid efforts.

Overlooking or disregarding organic channels of growth is another pitfall growth teams often fall into. Paid marketing is so easy to implement that it can sometimes weaken the resolve to seek more innovative solutions. In addition, organic growth channels generally take longer to generate results, which can lead teams to deprioritize them in favor of the faster paid channels. But organic channels can turn into crucial long-term growth drivers. For example, search engine optimization has been a critical component of growth for companies like TripAdvisor, Yelp, Zillow, and more. They did not start with the massive search advantages they now each have; their teams experimented intensively in order to achieve that success.

OPEN UP THE IDEATION PROCESS

Often the best remedy for a growth team that has stalled or is coming up short on ideas is bringing in a fresh perspective. Inviting people from other departments, teams, and individuals to contribute to the ideation process can produce a wealth of creative new ideas. Recall that at GrowthHackers we opened up the ideation process to the entire company, then to our board of directors and trusted advisers, and then to members of the community. And, in fact, several of the most successful experiments run by the team were suggested by one of our outside advisers, such as changes to our site that improved our position in Google search results for key terms.

Teams can seek such cross-fertilization of ideas in many ways. Ankur Patel, principal growth hacking lead at Microsoft, regularly brings together product managers, engineers, and designers from different teams at Microsoft to share new thinking and insights to spur bursts of new ideas for his team to test. At Science, a start-up incubator where Morgan worked, information about winning experiments that one start-up had tried were shared so others could also consider them.

TAKING MOONSHOTS

One of the biggest challenges for companies in continuing to pursue growth is breaking out of the bounds of currently successful ways of operating: the "if it ain't broke, don't fix it" mentality. Growth teams can play a crucial role in helping companies think out of the proverbial box to break the mold and find ways to go beyond what's "not broke" to in fact find something that works better.

A good place to start is by testing significant redesigns of features or of the company's marketing or products that have been successful, to see if they might not be substantially reenvisioned. Teams can start relatively small, by challenging whether features or screens that seem to have been optimized might not be even more effective if overhauled. Think of this as the principle of pushing past the plateau of a *local maximum*. A *local maximum* is defined as the highest value in a current set of points, but not the highest point overall. For example, running experiments on the same pricing page over the course of a year can lead you to a local maximum for the performance of that pricing page. But for even higher performance, the team should eventually experiment with a whole new style of pricing page. Getting beyond such local maximums is essential to continuing to unlock new growth.

A growth team should regularly schedule experiments that go beyond optimizing to innovating bigger changes. These moonshot bets are a company's best defense against the incremental thinking about innovation that so often leads to growth stalls. Of course these larger efforts generally take longer to prepare. The best approach is to slate big swings in between incremental optimizations. Recall how Pinterest's Copytune machine learning optimization software represented a massive leap beyond simple A/B testing to engage millions more users. Similarly, when Uber decided to make the radical move of testing a flat-fee-per-ride version of its service, rather than the variable rates depending on the demand for cars (which as of the time of this writing was in limited testing in San Francisco only), it was a noteworthy leap from other growth experiments. Such bold experimenting on a regular basis is vital. In tandem with continual optimization efforts, these bigger bets can lead to huge leaps forward.

We believe that growth hacking is so much more than a business strategy, or even an ongoing process. It's a philosophy, a way of thinking, and it's one that can be adopted in any team or company, big or small. Hopefully this book has inspired you to make it yours.

We wish you many wins along your way to unstoppable growth.

ACKNOWLEDGMENTS

Hacking Growth is based on the learning that we've assembled throughout our careers, so I want to thank those who have given me an opportunity to learn. First, to my family for bearing with me through long days in the start-up testing trenches. And also to the founders and CEOs who have given me the trust to experiment on their start-ups and with their precious early customers. In particular Mike Simon of LogMeIn and Uproar, who took a risk on me and mentored me through my early career, and David Weiden, Adam Smith, and Matt Brezina of Xobni; Drew Houston of Dropbox; Kevin Hartz of Eventbrite; and John Hering of Lookout, who all accepted my unconventional desire to work in interim executive growth roles at the most fragile stages of their start-ups. I also want to thank David Barrett of Polaris Partners and Tony Conrad of True Ventures, the VCs who've backed me as a founder and allowed me to accelerate my learning with Growth Hackers.com.

Finally, I want to thank the awesome team that helped make this book a reality. First to my coauthor, Morgan Brown, whose dedication and hard work have kept this book on track from the beginning. And to our supportive and talented team, including Lisa DiMona, Emily Loose, and Talia Krohn, who helped us take *Hacking Growth* to the next level.

—Sean

There are so many people to thank at the end of a process and journey like this. This book has been in the making for the better part of three years, and of course, is the result of everything I've learned in my career to date. The first people who deserve thanks are my family: my wife, Erika, and children, Banks and Audrey Grace. They have given up so many evenings, dinners, and weekends in service of me writing that I'm terrified to think of all the time traded with them to make *Hacking Growth* happen. I hope that it has been time well spent and that they know that it was done for them, with love. I am grateful to them for creating the space to allow me to do this. Thank you, Erika, especially for being selfless and understanding and kind along the way. You are an incredible partner and I could not have done this without your love and support. I love you, *mon ange*.

To Sean, my coauthor, who was trusting enough to bring me on as his partner in this project and to share his wisdom and learning with me along the way. It is hard to measure the impact working with you has had on my career, and I am forever grateful for the opportunity to work with and learn from you. It's hard to find good mentors and I'm a lucky one in that way.

Books aren't just written, they're written and rewritten, torn down and reshaped. This isn't the work of two people but of many, and they all deserve recognition. First, to Lisa, our agent, who saw a great idea within a bad proposal and took the time to help us get it straightened out and in the right hands. This book doesn't happen without her vision to see it early on. To Emily, our developmental editor and coconspirator, who took our rough-hewn phrasing, confusing logical leaps, and inside-baseball jargon and helped us turn it into a breezy narrative that read like it should. To Talia and Tina and the entire team at Crown Business, who believed mightily in this book and helped bring it to be, we are grateful for your trust in us, belief in the book, and vision and teamwork to make it happen.

Hacking Growth is really a love letter to the growth community. In it, I tried to articulate the skill and rigor you bring to the process of growing something and the real value your sweat equity creates. I hope it comes across that way. *Hacking Growth* is designed to shine a bright light on the tremendous value you create for companies everywhere and the work you do to bring promising and worthy new ideas the attention they deserve. It was written to highlight your smart thinking, innovation, and passion, and to share your incredible thinking and craft with an audience that desperately needs to hear and heed it. Thank you to everyone in our small circle who inspires, teaches, shares, and champions the crucial role that growth plays in a company's success. You inspire me daily and I'm honored to call you colleagues, peers, and friends. To the people in this book who are highlighted, thank you for being visible, giving, and admirable leaders in our field.

This book comes after seventeen years working in digital marketing, from my first start-up job out of college at SalesMountain.com to all the start-ups and companies I've had the privilege of working at since then. My motto when choosing each new venture has been "optimize for team over everything else," and in doing so I have had the honor of working for and alongside many incredible people. There are so many people to thank over the course of a career, and for me it is no different. I stand on the shoulders of giants and I am grateful for the time and wisdom they have given me. These are but a few of the many people to whom I owe deep thanks: Jack Abbott, thank you for teaching me about the art of hustle, of creating something from nothing, and for pushing to create value always. Mark Affleck, your guidance on how to be confident in my ability and lead from my strengths fuels my growth every day. Laura Goldberg, your standard of excellence and insistence on being data driven has had a profound impact on how I operate and lead. And Brad Inman, who has taught me that there is no surer way to success than waking up hungry to run down the next opportunity.

Last, but certainly not least, a sincere thank you to my family. For without them there isn't a me to write this book. To my Mom, thank you for being an unfailing champion, even in times when I probably didn't deserve it. Your never-ending love is a true gift. To my Dad, who has always driven me to expect more of myself and do the best I could, I am grateful to have your standard to live up to. And to my brother, Graeme, my best friend, thanks for a lifetime of friendship and memories. I love you all.

—Morgan

INTRODUCTION

1. Eric Ries, "How Dropbox Started as a Minimum Viable Product," Tech-Crunch, October 19, 2011, techcrunch.com/2011/10/19/dropbox-minimal-viable-product/.
2. I'd then moved over to work on growth at LogMeIn, a service started by the Uproar founder that allowed users to access their files, email, and software from any computer in the world. We managed to turn the company into the market leader despite a massive marketing campaign waged by its main competitor, GoToMyPC. What was the secret? In addition to drawing on my knowledge of marketing and sales tactics, I worked with the engineers to utilize technology for what was, to them, a novel purpose: to craft novel methods for finding, reaching, and learning from customers in order to hone our targeting, grow our customer base, and get more value from our marketing dollars.
3. Steve Jurvetson and Tim Draper, "Viral Marketing: Viral Marketing Phenomenon Explained," January 1, 1997, DFJ blog, accessed September 13, 2016, dfj.com/news/article_26.shtml.
4. Eric M. Jackson, *The PayPal Wars: Battles with eBay, the Media, the Mafia, and the Rest of Planet Earth* (WND Books: 2012), 35–40.
5. Josh Elman, "3 Growth Hacks: The Secrets to Driving Massive User Growth," filmed August 2013; posted on YouTube August 2013, youtube.com/watch?v=AaMqCWOfA1o.
6. "Conversation with Elon Musk," online video clip, Khan Academy, April 17, 2013. Accessed September 13, 2016.

7. LeanStartup.co, "Dropbox @ Startup Lessons Learned Conference 2010," July 2, 2014, youtube.com/watch?v=y9hg-mUx8sE.

8. Douglas MacMillan, "Chasing Facebook's Next Billion Users," Bloomberg .com, July 26, 2012, bloomberg.com/news/articles/2012-07-25/chasing -facebooks-next-billion-users.

9. Chamath Palihapitiya, comment on question "What are some decisions taken by the 'Growth team' at Facebook that helped Facebook reach 500 million users?" Quora, May 13, 2012; accessed September 13, 2016, quora.com/ What-are-some-decisions-taken-by-the-Growth-team-at-Facebook-that -helped-Facebook-reach-500-million-users; Yishan Wong, December 12, 2010, comment on question "What was the process Facebook went about getting their website translated into different languages?" Quora website, accessed September 13, 2016, quora.com/What-was-the-process-Facebook -went-about-getting-their-website-translated-into-different-languages.

10. Andrew Chen, "Growth Hacker Is the New VP Marketing," @*andrewchen* (blog), accessed September 13, 2016, andrewchen.co/how-to-be-a-growth -hacker-an-airbnbcraigslist-case-study/.

11. Michael Carney, "Brian Chesky: I Lived on Cap'n McCain's and Obama O's Got Airbnb Out of Debt," January 10, 2013. *Pando* (blog), accessed September 13, 2016, pando.com/2013/01/10/brian-chesky-i-lived-on-capn -mccains-and-obama-os-got-airbnb-out-of-debt/; Chen, "Growth Hacker Is the New VP Marketing"; Dave Gooden, "How Airbnb Became a Billion Dollar Company," *Dave Gooden* (blog), June 31, 2011, accessed September 13, 2016, davegooden.com/2011/05/how-airbnb-became-a-billion-dollar -company/; Rishi Shah, "Airbnb Leverages Craigslist in a Really Cool Way," *GettingMoreAwesome* (blog), November 24, 2010, gettingmoreawesome.com/ 2010/11/24/airbnb-leverages-craigslist-in-a-really-cool-way/.

12. Matthew S. Olson, Derek van Bever, and Seth Verry, "When Growth Stalls," *Harvard Business Review*, March 2008.

13. Aatif Awan, "Lessons Learned from Growing LinkedIn to 400m Members," GrowthHackers.com video of talk, February 18, 2016, https://growthhackers.com/videos/gh-conference-16-aatif-awan-head -of-growth-linkedin-lessons-learned-from-growing-linkedin-to-400m -members.

14. Amir Efrati, "The People Who Matter at Uber," *The Information* (blog), August 30, 2016, theinformation.com/the-people-who-matter-at-uber.

15. General Electric *2013 Annual Report*, 6.

16. Michael Porter and James E. Heppelmann, "How Smart, Connected Products Are Transforming Competition," *Harvard Business Review*, October 2015.

17. Fred Lambert, "Tesla Is Building a New Growth Team 'From Scratch'

Ahead of the Model 3 Launch, Hires from Facebook and Uber," *Electrek* (blog), May 9, 2016, electrek.co/2016/05/09/tesla-growth-team-model-3 -launch-hires-facebook-uber/.

18. http://original.livestream.com/f8industry/video?clipId=pla_a093cf1f -2d34-4e74-8377-9e54bc65d8e9.

19. Interview by author, February 17, 2016.

20. "Internet Users by Country (2016)," Internet Live Stats website, accessed September 13, 2016, internetlivestats.com/internet-users-by-country/.

21. Aaron Smith, "U.S. Smartphone Use in 2015," Pew Research Center website, April 1, 2015, pewinternet.org/2015/04/01/us-smartphone-use-in -2015/.

22. Anne Freier, "Ad Blocker Adoption Jumped Over 34% in 2016," *Moby- affiliates* (blog), June 23, 2016, mobyaffiliates.com/blog/ad-blocker -adoption-jumped-over-34-in-2016/; "Nearly Two in Three Millennials Block Ads," eMarketer blog, September 21, 2015, emarketer.com/Article/ Nearly-Two-Three-Millennials-Block-Ads/1013007.

23. Nathalie Tadena, "Streaming Video Subscriptions Are Now Just as Popular as DVRs," *Wall Street Journal* website, updated June 27, 2016, 12:29 p.m. ET, accessed September 13, 2016, wsj.com/articles/streaming -video-subscriptions-are-now-just-as-popular-as-dvrs-1467032401.

24. Eric Kutcher, Olivia Nottebohm, and Kara Sprague, "Grow Fast or Die Slow," McKinsey & Company website, April 2014, accessed September 13, 2016, mckinsey.com/industries/high-tech/our-insights/grow-fast -or-die-slow.

25. "73% of CEOs Think Marketers Lack Business Credibility," Fournaise Marketing Group website, media release, June 15, 2011, accessed September 13, 2016, fournaisegroup.com/marketers-lack-credibility/.

26. Graham Charlton, "Why Are Conversion Rates So Low? [Info- graphic]," *Econsultancy* (blog), October 18, 2012, accessed September 13, 2016, econsultancy.com/blog/10914-why-are-conversion-rates-so-low -infographic/.

27. quora.com/What-are-some-decisions-taken-by-the-Growth-team-at -Facebook-that-helped-Facebook-reach-500-million-users.

CHAPTER ONE

1. Carolyn Dewar, Scott Keller, Johanne Lavoie, and Leigh M. Weiss, McKinsey & Company, Organization Practice, "How Do I Drive Effec- tive Collaboration to Deliver Real Business Impact?" September 2009.

2. Adam M. Kleinbaum, Toby E. Stuart, and Michael L. Tushman, "Com- munication (and Coordination?) in a Modern, Complex Organiza- tion," Harvard Business School's *Working Knowledge* blog, July 31, 2008,

hbswk.hbs.edu/item/communication-and-coordination-in-a-modern
-complex-organization.

3. Ranjay Gulati, "Silo Busting: How to Execute on the Promise of Customer Focus," *Harvard Business Review*, May 2007.

4. Ben Horowitz, "Good Product Manager/Bad Product Manager," Andreessen Horowitz website (no exact date given), a16z.com/2012/06/15/good-product-managerbad-product-manager/.

5. Noah Kagan, "What Happens After You Get Shot Down by Mark Zuckerberg?" Fast Company, July 24, 2014, fastcompany.com/3033427/hit-the-ground-running/what-happens-after-you-get-shot-down-by-mark-zuckerberg.

6. Harry McCracken, "Inside Mark Zuckerberg's Bold Plan for the Future of Facebook," *Fast Company, Long Read/Behind the Brand* (blog), November 16, 2015.

7. "Fireside Chat: Defining True Growth—How Do You Find Your North Star Metric," GrowthHackers, https://growthhackers.com/videos/gh-conference-16-fireside-chat-with-nate-moch-vp-product-teams-at-zillow-and-morgan-brown-coo-at-inman-news.

8. Andrew McInnes, "How Do You Choose the Best Growth Team Model?," Medium, October 19, 2015, medium.com/swlh/how-do-you-choose-the-best-growth-team-model-632ad5a85be9#.955lnqbgc.

9. John Egan, "How We Increased Active Pinners with One Simple Trick," Pinterest Engineering blog, March 18, 2016, engineering.pinterest.com/blog/how-we-increased-active-pinners-one-simple-trick.

10. Anand Rajaraman, "Goodbye, Kosmix. Hello, @WalmartLabs," @WalmartLabs blog, May 3, 2011, walmartlabs.blogspot.com/2011/05/goodbye-kosmix-hello-walmartlabs.html.

11. Josh Schwarzapel, "How to Start a Growth Team: Lessons Learned from Starting the Yahoo Growth & Emerging Products Team," Medium, July 9, 2015.

12. McInnes, "How Do You Choose the Best Growth Team Model?".

13. Morgan interview with Josh Elman, April 26, 2016.

14. Morgan interview with Lauren Schafer, March 3, 2016.

CHAPTER TWO

1. Alice Z. Cuneo, "Microsoft Changes Its Marketing Tune for Lackluster Zune," *Advertising Age*, November 5, 2007.

2. Farhad Manjoo, "The Flop That Saved Microsoft," *Slate*, October 26, 2012.

3. Chamath Palihapitiya, "How We Put Facebook on the Path to 1 Billion

Users," posted at YouTube, January 9, 2013, youtube.com/watch?v=
raIUQP71SBU; Brian Roemmele comment on question "How did Yelp
gets its first 25 million reviews? What was the innovation to attract users
when they started?" Quora, July 31, 2013, quora.com/How-did-Yelp-get
-its-first-25-million-reviews-What-was-the-innovation-to-attract-users
-when-they-started/answer/Brian-Roemmele.

4. Amy Pack, "Is BranchOut a LinkedIn Killer," CNBC.com, June 14, 2012,
   cnbc.com/id/47736408.

5. Josh Constine, "How BranchOut Hit the Tipping Point and Grew
   from 1M to 5.5M Actives in 2 Months," TechCrunch, March 2, 2012,
   techcrunch.com/2012/03/02/branchout-growth/; Colleen Taylor, "Branch-
   Out Hits 25 Million Users, Nabs $25M in Series C Funding," Tech-
   Crunch, April 19, 2012, techcrunch.com/2012/04/19/branchout-25-million
   -users-funding-series-c/.

6. Marc Drees, "BranchOut Keeps Falling Down, Down," ERE Media,
   June 23, 2012, eremedia.com/ere/branchout-keeps-falling-down-down/.

7. Colleen Taylor, "BranchOut CEO Rick Marini on Building a Company
   atop Facebook's 'Shifting Sands' [TCTV]," TechCrunch, August 10, 2012,
   techcrunch.com/2012/08/10/branchout-ceo-rick-marini-on-building-a
   -company-atop-facebooks-shifting-sands-tctv/.

8. Ingrid Lunden, "As BranchOut Team Goes to Hearst, 1-Page Buys BranchOut's Assets for $5.4M in Cash and Shares," TechCrunch, Novem-
   ber 18, 2014, techcrunch.com/2014/11/18/branchout-1-page/.

9. Growth @ Airbnb, "Driving User Growth at Airbnb," posted at YouTube,
   April 11, 2016, youtube.com/watch?v=03mc78lKOwI.

10. Newsweek Staff, "My Big Break: Yelp's Jeremy Stoppelman," Newsweek,
    October 21, 2009, newsweek.com/my-big-break-yelps-jeremy-stoppelman
    -81133; Erick Schonfeld, "Citysearch Recasts Itself as CityGrid Media,"
    TechCrunch, June 2, 2010, techcrunch.com/2010/06/02/citysearch-recasts
    -itself-as-citygrid-media.

11. JP Mangalindan, "The Trials of Uber," Fortune, February 2, 2012, tech
    .fortune.cnn.com/2012/02/02/the-trials-of-uber/.

12. Andrew Chen, "New Data Shows Losing 80% of Mobile Users Is
    Normal, and Why the Best Apps Do Better," Andrew Chen blog (n.d.),
    andrewchen.co/new-data-shows-why-losing-80-of-your-mobile-users-is
    -normal-and-that-the-best-apps-do-much-better/.

13. Downloadable Library of SaaS Resources, Pacific Crest Securities, pacific
    -crest.com/saas-survey-file-vault/.

14. Lisa Jennings, "Study: Restaurants Improve Customer Retention Rates,"
    Nation's Restaurant News, June 8, 2012.

15. Tony Boobier, "Keeping the Customer Satisfied: The Dynamics of Customer Defection, and the Changing Role of the Loss Adjuster," CILA report, July 2013.

16. Ash Maurya, "The Achilles Heel of Customer Development," Lean Stack, August 2009, leanstack.com/customer-development-getting-started/.

17. Danielle Maveal, comment on Quora question "How did Etsy get its first batch of independent sellers when it started?" August 21, 2014, quora .com/How-did-Etsy-get-its-first-batch-of-independent-sellers-when-it -started.

18. Etsy registration statement, sec.gov/Archives/edgar/data/1370637/00011 9312515077045/d806992ds1.htm.

19. Ibid.

20. Bryan Hackett, "Tinder's First Year User Growth Strategy," Parantap Research & Strategy blog, March 3, 2015.

21. Ibid.

22. Issie Lapowsky, "How Tinder Is Winning the Mobile Dating Wars," *Inc.*, May 23, 2013.

23. Jackson, *PayPal Wars*, 35–40.

24. Margaret Kane, "eBay Picks Up PayPal for $1.5 Billion," CNET, August 18, 2002, cnet.com/news/ebay-picks-up-paypal-for-1-5-billion/.

25. Josh Muccio, "Brian Balfour of HubSpot—The Minimum Viable Test and How to Grow Your Startup," Dailyhunt, April 27, 2015, dailyhunt .thepitch.fm/hubspot.

26. "How to Increase Signups by 200%," Treehouse blog, July 21, 2009, blog .teamtreehouse.com/how-to-increase-sign-ups-by-200-percent.

27. David Carr, "Giving Viewers What They Want," *New York Times*, February 24, 2013, nytimes.com/2013/02/25/business/media/for-house-of -cards-using-big-data-to-guarantee-its-popularity.html?_r=0.

28. Robert J. Moore, "Applying the Lessons of 'Moneyball' and 'Golden Motions' to Your Business," *Boss* (blog at *New York Times*), boss.blogs.nytimes .com/2014/06/10/applying-the-lessons-of-moneyball-and-golden -motions-to-your-business/.

29. Keith Sawyer, *Zig Zag: The Surprising Path to Greater Creativity* (Jossey-Bass, 2013), 22–3.

30. Simone Baribeau, "The Pinterest Pivot," *Fast Company*, October 23, 2012, fastcompany.com/3001984/pinterest-pivot.

31. Leah Goldman and Alyson Shontell, "Groupon's Billion-Dollar Pivot: The Incredible Story of How Utter Failure Morphed Into Fortunes," *Business Insider*, March 4, 2011, http://www.businessinsider.com/groupon -pivot-2011-3?op=1.

32. Jawed Karim, University of Illinois commencement address, May 13, 2007, https://youtu.be/24yglUYbKXE.

33. David Skok, "SaaS Metrics 2.0—A Guide to Measuring and Improving What Matters," *For Entrepreneurs from David Skok* (blog) (n.d.), forentrepreneurs.com/saas-metrics-2/.

CHAPTER THREE

1. Sarah Perez, "Everpix: All Your Photos, Automatically Organized and Accessible from Anywhere," TechCrunch, September 12, 2011, techcrunch.com/2011/09/12/everpix-all-your-photos-automatically-organized-and-accessible-from-anywhere/.

2. "The Truth About Conversion Ratios for Downloadable Software," *Successful Software* (blog) (n.d.), successfulsoftware.net/2009/04/23/the-truth-about-conversion-ratios-for-software/.

3. Casey Newton, "Out of the Picture: Why the World's Best Photo Startup Is Going Out of Business," The Verge, November 5, 2013, theverge.com/2013/11/5/5039216/everpix-life-and-death-inside-the-worlds-best-photo-startup.

4. Andy Johns, "Indispensable Growth Frameworks from My Years at Facebook, Twitter and Wealthfront," *First Round Review* (blog) (n.d.), firstround.com/review/indispensable-growth-frameworks-from-my-years-at-facebook-twitter-and-wealthfront/.

5. Ibid.

6. Ibid.

7. Elman, "3 Growth Hacks."

8. Alex Schultz, "Lecture 6: Growth," *How to Start a Startup* (blog), startupclass.samaltman.com/courses/lec06/.

9. Palihapitiya, "Facebook on the Path to 1 Billion Users."

10. Jordan Crook and Anna Escher, "A Brief History of Airbnb," slideshow at TechCrunch (n.d.), techcrunch.com/gallery/a-brief-history-of-airbnb/; "How Design Thinking Transformed Airbnb from a Failing Startup to a Billion Dollar Business," *First Round Review* (n.d.), firstround.com/review/How-design-thinking-transformed-Airbnb-from-failing-startup-to-billion-dollar-business/.

11. Austin Carr, "19: Airbnb," *Fast Company*'s Most Innovative Companies 2012, February 7, 2012, fastcompany.com/3017358/most-innovative-companies-2012/19airbnb.

12. Schultz, "Lecture 6: Growth."

13. Jack Dorsey, "Instrument Everything," eCorner (Stanford University), February 9, 2011, ecorner.stanford.edu/videos/2643/Instrument-Everything.

14. Alex Schultz and Naomi Gleit, Facebook F8, "Ready to Grow" Breakout Session, April 21, 2010, original.livestream.com/f8industry/video?clipId=pla_a093cf1f-2d34-4e74-8377-9e54bc65d8e9.

15. Rob Sobers, "$9 Marketing Stack: A Step-by-Step Guide," Rob Sobers blog (n.d.), robsobers.com/9-dollar-marketing-stack-step-by-step-setup-guide/.

16. Willix Halim, "Create a Full Company Growth Culture," GrowthHackers Conference, February 18, 2016, https://growthhackers.com/videos/gh-conference-16-william-halim-svp-growth-freelancer-create-a-full-company-growth-culture.

17. John Egan, "The 27 Metrics in Pinterest's Internal Growth Dashboard," John Egan blog, January 22, 2015, jwegan.com/growth-hacking/27-metrics-pinterests-internal-growth-dashboard/.

18. Avinash Kaushik, "The Difference Between Web Reporting and Web Analysis," *Occam's Razor* (Avinash Kaushik's blog) (n.d.), kaushik.net/avinash/difference-web-reporting-web-analysis/.

19. Josh Elman, "3 Growth Hacks," https://www.youtube.com/watch?v=AaMqCWOfA1o.

CHAPTER FOUR

1. Associated Press, "College Football Games Are Getting Longer; Are They Too Long?" *OregonLive* (blog at the *Oregonian*), December 26, 2014, oregonlive.com/collegefootball/index.ssf/2014/12/college_football_games_are_get.html; Phil Steele, "Offensive Plays per Game/Pace," Phil Steele blog, January 14, 2016, philsteele.com/blogs/2016/JAN16/DBJan14.html.

2. Frederick F. Reichheld and Phil Schefter, "The Economics of E-loyalty," Harvard Business School archives, July 10, 2000, hbswk.hbs.edu/archive/1590.html.

3. Bryan Eisenberg, "3 Steps to Better Prioritization and Faster Execution," Bryan Eisenberg website, December 3, 2010, bryaneisenberg.com/3-steps-to-better-prioritization-and-faster-execution/.

4. "PIE Framework," WiderFunnel blog, August 28, 2015, widerfunnel.com/case-studies/telestream-case-study/pie_2015_v1/.

5. Lars Lofgren, "My 7 Rules for A/B Testing That Triple Conversion Rates," Lars Lofgren blog (n.d.), larslofgren.com/growth/7-rules-for-ab-testing.

CHAPTER FIVE

1. Ginny Marvin, "US Digital Ad Revenues Top $59.6 Billion in 2015, up 20 Percent to Hit Another High," Marketing Land blog, April 21,

2016, marketingland.com/us-digital-ad-revenues-60-billion-2015-iab-174043.

2. "Slowing Growth Ahead for Worldwide Internet Audience," eMarketer blog, June 7, 2016, emarketer.com/Article/Slowing-Growth-Ahead-Worldwide-Internet-Audience/1014045.

3. Sarah Frier, "Fab.com's Ascent to $1 Billion Valuation Brings Missteps," Bloomberg Technology blog, June 24, 2013, bloomberg.com/news/articles/2013-06-24/fab-com-s-race-to-1-billion-valuation-brings-missteps.

4. James Currier, "[500DISTRO] Do You Speak Growth? Examining the Language Behind What Users Want," August 12, 2014, retrieved from: youtube.com/watch?v=FI52Z-fDM5c.

5. Consumer Insights group, Microsoft Canada, "Attention Spans," Spring 2015, advertising.microsoft.com/en/WWDocs/User/display/cl/researchreport/31966/en/microsoft-attention-spans-research-report.pdf, 6.

6. Alyson Shontell, "How to Create the Fastest Growing Media Company in the World," *Business Insider*, November 5, 2012; Upworthy, "The Sweet Science of Virality," March 18, 2013 [slideshare], retrieved from: slideshare.net/Upworthy/the-sweet-science-of-virality.

7. Currier, "[500DISTRO] Do You Speak Growth?"

8. Video of Febreze advertisement from 1998, viewed at: youtube.com/watch?v=4 kAIHN6qYY.

9. Charles Duhigg, "How Companies Learn Your Secrets," *New York Times Magazine*, February 16, 2012.

10. Video of Febreze advertisement from 1999, viewed at: youtube.com/watch?v=ZTPNtruSIU0.

11. Molly Young, "Be Bossy: Sophia Amoruso Has Advice for Millennials and a Bone to Pick With Sheryl Sandberg," *New York* magazine, *The Cut* (blog), May 26, 2014, nymag.com/thecut/2014/05/sophia-amoruso-nasty-gal-millennial-advice.html.

12. Blake Masters, "*Peter Thiel's CS183: Startup—Class 9 Notes Essay*," Blake Masters blog, May 4, 2012, blakemasters.com/post/22405055017/peter-thiels-cs183-startup-class-9-notes-essay.

13. Awan, "Lessons Learned from Growing LinkedIn."

14. Brian Balfour, "5 Steps to Choose Your Customer Acquisition Channel," *Coelevate* (blog), May 21, 2013, coelevate.com/essays/5-steps-to-choose-your-customer-acquisition-channel.

15. Ivan Kirigin, "[500DISTRO] Sharing Lab Notes: 27 Referral Program Hack-tics in 20 Minutes," August 13, 2014, retrieved from: youtube.com/watch?v=KMGnOU3lwQg.

16. Shontell, "Fastest Growing Media Company."

17. David Skok, "Lessons Learned—Viral Marketing," *For Entrepreneurs from David Skok* (blog) (n.d.), forentrepreneurs.com/lessons-learnt-viral-marketing/.

18. Schultz, "Lecture 6: Growth."

19. Eventbrite, "Social Commerce: A Global Look at the Numbers," Eventbrite blog, October 23, 2012, eventbrite.com/blog/ds00-social-commerce-a-global-look-at-the-numbers/.

20. Elman, "3 Growth Hacks."

CHAPTER SIX

1. AdRoll, "What Is Retargeting?" 2016, adroll.com/getting-started/retargeting; Chen, "Losing 80% of Mobile Users Is Normal."

2. Ibid.

3. Neil Patel, talk at Search Engine Journal Summit, Santa Monica, California, February 24, 2015, retrieved at: slideshare.net/SearchEngineJournal/1-neil-patel-final.

4. Ibid.

5. Growth@ Airbnb, "Driving User Growth at Airbnb," April 11, 2016, retrieved at: youtube.com/watch?v=03mc78lKOwI.

6. Elman, "3 Growth Hacks."

7. John Egan, "Measuring for Engagement: Understanding User Gains, Losses & Levels of Interaction," August 12, 2014, retrieved at: youtube.com/watch?v=NghOllGvv4E.

8. Neil Patel talk at Search Engine Journal Summit, slideshare.net/SearchEngineJournal/1-neil-patel-final.

9. "How Adobe Converted Free Trial Downloads into Satisfied Customers," *Bunchball* (blog), 2016, bunchball.com/customers/adobe.

10. Adam Kleinberg, "Brands That Failed with Gamification," iMedia, July 25, 2012, imediaconnection.com/articles/ported-articles/red-dot-articles/2012/jul/brands-that-failed-with-gamification/.

11. Gabe Zichermann, "Cash Is for SAPS," *Gamification* (blog), October 18, 2010, gamification.co/2010/10/18/cash-is-for-saps/.

12. Jen Wieczner, "Starbucks Cards Now Have More Money Than Some Banks," *Fortune*, June 10, 2016.

13. BJ Fogg's Behavior Model, "What Causes Behavior Change?" behaviormodel.org.

14. Andrew Chen blog, "New Data Shows Up to 60% of Users Opt-Out of Push Notifications (Guest Post)," andrewchen.co/why-people-are-turning-off-push/.

15. John Egan, "Long-Term Impact of Badging," John Egan blog, February 13, 2015, jwegan.com/growth-hacking/long-term-impact-of-badging/.

16. Adam Marchick and Thue Madsen, "How to Craft Push Notifications That Users Actually Want to Receive," Kissmetrics blog, 2016, grow .kissmetrics.com/webinar-93.

17. BJ Fogg's Behavior Model, "Triggers Tell People to 'Do It Now!'" behaviormodel.org/triggers.html.

18. Kyle Rush, "Optimization at the Obama Campaign: A/B Testing," Kyle Rush blog, December 12, 2012, kylerush.net/blog/optimization-at-the -obama-campaign-ab-testing/.

CHAPTER SEVEN

1. Peter Drucker, *Management: Tasks, Responsibilities, Practices* (New York: Routledge, 2012), 57.

2. Fred Reichheld, "Prescription for Cutting Costs," Bain & Company report (n.d.), bain.com/Images/BB_Prescription_cutting_costs.pdf.

3. Ellen Huet, "What Really Killed Homejoy? It Couldn't Hold On to Its Customers," *Forbes*, July 23, 2015.

4. Daniel B. Kline, "Amazon Prime Improves Its Customer Retention Rate," June 1, 2016, fool.com/investing/2016/06/01/amazon-prime-improves-its -customer-retention-rate.aspx.

5. Jules Maltz and Daniel Barney, "Should Your Startup Go Freemium?" TechCrunch, November 4, 2012, techcrunch.com/2012/11/04/should -your-startup-go-freemium/.

6. Brian Balfour, "Growth Is Good, but Retention Is 4+Ever," May 10, 2015, retrieved at: youtube.com/watch?v=ch7aps2h8zQ.

7. Alistair Croll and Benjamin Yoskovitz, *Lean Analytics: Use Data to Build a Better Startup Faster* (Sebastopol: O'Reilly Media, Inc., 2013), 73.

8. Dharmesh Shah interview with Morgan Brown, March 1, 2016.

9. Balfour, "Growth Is Good, but Retention Is 4+Ever."

10. Daniel B. Kline, "Amazon Improves Its Customer Retention Rate," *The Motley Fool*, June 1, 2016, http://www.fool.com/investing/2016/06/01/ amazon-prime-improves-its-customer-retention-rate.aspx.

11. Christoph Janz, "From 'A as in Amiga' to 'Z as in Zendesk,'" *The Angel VC* (blog), July 16, 2016, christophjanz.blogspot.com/2016/07/from-as-in -amiga-to-z-as-in-zendesk.html.

12. Nir Eyal, *Hooked: How to Build Habit-Forming Products* (Portfolio: 2014), 5–10.

13. Brad Stone, *The Everything Store: Jeff Bezos and the Age of Amazon* (Little, Brown: 2013), 187.

14. Brad Stone, "What's in Amazon's Box? Instant Gratification," Bloomberg, November 24, 2010, bloomberg.com/news/articles/2010-11-24/whats-in -amazons-box-instant-gratification.

15. Dave Kim, comment on question "How did Yelp get initial traction and overcome the critical mass problem?" Quora, March 10, 2011, quora .com/How-did-Yelp-get-initial-traction-and-overcome-the-critical-mass -problem.

16. Zhongmin Wang, "Anonymity, Social Image, and the Competition for Volunteers: A Case Study of the Online Market for Reviews," April, 2010, https://editorialexpress.com/cgi-bin/conference/download.cgi?db_name= IIOC2010&paper_id=336.

17. Sarah Silbert, "The Inside Scoop on the Amex Centurion (Black) Card," *The Points Guy* (blog), October 14, 2015, thepointsguy.com/2015/10/amex -centurion-black-card/.

18. Sarah Buhr, "theSkimm on How to Rapidly Grow an Audience of Engaged Millennials," TechCrunch, May 9, 2016, techcrunch.com/ 2016/05/09/theskimm-on-a-better-way-to-serve-the-news-to-young -professionals/.

19. Justin Ellis, "How theSkimm's Passionate Readership Helped Its Newsletter Grow to 1.5 Million Subscribers," Nieman Lab blog, August 18, 2015, niemanlab.org/2015/08/how-the-skimms-passionate-readership-helped -its-newsletter-grow-to-1-5-million-subscribers/.

20. Jimmy Daly, "Behavioral Emails That Keep Customers Coming Back (with Examples from My Inbox)," Unbounce blog, March 9, 2015, unbounce .com/email-marketing/behavioral-emails-keep-customers-coming -back/.

21. Shouvick Mukherjee interview with Morgan Brown, March 10, 2016.

22. Cara Harshman, "The Homepage Is Dead: A Personalization Story," Call To Action Conference, June 20, 2016, http://calltoactionconference .unbounce.com/speakers/2016-cara-harshman.

23. Egan, "How We Increased Active Pinners."

24. Bing Gordon, "Five Things to Know About Retention Hacking," KPCB blog, November 17, 2014, kpcb.com/blog/five-things-to-know-about -retention-hacking.

25. Debora Viana Thompson, Rebecca W. Hamilton, and Roland T. Rust, "Feature Fatigue: When Product Capabilities Become Too Much of a Good Thing," Marketing Science Institute blog, 2005, msi.org/reports/ feature-fatigue-when-product-capabilities-become-too-much-of-a-good -thing/.

26. David Pogue, "Simplicity Sells," TED Talk, filmed February 2006, retrieved at: ted.com/talks/david_pogue_says_simplicity_sells?language=en.

27. Jordan T. McBride, "Dan Wolchonok on Running Retention Experiments," *ProfitWell* (blog), January 21, 2016, blog.profitwell.com/saasfest
-recap-dan-wolchonok-on-running-retention-experiments.

CHAPTER EIGHT

1. Monetate, "Monetate Ecommerce Quarterly for Q1 2016," 2016, retrieved at: info.monetate.com/EQ1_2016.html.
2. Croll and Yoskovitz, *Lean Analytics*, 113–19.
3. Colin Zima, "Growth Hacking with Data—How to Uncover Big Growth Opportunities with Deep Data Dives," GrowthHackers.com, September 8, 2014, retrieved at: https://growthhackers.com/videos/growth-hacking
-with-data-how-to-uncover-big-growth-opportunities-with-deep-data
-dives/.
4. Elena Verna, "Product Experience Usability to Improve Growth," Growth Hackers.com, February 18, 2016, retrieved at: https://growthhackers.com/
videos/elena-verna-vp-growth-at-surveymonkey-product-experience
-usability-to-improve-growth.
5. Annabell Satterfield (Growth at BitTorrent), "Engaging Customers to Find Your Next Big Growth Opportunity," GrowthHackers.com, February 18, 2016, retrieved at: https://growthhackers.com/videos/gh conference-16
-annabell-satterfield-growth-at-bittorrent-engaging-customers-to-find
-your-next-big-growth-opportunity.
6. Colin Zima, "Recommendations Are Easier Than You Think," *Looker* (blog), December 22, 2014, looker.com/blog/recommendations-are-easier
-than-you-think.
7. Charles Duhigg, "How Companies Learn Your Secrets," *New York Times Magazine*, February 16, 2012, retrieved at: nytimes.com/2012/02/19/
magazine/shopping-habits.html?_r=0.
8. William Poundstone, *Priceless: The Myth of Fair Value (and How to Take Advantage of It)* (Hill and Wang: 2011), 185–92, retrieved at: books.google.com/
books?id=4Fs1TrLjWhUC&lpg=PT156&dq=poundstone%20charm
%20pricing&pg=PT156#v=onepage&q=poundstone%20charm%20pricing
&f=false.
9. "The Price Is Right: Essential Tips for Nailing Your Pricing Strategy," First Round Review (n.d.), retrieved at: firstround.com/review/the-price
-is-right-essential-tips-for-nailing-your-pricing-strategy/.
10. Patrick Campbell, "The Value Metric: Optimize Your Pricing Strategy for High Growth," Price Intelligently, March 12, 2014, retrieved at:
priceintelligently.com/blog/bid/195287/The-Value-Metric-Optimize
-Your-Pricing-Strategy-for-High-Growth.
11. Dana Mattioli, "On Orbitz, Mac Users Steered to Pricier Hotels,"

Wall Street Journal, August 23, 2012, retrieved at: wsj.com/articles/ SB10001424052702304458604577488822667325882.

12. Dan Ariely, *Predictably Irrational, Revised and Expanded Edition: The Hidden Forces That Shape Our Decisions*, (Harper Perennial: 2010), 1–6, retrieved at: books.google.com/books?id=44ecn9XukOoC&lpg=PA1&dq=%22the %20economist%22%20subscription&pg=PT21#v=onepage&q=%22the %20economist%22%20subscription&f=false.

13. Steve Young, "How a Made-Up Product Increased Conversions by 233%," Unbounce, August 14, 2012, retrieved at: unbounce.com/conversion-rate -optimization/made-up-product-increased-conversions/.

14. Stuart Hall, "An App Store Experiment," StuartKHall.com, June 20, 2013, retrieved at: stuartkhall.com/posts/an-app-store-experiment.

15. "Top Apps on iOS Store, United States," App Annie, September 16, 2016, retrieved at: appannie.com/apps/ios/top/.

16. Sarah Needleman, "How Mobile Games Rake In Billions," *Wall Street Journal*, July 28, 2106, retrieved at: wsj.com/articles/how-mobile-games -rake-in-billions-1469720088.

17. Joe Pinsker, "The Psychology Behind Costco's Free Samples," *The Atlantic*, October 1, 2014, retrieved at: theatlantic.com/business/archive/2014/ 10/the-psychology-behind-costcos-free-samples/380969/.

18. Steve J. Martin, Noah Goldstein, and Robert Cialdini, *The Small BIG: Small Changes That Spark Big Influence* (Grand Central Publishing: 2014), 1–2, retrieved at: books.google.com/books?id=3a5gAwAAQBAJ&lpg= PT10&dq=the%20small%20big%20HMRC&pg=PT10#v=onepage&q= the%20small%20big%20HMRC&f=false.

19. Angie Schottmuller, "Social Proof Power Plays," March 30, 2016, retrieved at: inbound.org/discuss/conversionxl-live-notes-slides-and-q-a -slideshare-s-now-included#angieschottmuller.

20. "Conversion for E-commerce: Two Winning Tests for a Multilingual Online Florist," Conversion Rate Experts (n.d.), retrieved at: conversion -rate-experts.com/daflores-case-study/.

21. Aileen Lee, "Social Proof Is the New Marketing," TechCrunch, November 27, 2011, retrieved at: techcrunch.com/2011/11/27/social-proof-why -people-like-to-follow-the-crowd/.

22. Paras Chopra, "Focus Matters on a Landing Page and Here's Why: 22% Increase in Sales," Visual Website Optimizer, October 24, 2012, retrieved at: vwo.com/blog/call-to-action-increase-sales/.

23. Jason Bosinoff, "Hacking Word-of-Mouth: Making Referrals Work for Airbnb," Airbnb, March 27, 2014, retrieved at: nerds.airbnb.com/making -referrals-work-for-airbnb/.

CHAPTER NINE

1. Facebook, September 16, 2016, retrieved at: newsroom.fb.com/company -info.
2. Matthew S. Olson, Derek van Bever, and Seth Verry, "When Growth Stalls," *Harvard Business Review*, March 2008.
3. Jon Russell, "Viddy, Once Touted as 'The Instagram for Video,' Will Shut Down on December 15," TechCrunch, November 4, 2014, retrieved at: techcrunch.com/2014/11/04/viddy-once-touted-as-the-instagram-for -video-will-shut-down-on-december-15/.